Even the Dead
are Coming

Mike Robbins

BROADS

BOOKS

The moral right of the author has been asserted

All photographs by the author

ISBN 978 0 578 03569 7

broadsbooks@gmail.com

Contents

Foreword

In November 1987 I travelled to Sudan to work as a development volunteer with the Refugee Settlement Administration on the Ethiopian frontier. This book describes the two years I spent there, and what I saw. My work was not really important. I did not save anyone's life (although I met people who did). If this book is of interest, it may be because it describes a little of what happened to hundreds of thousands of refugees when the world had moved on after the 1984-85 emergency in the Horn of Africa.

I hope this book will also allow the reader to form a more rounded picture of Sudan. The behaviour of its government in recent years is not excused, but the achievement of the Sudanese in coping with the emergency of the 1980s deserves to be acknowledged.

If the book has another purpose, it is to describe what life was like for one volunteer in Africa. It will be clear that I had my frustrations; we all did, but looking back 20 years, I am not sorry I went. It would be a pity not to have tried Ethiopian gin. The pit latrines were at least an education. And I met some very nice people indeed.

Of course Sudan has moved on in the intervening years, even if its government has not changed. Wars have ended and others have begun; oil has flowed; there is now a plan to redevelop the Mogren with a huge 21st century business centre. The war in Ethiopia is long over (although there are clearly still refugees in the Eastern Region). I have not attempted to update this book, however; it might as well stand as what it is, a memoir of a time and place.

Many people helped me immeasurably with my work in Sudan; without them, there would be no book to be written. It would be invidious to name some but not others. They know who they are.

Chapter One

November 1987: *Beginnings and a journey*

WHEN I rose at five, it had been black night; when I left the hotel half an hour later it was light, a very delicate pink from the sun beginning to spread across a pale, luminous blue. It wasn't cold. It was only mid-November, and the mornings wouldn't chill you until near Christmas; and then for three or four weeks at most. Still, it was mild, and as I lifted my heavy suitcase down the steps of the small hotel in Abdul Rahman Street, I barely broke into a sweat.

I had no problem hailing a taxi at that hour. People start early in many Third World cities, ready to struggle with overcrowded and irregular buses. The Hillman Arrow that stopped for me dropped me at the main bus station at Souk-el-Shaabi at six-fifteen. It was now quite light, although the buildings and buses were still in shadow. But after another quarter of an hour the sun had risen completely, warming my shoulders through the thin, worn cotton of my shirt. I started to feel better.

I had not been happy earlier. I hadn't slept much. I knew that there was a tarmac road all the way to the small town near the Ethiopian frontier, making me far luckier than many travellers in Africa. But I was worried about what I would find there; moreover, the sound of the zinc doors of the hotel clanging and scraping had reverberated all night, mingling with the relentless hawking of the Saudi in the room next door. He had either a chest complaint, a revolting habit, or both. My other neighbour was doing something active with a number of steel pails and much fluid, a performance that continued until after three. I suspected he was producing bootleg liquor. I don't think I should have enjoyed drinking with him. He was a sinuous man, rubbery, creepy, hairless, somewhat akin to an eel; I had passed him once or twice in the corridor and felt the tang of evil in his presence, as if he were conjuring up *djinns* rather than gin or concocting nightmares that, released, would roam the streets of the city, poisoning people's sleep. After an hour or so I had started to feel uncomfortable, and tossed and turned in bed; I told myself not to be absurd. But then the sounds of shots rang out in Abdel Rahman Street, and continued for half an hour. I was aware of the coup rumours, but felt cheated; surely they might have allowed me a little time to acclimatise? Then I guessed that they were shooting stray dogs, a guess confirmed by a squeal of shock and pain as some unloved animal died in the dust outside the hotel. All in all, I closed my eyes for less than an hour.

*** *** ***

SOUK-el-Shaabi bus station lay beyond the busy suburb of Souk Saggana, itself four or five miles from the city centre. Taxi was the only practical way at that time of the morning; I remember that the fare for the ride was S.20, about £2.00, but less than S.40 for the journey by coach that would take me for seven hours down the main artery of the country. And that was itself expensive; I could have done the journey for half the sum although, when I saw some of the buses on the road, I realised that that would have been unwise.

There was just one sealed road of any length, and it carried most of the country's imports. In the north, there was very little road; just a railway on which the service was highly irregular. There was just one other strip of sealed road, and that did not go far.

I awaited the bus, surrounded by ragged boys who looked fourteen but, I later realised, were probably four or five years older. They wished to guard my case, see me onto the bus, load my luggage; all of which, I felt, I had best do myself. When at a quarter to seven the bus had not turned up, they became desperate in their search for services to offer me. Exasperated, I gave them cigarettes, which I knew they could trade; raw Cleopatras from Egypt. They fell silent then but stayed close to me, like tick-birds.

Now, the sun was really warm. In two more hours the temperature would pass 100 deg. F in the shade, and there were no clouds in the sky. There would be none until June, seven months hence. I fidgeted. Along with other passengers, I was standing on one of eight or nine pavement-bays near the booking-office; these were where the Western-style coaches stopped to load. But the bus-station was enormous, and already it was crammed with vehicles of every kind. Some, like the blue MAN that would take me, and stood some yards away with no sign of life, were of a type familiar in Europe - albeit a little old. Most of the others were converted pick-up trucks, with rough wooden benches nailed to the back, and covered over with a souk-built framework that reminded me of wrought-iron gates in English suburbia. And then there was the closed, coachbuilt bus on an Austin chassis. Long, high in the back, with multiple rear wheels, it rather resembled the American school buses that were also common here. However, the Austins were immensely powerful, and hunted in packs. I think they must have been powered for the haulage of grain in the desert, then geared up at the differential to allow for their lighter load. Unlike the European coaches, they would cross hundreds of miles of desert in the North, drivers taking their direction from tangled tyre-tracks, stars and occasional, stunted trees.

A few minutes before seven, Souk-el-Shaabi became busier. There were families; middle-aged men in white *djellabiyas* reaching to the ankles, and *sirwals*, baggy trousers cut very low in the crotch, beneath. The women, sometimes with tribal scars in the form of horizontal or vertical slashes on their cheeks, looked almost to me as if someone had been at them with cattle-brands; but they wore no chadors. Rather, the city-dwellers wore Fifties-style dresses in bright colours, hidden usually below flowing, transparent *toabs* - white wraps of fine-ly-spun cotton that reached to the calves, and had hoods that could be lowered onto the shoulders. Their faces were never covered. Older women, and countrywomen, wore similar robes, but of many colours, light and thin, but drawn many times around the body. Sometimes, the women seemed very bulky, and moved with excruciating slowness. Later, I realised that the practice of female circumcision sometimes made movement very painful for them.

They made much noise and drank much tea, bought from men who crouched on the ground beside frames of iron that carried char-coal. Always, it seemed, these travellers were laden with possessions. When one goes somewhere, one acquires what cannot be bought at home. So it was here; people have reported passengers staggering aboard the ferry home from Aswan laden with everything from ket-tles to sofas. Certainly, at Souk-el-Shaabi, they had mattresses, clothes, pots and pans; and a posh stereo or two, bound perhaps for some place where there was power. Quickly the rooves of the Austins were piled high with booty, from trips to Egypt perhaps, or just to the Libyan Souk across the city.

"Kassala-Kassala-Kassala-KASSALA!"

The shouting pierced the canopy of chatter that arose from the passengers.

"Sennar! Sennar!"

"Rabak! Rabak!"

"Kosti-Kosti-KOSTI!"

9

The name Kosti I knew, given the town in memory of a Greek merchant, who had arrived to trade in goods and chattels in the days of slavery. Richard Dimbleby wrote that there was a Greek grocer in Khartoum with General Gordon, but I believe they were there before that.

I listened hard for my own destination, but it seemed that we were forgotten. Then, at five to seven, the blue MAN bus decided it was time to go. It yawned; stretched; scratched itself, and ambled over with a whiff of morning diesel. It was time to join the flow down the artery into the belly of the Sudanese beast.

*** *** ***

KHARTOUM'S suburbs were unlovely. The bus passed down Africa Road between lines of concrete blocks of flats, crudely built and often unfinished. It was the custom, as it was elsewhere, to leave steel wands protruding from the top storey, in case one should later wish to build above. Between buildings and potholed tarmac were wide dusty margins of nothing much, dotted here and there with tea-stands; or the odd boy selling cigarettes from behind a blue plywood box, on top of which there was always a jam-jar holding 'singles' for those who preferred to buy that way. Often they did; a packet of 10 cost half a day's wages for most urban Sudanese.

There were planning laws in Sudan but everyone ignored them, and many a multi-storey block had been thrown up wherever, maybe on land owned by someone who is quite unaware of the building's existence. To connect water and telephones, such as they were, without the correct *warriga* (any bit of bureaucratic bumph in Sudan is called a *warriga*) was illegal, but of course it happened. The city authorities were aware of the problem and it irked them. Nonetheless Khartoum grew and grew, and straggled deep into the Gezira, the cotton-growing belt to its south-east, so that leaving the city could take an hour or more on empty roads.

After Souk-el-Shaabi, this unattractive mess was strewn with petrol-stations. There were hundreds on the outskirts of Khartoum. But there was rarely much petrol. Even taxis were restricted to four gallons a day, and to get this, they queued. The queues outside a petrol-station could certainly be a mile long on a weekday morning and ran into and beside each other, mile after mile of bright yellow taxis, drivers resigned to spending the first two or three hours of their working day (which could begin at five) waiting for their lifeblood.

The souk-trucks, too, were preparing for the day. In the hinterland, we passed an enormous dust field with maybe 30 such vehicles, parked with their bonnets up so that the riding-boys could polish the engines. They were beautifully-kept, these souk-trucks, and could rumble on for several decades. They were built mostly on the Bedford TJ chassis; their round, postwar-style cabs were usually a bright royal blue and their bodywork had been painstakingly constructed in the souk, great slabs of steel painted matt-black, studded with a thousand rivets. Sometimes steel hoops protected the cargo, which might be loaded to twice the vehicle's height. The bodies were extremely heavy, and the lorries were said to be net consumers in the economy, so profligate were they with precious diesel. But they were impressive, polished to perfection, interiors tastefully upholstered in crushed velvet and hung with tassels; doors cut away and replaced with wooden balustrades as armrests; slogans painted, with care and symmetry, in a million designs that included expressions of religious faith, national flags, eyes - all overshadowing the drabness of the buses, which offered nothing more than posters of Bob Marley and, more frequently, Michael Jackson in their rear windows. (But whenever we played a tape of Michael Jackson to the Sudanese, they couldn't stand him.)

Khartoum came to an end eventually. We passed a police checkpoint, where the duty officer glanced inside the coach and saw me; he must have asked the driver where the white face was going and, satisfied, did not ask to see my permit to leave the capital. Later, things would be less relaxed.

We entered the Gezira. The original cotton plantations were irrigated around the time of the first world war, by the British; by the time they left the country in 1955, a million acres were under cultivation. It sounds impressive, but the Sudanese later doubled it. It was indeed impressive now. The price of cotton, however, was not. Still, the earth was rich and brown and amazingly fertile; palms grew, as did acacias; and there was a village every few miles.

It was as we passed these that I got my sense of place. It was a small thing that did it; it usually is. Every village had its school, and they were not far apart. At eight there was morning assembly, and for some minutes I kept seeing long, neat parallel lines of pupils in bright cotton uniforms, robes and pajama suits of bright blue or orange topped, in the case of the girls, by a white hijab, a cotton headscarf. I regressed 20 years and remembered my mouth thick with bacon and eggs and the cold breath clouding from me as I stood waiting to do calisthenics in the schoolyard; or my stomach playing up from breakfast as we opened our hymn-books in the oak-beamed hall. Here, they stood in dusty yards under a pale blue sky, but this is how a strange country clicks into place. A mass of curious sounds, beating sun and dust and broken pavements, becomes a man stirring tea with a spoon; or a squad of soldiers running, to barked orders, by the side of a road or a man resignedly reading his paper as he queues for petrol, or simply scratching his arse, like I do.

*** *** ***

AFTER nine, we passed through Hasaheisa. On the night of August 4, 1988, Hasaheisa would be the last dry place I would see on earth. On a bright November morning the previous year, it was the best view I had had so far of the Blue Nile, here nearing the end of its journey from Lake Tana in Ethiopia to the Mogren in Khartoum, where it joins the White Nile from Uganda.

Long before that junction it is majestic. A mile wide at Hasaheisa, it was there lined with trees, and a shady wood had grown up above the beach in the town; just opposite was the coach-stop with its restaurants where lumps of lean meat hissed on hot stones heated with charcoal. From Rufa'a, on the opposite bank, came a ferry; its ramp slapped down on the sand, and Toyota pick-ups struggled for the beach, hampered by hordes of white-clad men travelling to the market. Glimpsed; then gone, as was a felucca seen like a snapshot, gliding through the trees. We did not stop at Hasaheisa.

I once read a short story that referred to 'the stupefying plains of Sudan'. Stupefaction sets in after Hasaheisa. After Wad Medani has slipped past to the right and the bus has climbed the Blue Nile bridge outside that town, there is scarcely a feature in the landscape. It takes about an hour for stupefaction to become complete.

The endless baked-earth plain that accounts for most of Eastern Sudan is not what it appears, but in November the dry season had begun, and it was like a sheet of grey marble broken only by a skein of very fine cracks. Moreover it stretched, uninterrupted, as far as the eye could see, so that one had the impression that the earth had been turned inside-out, and you were crossing what had been the inside and was now the skin. Both earth and sky were infinite, leaving the eye to search for some point of reference and find none.

Except the mirages. These began at about ten, and seemed always to be on the horizon; at first, I thought that they were lines of trees. They were not simple shimmers such as one sees on an English summer's day, but great expanses of water floating across the landscape. So realistic were they that reflections of real objects, when there were any, could be seen as they passed. All this somehow added to the heat; by now all the curtains on my side of the bus were closed, so that I could only look out through a small crack by my seat-upright. In fact, the sun did not shine too fiercely into my side of the coach, for Ibrahim had thoughtfully booked me *fi'il dol* - in the shade; you can save a little money by sitting on the other side of the coach, but you will fry.

I didn't fry, but the heat was fierce and I welcomed the iced water brought round by the driver's mate. There wasn't much of it on board, however. Or perhaps it became tepid. I found out later that if something - water, Pepsi - is supposed to be served cold, then the Sudanese will only serve it cold; pride will not permit it to be given any other way, even if you are dying of thirst. So I dried out slowly and watched the empty world slip by outside, only the odd discarded tyre or fan-belt by the side of the road betraying the motion of the coach.

"The world is flat," I wrote to a friend a week or two later. "I know, because I've just fallen off the edge of it." I might have added that I had discovered a secret of the Creation; that God had baked the earth in a kiln. I knew too that he had forgotten to attend to parts of it afterwards, for I had crossed one such place, and discovered His omission.

*** *** ***

JEBEL is the Arabic word for either a hill or a mountain; to a European, a jebel is a low hill and that was what these were, barely a hundred and fifty feet. There were a number of them, clustered around that part of the road that twisted through Fau.

This was once the site of one of the biggest refugee camps of them all. A camp, Fau V, still existed, but Fau I and II had vanished in the dust, just three years on from the year of hunger in the Horn of Africa that saw the Tigrayans lead 400,000 of their people across the mountains to Sudan. Later, when they could, they led them back.

I did not know this then. But I certainly noticed Fau, for the jebels

13

*A visitor to Showak market greets
me through my office window*

were hauntingly weird; some round, and some jagged like snaggle-
teeth of witches; small ravines full of stones ran down their flanks.
One of them, two or three miles from the road, was so distinctive in
shape that I dubbed it Cathedral Rock, and in months to come it was
a landmark on many journeys that I made along this road.

In the shadow of the jebels, man and beast took shelter from the
furnace of the day. This was where I saw my first camels; first just two
or three, hobbled, one leg tied in an angle at the knee so that it would-
n't wander far. Then there were more and more, and there were goats
too, and stupid brown sheep with their long, silly tails and ears. Always
these animals seemed to be in the care of a single boy, who looked
about 10 to me but was probably 14; he was armed with nothing more
than a stick, and dressed in a simple white *djellabiya*. He would squat
below a solitary, windswept acacia, if he could find one, and would be
alone but for the herd, which might be a hundred strong. I have no
idea how he controlled them. Probably he did not know himself, and
would have been surprised that anyone should remark upon the matter. Sometimes, he would be at a *hafir*, an artificial lake or pond 50 or
60 feet across, constructed of banked earth on the surface of the
plain. They collected water in the rains, and held them a few weeks -
no more; already, after three weeks of drought, they were reduced to

a few murky puddles in a bowl of churned earth.

Near Fau we stopped for Pepsi. We had been on the road for four hours and I should have liked to relieve myself, but felt I could not do so when the other passengers were fanning out from the tea-shack to pray. I watched them prostrate themselves for a moment before I realised that they were actually squatting to urinate. I thought I'd feel an idiot standing, and decided to wait.

Pepsi was less of a problem. I was befriended by a tall Sudanese, dressed not in *djellabiya* but in slacks and sandals and Western-style shirt, which is what Sudanese office-workers wear during the day. (The shirts always have collars. No Arabic-speaking Sudanese wears a tee-shirt. Only Southerners of African origin do that.) The man fetched me a Pepsi, and we smoked cigarettes together. As always in that country, I was not allowed to pay.

There were many tumbledown shacks lining the road just south of Fau, and we would see more further east, near Gedaref. They are tea-houses and restaurants, with a few shops selling cigarettes and groceries; others sell petrol or *jazz* (diesel) from 44-gallon drums from which the fuel is pumped by hand.

Other shacks were brothels. The Sudanese attitude to prostitution appeared ambivalent; this is a Moslem society in which premarital sex is unimaginable for a woman (although the rules are broken more frequently than Westerners think). Thus a man obtains sex elsewhere, and does so until he is 30, as marriage is expensive and therefore late. So prostitution was not rare, and was a service industry in which Ethiopian refugees played a role.

The truck-stop was, in fact, a good place for a brothel. A lorry-driver's life in Sudan was a lonely one, and never more so than on the long tarmac road that stretches 1,000 kilometres from Khartoum to Port Sudan. The journey could be completed by coach in 19 hours, often with a single driver, who would go hard to make time. The truckers did likewise. There was an incentive; in 1988 a good truck-driver could earn S.250 for a haul from capital to coast and back. That was then about £75.00 at the official exchange rate. In real terms, given the cost of living, it was worth £250-£300. I heard of one man who regularly did three trips back and forth in a week, so that he must have spent about 120 hours at the wheel. He would, if he kept it up, have netted about S.3,000 a month. The average wage for a teacher or a junior civil servant, both of whom might have had a much-prized degree, was about S.400.

There was only one way for many of the drivers to survive such a punishing schedule - dope, or *bango*; a rolled leaf full of the stuff (which was strong) could be had for about S.35. I was told that many of the lorry-drivers were more or less constantly stoned out of their brains.

Even if this were untrue, fatigue and heat together would have wrought havoc on this road. Every mile or two there seemed to be a burnt-out coach, overturned souk-truck or flattened car. Months later, I travelled to the capital with a colleague from the finance department of our office, who had been trained as a glass technologist in Bulgaria but for some reason was now a wages clerk. We amused ourselves by counting off the wrecks at the side of the road, each crushed pick-up or bleached and mangled mechanical skeleton being greeted with ironic cheers. By the time we passed Wad Medani we had reached 17; at that point, we gave up and discussed Bulgarian glass-blowing instead.

The evidence of carnage did not discourage people from travelling at 150kph and more. At night, you were lucky if a lorry had more than one headlight. That would be pointing in the wrong direction, anyway. Tail-lights were often neglected; a problem, as the big Fiat trailer-trucks often rumbled through the night at 35-40kph or less. Any faster, and the one dim headlight would have been inadequate. But the truckers' most disconcerting habit was seen when they were standing still. In the event of a breakdown, a cairn would be erected some way behind the disabled vehicle, to warn oncoming drivers. The matter resolved, the truck would pull away, the cairn being left where it was - normally under your sump.

*** *** ***

THE JEBELS passed and there was again nothing to either side of us. There wasn't even much traffic; it was one, and many drivers had chosen to break their journeys. We had ourselves been travelling for six hours. With the noon came an uncomfortable dryness and a caking of dust upon the face, so that the eyelids felt as stiff as card.

The passengers were quiet. Earlier, there had been a cheerful group at the back of the bus. One had cried out: "Sudan *niish - aragi*!" Sudan finished - *aragi*! The latter was the local firewater, distilled from dates and, like all alcohol, illegal. Perhaps the cry was for my benefit. But now those passengers, too, were dozing. The sky was pale blue and empty, although I believe that once on that journey I did see a tiny white cloud; I can't be sure. An empty pan beneath a dome. Such emptiness can panic some people; to others it brings a sense of freedom.

Occasionally, however, the featurelessness was broken. Every half an hour, we would drift past a small corral of rush fencing, often broken or sagging. Within would be a group of perhaps four or five round straw huts, with conical thatch rooves tied at their peak. The walls of the huts, too, were often thin or damaged. These were called *tukls*, or *goateas*, depending on the region. Nothing stirred within the compounds; and there was just nothing there, save for an occasional *abrique*, a yellow moulded plastic jug with a handle and a long spout. This was used to keep water handy for washing, and was found in every house.

Two things puzzled me about these compounds. The first was the absence of movement or objects; the second, the distance of the compounds from any form of life. The mysteries would be solved. No-one stirs in the midday heat unless they really must, for it is dangerous to expose yourself to it (although labourers do, perforce, during the harvest). As to how anyone could live on a slab of baked earth 80 kilometres from the nearest means of making a living, I would find this out during the rains. Yet the strangeness of such a life never ceased to impress me.

*** *** ***

WE APPROACHED the city of Gedaref at two. It is a place of 300,000 people, but there are few high buildings; only a massive grainstore that can be seen half an hour away. Gedaref is the granary of Sudan.

We entered the city. My memory is of mile after mile of straggling suburbs consisting of compounds of *tukls*, the perimeter walls becoming steadily more elaborate as we neared the centre. Simple holes for people to pass through were replaced with slabs of corrugated iron set in crude frames of wood, protruding above hedges of mesquite. These gave way to walls of *biriish*, matting woven from dura stalks. There were still few people to be seen. Work had finished for the day at half-past one or two, and it was time for lunch, followed by sleep until after four. Then the shops would reopen for several hours. For now the city of Gedaref seemed ghostly, but one other thing struck me at once. The taxis: almost without exception, they were royal blue Mark Three Consuls and Zephyrs with sweeping, finned rear wings. Why? I never found out.

We paused for Pepsi and passengers in the shadow of the huge television aerial, surrounded by compounds that had not, essentially, changed in appearance since the time of Elizabeth I. My companion and I drank Pepsi together and chatted as best we could with the 10 or 20 words of Arabic and English we had in common. The language difficulty did not bother us. Together we watched the passengers leaving the coach, hauling luggage slowly through the narrow door, the older, fatter women clumsy as before in their movements. My friend explained that the coach would go to Kassala, but would pass the town of Showak en route, in about 30 or 40 minutes. There I would leave it, if the driver remembered to stop.

The word Showak, a colleague was to tell me, meant yearning. But others said that it meant fork, and indeed it was on a bend in the river Atbara. Showak, yearning or a fork.

The road wound out of Gedaref up a shallow slope, but after five minutes the unrelieved flatness of the land returned. It was not so empty, though. Within 10 minutes a village appeared, and then another; large and prosperous, with squat one-storey brick houses, many large compounds, tractors, and the tall square water tanks with their chequerboard pattern that were a common sight all over the region.

And then there was a wood. This puzzled me. It looked large, but in fact spread only a quarter of a mile on either side of the road, a remnant of the forests and savannahs that had characterised the area until the 1960s. In the woods, herdsmen, for some reason older now, had hobbled their camels for the midday heat, and let their flocks graze in the shade. Often these were goats, whose constant nibbling was destroying what was left of the trees. Some of the men looked villainous, and I was later to learn that this stretch of road was not advised at night - although by then I had already made several journeys down it in the hours of darkness.

There was a haze within the woods, and a hint of green; for a moment I couldn't place it, although I noticed the mixture of red and silver tree-barks, both of which gave gum arabic, and the vegetation on the forest floor. I was curious; it was November 14 and we were 1,000 miles north of the equator. Only later did I realise that the *kha-reej*, or rainy season, had just ended, and that the trees were not in bud; rather, the leaves had died and were shrivelling, parched, on the

18

branches. Nothing was ever quite what it appeared in Sudan.

*** *** ***

MY JOURNEY had really begun about two years earlier, through a sequence of events and thoughts that seemed unconnected at the time. I was 28 in 1985, and had a vague sense of unease about the world and my lack of knowledge of it; but it had yet to crystallize, and I had no thought of travelling.

I had worked for a year as a press officer and traffic broadcaster at the RAC Press Office, opposite the Royal Automobile Club in Pall Mall. I enjoyed broadcasting, and I think I still would. My home life, in a shared rented house in an Edwardian terrace in South London, was comfortable enough. I was even able to erect my darkroom in the boiler-room, and indulge my passion for black-and-white printing. On warm evenings (the summers of 1982 and 1983 had been unusually fine), I could drink wine and chat to friends in a pleasant patch of garden, sometimes accompanied by the singing of an Italian baritone neighbour singing in an adjoining garden. His rich, smooth notes floated across the mid-Victorian rooves of South London, mingling with the summery scent of roses.

I worked shifts. Sometimes that summer I biked across Lambeth Bridge in the delicate light of dawn and saw the Houses of Parliament reflected in the still river, every cornice perfectly mirrored; and then swept through Parliament Square and down Horse Guards through the early mist still rising from St. James's Park. Then on through The Mall and into the office to make real coffee in the percolator, and compose my first broadcast from bits and pieces given me by a sleepy duty officer at Scotland Yard, himself just beginning his day. During that summer I also moonlighted as a press officer and photographer to a fringe theatre company in Camden Town, where a friend was directing a wonderfully tense version of *A Long Day's Journey Into Night*.

Looking back across the years, that summer has an elegiac feel, a sort of land of lost content just before life changed forever. It was nothing of the sort. I was often broke, and in any case, at the end of 1985 almost everyone in the RAC press office was made redundant. Not long afterwards, we were forced to leave the South London house. I found another job quickly enough, and a new flat, shared with a friend; but it was at this stage that I first thought of volunteering to work overseas as a way of making my life a more open question.

But it was a year before I got around to filling in the application forms. In the meantime, I had become a reporter on the weekly newspaper for the commercial fishing industry. The editor had once been a Hull trawlerman, working Arctic waters. He sent me on fishing trials in the North Sea; to a fish festival in the North-East; to see boatbuilders on the South Coast; and out to the little yards on the Medway where skilled men could double the length of a boat in a fortnight's work. Every week or so we would travel north to do a press pass, working with the typesetters in the gloomy castle of the *Nottingham Evening Post*, where Graham Greene had begun his career half a century earlier. Things were looking up, and the application made to Voluntary Service Overseas (VSO) had been forgotten.

One hot day in June 1987 I was sitting at my desk overlooking Farringdon Lane, reading a press release from the Ministry about haddock quotas, when the 'phone rang.

"I can't tell you much over the 'phone," said a cultured female voice, "but we think it may be Java. Are you still interested?" I had heard nothing from the voluntary service organization VSO since putting in my application nine months earlier. But there was little to lose from listening, so I said that I might be. On the hottest, muggiest day I can remember that year, I donned my best grey suit and made the short journey to VSO's headquarters, then still in Belgravia. A series of three interviews followed.

The first was businesslike and friendly. The second, to assess my personality, was odd. I was asked briefly if I could cook.

I replied that it got a bit expensive if you couldn't.

"Good," she replied, and asked me whether I drank or smoked. I owned up to two or three pints of beer a day, and about 20 cigarettes.

"You'll have to watch the smoking," I was told. "Everyone smokes a lot abroad." The remainder of the quiz was given over to a quiz on racism and sexism, and I confess I told the interviewer what I thought she wanted to hear. It was, I think, also the truth; but she can hardly have known that. The third and final interviewer, in contrast, gave me what seemed like a gentle grilling on my professional qualifications. When I read her assessment afterwards, I was astonished by its accuracy.

Oddly, Java was not mentioned, although Thailand was, briefly. A week later I received a duplicated letter telling me that I had been accepted for VSO. "Many trials and tribulations lie ahead," it warned darkly, and went on to explain how I should get myself inoculated against everything from rabies to the Black Death.

There was also a job description for a post at the headquarters of the Refugee Settlement Administration of the Commissioner for Refugees (COR) at Es Showak, Sudan, near the border with Ethiopia, Eritrea and Tigray.

"It is rather an embarrassing situation," Cultured Voice had scribbled at the bottom, "as the employer has asked for a specific volunteer and she was not accepted by VSO. Please let me know as soon as possible whether you can accept this post." Nothing about Java.

I kept them waiting for four weeks for a decision. They wanted a sub-editor to help produce a quarterly magazine about the Administration's work, a job which seemed to have possibilities. My doubts centred on my ability to cope with extreme heat and illness - and a strong sense of feeling cheated, for which I make no apology. What had VSO been playing at? Had this been the intention all along? I later got to know the owner of the cultured voice, Pam, quite well and decided it hadn't. But I was annoyed.

By early August, however, I had made up my mind. Pam, pleased, invited me to attend a training course in Bristol later that month. It lasted a week; I liked everyone I met, and decided that I was going away with good people. I was less sure about the course, a long series of encounter groups and participation games designed to improve interpersonal relationships. I felt that I should have been better off learning how to do simple repairs to a Land-Rover. My view was widely, though not universally, shared. No-one protested, as VSO has been known to reassess volunteers who questioned the wisdom of such courses, although I do not know if they would really have held anyone back for that reason. Because of my late interview, I never attended the post-selection course on (mainly) racism, but those who did later told me that they had found it insulting, being lectured about their supposed prejudices for a weekend by sometimes aggressive people who did not know them. The subject raised hackles among volunteers of all ages and skill backgrounds, although I do not know if it does now.

Preparations continued throughout September. I visited my GP, who passed me as fit and refused to charge me for inoculations. I didn't know that he himself was interested in Africa. A trip to the Royal Dental Hospital in South London disposed of wisdom teeth I did not wish to take abroad. It was a painful business. ("I say, this one's enormous," said the dentist cheerfully, peering at the X-ray. "It's lying on its side. God, it's like the *Titanic*.") I drove off to King's Lynn the next day to see a cockle merchant, blood pouring from my gum, and lost my way, cursing.

The departure date kept being pushed back. Most of the people on the course bound for Sudan flew on October 1, themselves late. Not knowing when I would leave, I was still at work, and went that day to Weymouth to see a ship's chandler in the town. It was very fine weather, one of those last stabs at summer, but mellowed by the progress of the year; the sky was a deep blue and it was gently warm. The chandler and I hitched a lift up the harbour in a fishing-boat that was going our way. The water was calm, with a slight breeze. It was my last outing for *Fishing News*. The following week I said goodbye to everyone and left London, I thought perhaps for ever.

I arrived at my parents' home in Oxford to find that my departure date had been put back again, this time by a week. I decided just to enjoy a month's break.

*** *** ***

DURING this time I tried to read as much about Sudan as possible. There was relatively little literature; but what there was, was good. Anyone interested would do well to start with the two books by Alan Moorehead, *The White Nile* and *The Blue Nile*. However, a brief introduction here will be useful.

In the 19th century, Sudan emerged from the dominance of the old Ottoman Empire, the influence of which was also waning in Egypt. Internally, Sudan was then a chaotic mix of Arab tribes and traders with Nilotic, Negroid people; and the majority of Arabic-speaking, Moslem people in the northern half of modern Sudan are not obviously Arabs as we think of them. To some extent this reflects the intermingling of Arabs and Africans in the region, partly a consequence of slavery.

The British came to the African interior in the mid-19th century, and found a power vacuum. With the zeal of converts - Wilberforce was recent - they determined to stop slavery. But for the time being, the British simply became another element in the confusion, without dominating it. This era ended in the 1880s with the Mahdist war, a religious-nationalist uprising; the Mahdist siege of Khartoum and the death, at their hands, of General Gordon in 1885 represented the end of the interregnum that had followed the fading of Ottoman power.

There was pressure on successive British governments to avenge the death of Gordon. But it was not inevitable that they would do so. Sudan is not accessible even now; there is no road link with Egypt, and no railway across the border. Gordon himself had regarded it, in Imperial terms, as a 'useless possession'. But the French were interested in the region, and if they were to run an empire from the Atlantic to the Red Sea, any British notion of doing the same from Cairo to the Cape could be abandoned. The Kitchener expedition that advanced south down the Nile and overthrew Mahdist rule in 1898 helped ensure that the French did not succeed.

Britain thus found itself in control of the 'useless posession'; although, like the expedition itself, Sudan was a condominium ruled jointly by Egypt and Britain together. Moreover, not all this vast country was under its control; much of the south was unexplored, while in the far west, local emirs retained control until the British deposed the last ruler of Darfur in 1916. Elsewhere, however, Britain took control more quickly, working through a combination of friendly local sheikhs and, increasingly, after the First World War, the Sudan Political Service (SPS).

This was not part of the colonial service, as Sudan was not a colony. Its recruitment criteria, however, were if anything higher. Members were recruited almost entirely from Oxford and Cambridge, and were selected on both academic and sporting achievement. The latter standard was not an elitist joke, but a way of ensuring that the recruits would survive the climate; a rowing or rugby blue was particularly welcome. Accompanying wives were not allowed until the 1930s, and even then marriage was outlawed for the first two years of service. According to Rosemary Kenrick's excellent book, *Sudan Wives*, fewer than 400 men served in the SPS during the entire Condominium period. There would, obviously, have been fewer at any one time. Despite this, the SPS appears to have kept order without recourse to violence, and to have taken a considerable interest in local industry and agriculture (in the south, this did not always have happy results).

It seems that it was, for the most part, benevolent. In Khartoum, my teacher of Arabic, Abdel Moneim, once told me of a governor of Omdurman who patrolled the streets on horseback in the 1930s to ensure that no-one broke the Moslem sabbath (Friday). Offenders, it seemed, were horsewhipped. According to Moneim, people were sufficiently impressed with this cross-cultural cooperation to remember him to this day. I reflected inwardly that I should not have liked being horsewhipped by an infidel for breaking my own Sabbath. But the country seems, in the main, to have been ruled with a light hand.

However, such economic development as there was tended to be geared to the world economy and thus, in the end, to the benefit of the British. So ran the argument of young Sudanese I spoke to, who pointed out that the largest single development-the Gezira project-was designed to grow cotton, an international cash crop, while the other great advance - the railway - took it for export to Port Sudan, itself built by the British in 1905.

Moreover, although the Condominium does not seem to have been oppressive, it was not freedom. By the 1940s, more and more educated Sudanese wanted the British out; and indeed they had never planned to stay for ever (no foreigner was permitted to acquire land, for example). The difficulty was to persuade Egypt that Sudan should become independent, rather than be incorporated into Egypt; the British did not think that the Sudanese wanted that. There was a second problem; the African south of the country was administered separately and radically different in character, and most British observers probably believed it should be incorporated not into Sudan but into Uganda. It is unlikely Egypt would ever have agreed to that. However, the Egyptian ruler, General Naguib, who had been born and spent his childhood in Sudan, and had a Sudanese mother, did agree to Sudanese independence if the British withdrew within three years. They left at the end of 1955. The second problem, the differing character of the South, remained unresolved.

The nation that came into being on January 1, 1956 was the largest country in Africa, and one of the largest in the world. But its population was small; even when I arrived in 1987, it was only 23 million. The northern half was flat and most of it was desert, but south and east of Khartoum there were areas of savannah and of relatively rich rainfed wheat- (or dura) growing plains, with stretches that were partially forested. In the south, the huge swamp of the Sudd in a crook of the White Nile made navigation southwards difficult. There were 117 languages (some estimates were higher). The southerners were the most diverse of the lot, ranging from the quarrelling Nuer and Shilluk peoples to the towering Dinka, cattle-rearing warriors for whom six foot six was quite a normal height.

Religion was a more unifying factor, but could also be a divisive one. In the northern half of the country, almost everyone professed the Moslem faith. In the south, only 10-15% did; about 70% were Christian, and the balance often held to pagan or animist beliefs. Already there was trouble in the region, where ill-advised attempts by the British to move tribes to what they considered to be healthier grazing-grounds had caused a rebellion in 1955. This was still going on, and was the genesis of one of the longest wars in Africa.

Economically, the country was based largely on subsistence farming, but with a growing tendency towards large-scale mechanized farming in the east. This did produce a cash crop, as did the Gezira project; exports of cotton were healthy, as were those of gum arabic (essential binding for products such as sweets and pills), and karkadee, or hibiscus (still exported in large quantities to Germany for soft drinks of the Ribena kind).

There was extensive illiteracy, to be sure, but at its top end Sudanese society was educated and organized. But the continuing insurrection in the south was a constant drain on the country. In 1969 control of Sudan passed to Jaafar Nimeiri, leader of a group of young turks dedicated to building socialism. Reviled in Sudan in the 1980s as the cause of many of its problems, Nimeiri nonetheless managed, by 1972, to end the 17-year civil war and build the country's first really long tarmac road, from Khartoum to Port Sudan. But as the years went by Nimeiri espoused not socialism but, increasingly, Moslem fundamentalism.

This was a growing trend in the region. When I asked Sudanese friends why, in what is elsewhere a secular age, they explained that it was also the age of nationalism in the Third World, and that Moslem fundamentalism is that in a sense; a pan-Arab nationalism developed to replace the distinctive pan-Arabism of Nasser.

This had been, in a sense, social nationalism. It had taken Nasser as a focus in the years after Suez. But the Six Day War, my friends told me, had broken Nasser, and the students and the young - infuriated by America's support for Israel - had searched for a replacement. In Islamic fundamentalism they found it, a different beast in the same pan-Arabic burrow.

In 1983 Shari'a, Islamic law, was promulgated in Sudan. It was not, in truth, genuine Koranic law. That is stricter yet, but has safeguards built in for the innocent that can make it hard to get a conviction for anything. Indeed, one who bears false witness may suffer the savage penalty he has sought for the acquitted. Nimeiri lacked the stomach for this. But certainly amputation for theft was introduced, as was public flogging for certain crimes (including drunkenness). Alcohol for consumption became completely illegal. The only exception was Holy Communion. It was a blow to the Camel Brewery, which had just opened a new factory in Khartoum. The police poured huge quantities of alcohol into the Nile - although it was said that they quietly buried much of it, intact, around Port Sudan and it was slowly retrieved by scavengers over the next few years, so that slightly sandy bottles of Johnny Walker kept turning up in unlikely places.

Many Sudanese, while not necessarily wanting alcohol banned, did regard drinking with distaste. Judicial amputation, however, was regarded as cruel and unnatural; it was also hypocritical, being applied to petty thievery rather than grand larceny. The excellent Government magazine *Sudanow* made the point with elegance after Nimeiri had gone by printing a shot of three amputees, with the caption: "Better off stealing S.75 million from a Ministry..."

Meanwhile, after 11 years of peace, a combination of oil, water and religion restarted the civil war in the south.

In the early 1980s Chevron found large deposits of oil at the railhead near Babanusa, in the northern part of southern Sudan. The people of the region asked whether they could expect any real benefit from this while Sudan remained a unitary state. At the same time, international assistance was being poured into the construction of the Jonglei Canal. This would bypass and thus drain the Sudd, ease navigation and prevent the loss of millions of gallons from the White Nile through evaporation. However, southerners argued that the destruction of the Sudd would rob some people of their homes and might radically alter the pattern of rainfall in the region. Finally, there was the imposition in August 1983 of Islamic law on the non-Muslim south. The Sudan People's Liberation Army (SPLA) emerged under a renegade Army officer, Colonel John Garang. It kidnapped the foreign experts working on the Jonglei Canal project as the opening shots in the new civil war. By 1990, the war would have claimed perhaps a million victims through murder, fighting, starvation and epidemics.

*** *** ***

THERE was a further challenge to the country's stability, this time in the north. This was the growing number and changing composition of the refugee population. Ethiopia, too, had been in a state of civil war, in Tigray and in the then northern province of Eritrea. In 1977, it had first nearly lost and then nearly won this war; and then in 1984 came the great famine.

Before the famine there were already about 750,000 Ethiopians, Eritreans and Tigrayans in Eastern Sudan, and they were destabilizing the economy. Since 1970, wages had risen by a factor of 30 in the region, but the cost of living had risen by a factor of 40, as the growing weight of skilled labour swelled the flow after the Ethiopian revolution of 1974, competing with nationals for jobs in Kassala, Gedaref and Port Sudan. From 1968, Sudan had resorted to putting all those who would cooperate into rural, self-contained settlements. There were now about 30 of these, administered by the Refugee Settlement Administration centred mostly on Showak. Each settlement contained between 2,000 and 20,000 people.

During 1983, members of NGOs (non-Government organizations, or charities) and others in Ethiopia realized that a serious food crisis was developing, but their messages seem to have been largely ignored; a story recounted in Peter Gill's *A Year in the Death of Africa* (Paladin, 1986). In fact, the disaster that struck sub-Sahelian Africa in 1984 had deep roots. Mechanized farming, begun by the British in the 1920s in the eastern region of Sudan, contributed; soil erosion in the mountains of Tigray was not new either. Nimeiri's own policy of turning Sudan into the 'breadbasket of Africa' had also filled the sky with topsoil.

In late 1984 the scale of the crisis started to become known to the public in Europe. In Ethiopia, the government, preoccupied as it was with the war and with crushing dissent, realised that something would must be done. Large-scale feeding-centres were set up in the mountains, but many Tigrayan peasants reached them only to die in them. Others were shovelled onto transports for forced 'resettlement' in strange parts of Ethiopia, where they knew neither the language nor the land. Against this background, the Tigrayan rebel relief organization, REST, decided to move 400,000 of its civilians across the mountains to the relative safety of Sudan, rather than let them be forced to go to Korem. Walking at night to avoid air attack, weakened by hunger, and unable to see in the dark due to Vitamin A deficiency through a shortage of red pepper, they lost many on the way. More died when they reached Sudan. Wad Kowli, the chief reception centre run by the Commissioner for Refugees with UN and aid-agency assistance, was hundreds of kilometres from the nearest tarmac road. Keeping it supplied was difficult, even in the dry season. In January 1985 300 Tigrayans a day died as measles swept through the camp.

Similar things were happening on a smaller scale in Darfur, in the far west of Sudan. There, 125,000 refugees from civil war in Chad had taken shelter. They joined villagers from Sudanese communities whose own crops had failed. The disaster had spread right through Sudan's own agriculture. As the famine tightened its grip on the countryside, internal and Ethiopian refugees poured into Khartoum and other major cities. Sudan's export potential, heavily dependent on cash crops, was badly damaged. In 1985 alone, according to The Economist Intelligence Unit, GDP declined by 11.5%. This worsened the decline of the Sudanese pound, the *gineih*. Anything that could not be produced domestically became unaffordable or unobtainable.

Meanwhile Nimeiri used the provisions of Koranic law that permits the execution of apostates from Islam to put to death a prominent theologian. Then, in April 1985, he announced major austerity measures just before travelling to Washington for consultations. In his absence, against a background of urban violence, civic leaders persuaded the Army to depose him, although the generals first extracted a promise that they should not be asked to harm him personally. (In fact, he remained in Cairo until 1999.) In May 1986 the Army organized elections that were generally agreed to have been fair. Office was restored to a descendant of the Mahdi, former Prime Minister and religious leader, Sadiq al-Mahdi. Amputations ceased, but other provisions of Shari'a remaned, including the ban on alcohol.

By the time I arrived on November 3, 1987, the war was fiercer than ever. Travel to south Sudan, except by air to Juba and sometimes to Babanusa, was not possible. In the east, the number of refugees had swollen to 1.2 million. Many Sudanese regarded this as an underestimate.

*** *** ***

I RECOGNISED the town from the cylindrical water-tanks that towered above the United Nations compound like Wellsian tripods. There was nothing else; I could see few buildings apart from the odd shack. By the time I had realised where we were, the bus was three kilometres up the road, passing the bus-station, a series of broken-down shacks in the plain.

Dancing in Abuda refugee settlement, February 1989

"Showak!" I gurgled.

"Showak!" yelled my friend.

"Showak!" cried my neighbour, a clerkly figure in razor-crease slacks and shirt, waking suddenly from the deep sleep in which he had been for the previous four hours.

"Showak! Showak!" yelled everybody, snapping their fingers and stamping their feet to attract the attention of the driver, who, they realised, had forgotten to stop for me. Now he did so, with reluctance, a kilometre or so beyond the bus-station. The riding boy helped me to take my suitcase from the locker in the vehicle's side. I did not tip him - you do not, in Sudan - but thanked him; he grunted and climbed aboard again, and the blue MAN pulled away, and out of my life forever.

I looked around me. There was no traffic whatsoever. Nothing stirred. The landscape was not so flat as it had been before Gedaref, but it was still plain, and for the most part featureless. I could see the bus-station in the distance, and wondered if I could walk to it with my luggage in the sun that beat down on the parched earth. There was no sound. It was peaceful, as it must be for a chicken when it is finally in the oven.

Far away, a white shape detached itself from the bus-station. It came slowly towards me as I watched, standing in the dust beside the empty road. It did not speed up but approached in third gear, the whining of the transmission coming clearly to me through the empti-ness. It was a pick-up truck. I wondered if I had arrived, by mistake, in a small Texan town; and whether the driver wore a stetson.

He wore no stetson, but looked thoroughly evil. He was a driver for the Commissioner for Refugees workshop in the town. He was also, it was said, a part-time secret policeman and was rumoured to carry a gun in his glovebox. I never confirmed this, but he was cer-tainly strangely wealthy, with a penchant for European three-piece suits which he wore on cold winter mornings - the only time when they did not boil him to death. But he was always kind to me.

I digress. I knew nothing, then, of this; nothing indeed about any-thing much. It was three in the afternoon of Saturday, November 14, 1987. It was 110 deg F in the shade. There was no shade. There was nothing much of anything. I could see no town.

"Oh, my God," I muttered. "Am I spending two years *here?*"

Chapter Two

November 1987: *A small town in Africa*

I had been pessimistic about Showak. Had I looked carefully when I climbed into the pick-up's cab that blazing day, I should have seen a slight hollow in the ground, four or five kilometres away towards the cleft made by the Atbara river. Therein lay the town of 15,000 that was Showak, yearning, or a fork.

It was the tree-shaded compound in which I lived that was the saving grace. Built at the top of a slight rise, it consisted of four tukls that had been built of brick, instead of the rush construction normally used. This was not uncommon; if someone could afford to build of brick, they did so, and sealed it down afterwards with a mixture made of donkey-dung. The rooves were thatched. Our tukls were oblong rather than round, and had originally been divided into two, giving eight rather cramped little homes. The building of a new, square-block compound down the road, and the decline in the number of volunteers since the 1985 Emergency, had made it possible to knock them all into one, although mine retained a partial divide, so that there were two rooms. It was just the right size for me, cool, dim, with concrete floors that were easily swept clean of the dust that deposited itself on every surface, even when there were no dust-storms as such. A litter of plywood furniture, crude but adequate, completed the picture, along with an enormous concrete slab of a bed built by my predecessor; at first, this had been hollow, but had been filled in, as the roof was never quite watertight and he had found that the mattress was always damp in the rainy season, the water collecting in the concrete depression. What was now left was a sort of platform with ample room for three. Over this, he had rigged a mosquito-net, made from two single ones; I kept this, and in the night, when the room was lit by a single Bulgarian low-watt lightbulb, the effect was that of a translucent tent into which one could slip and dream of Sinbad and Scheherezade.

We had electricity; sporadic, with voltage fluctuations, but it was there. The wiring was crude, and indoor light-fittings were used throughout, even in the open; thus in the rains a rubber-handled pair of pliers was kept to hand, to cut the power at source as soon as the first drops were felt. There was no glass in the windows (Sudanese buildings rarely use it). Instead, a wire net to keep out the mosquitoes covered the aperture in front of the wooden shutters. For coolness, I kept my door open during the day, and derived privacy from the rush enclosure that ran round the space a few feet in front of it. A rakuba across the top of this provided extra shade. A hedgehog sometimes came in the evenings to bask in the pool of light outside the door; once, it got into my room at midnight. I was puzzled by a scuffling, snuffling sound, and turned on the light. Then I looked under the ply-wood cupboard, and saw the hedgehog, rolled tightly into a ball. I fished it out as gently as I could and deposited it outside; it had been looking for the exit.

This was not the only nocturnal noise. The chickens could fly well enough to reach my roof, and spent many happy hours nesting in the thatch. Any droppings were deflected by the mosquito-net, and the rustling in the straw above became almost a comfort. I was less happy with the dogs. Every house had a guard-dog, and at night they ran wild, barking incessantly, so that towards the end of my time there I took to going out in the early hours and lobbing stones at any shad-owy presence within range.

In fact, they had been too far away to trouble me at first. But then we acquired a guard-dog of our own. Shaggy was a mongrel bitch; when she arrived, she was nothing more than a small soft mound of fur, rather plump, and very shy, although she was greeted with horror and much spitting from the many cats that hung around the com-pound. As she approached maturity she became more sociable, luring the dogs of the town to our gate, where they knew they would find a warm reception. Before long, Hamid our guard, told us, Shaggy was a good time had by all. This was the cause of the barking that drove me crazy.

Dogs were not the only animals that presented problems. The compound was surrounded by a scrappy hedge of mesquite, a tough, wiry bush that thrives in desert lands. It ran round the outside of a biriish wall that was constantly falling down or being split or ruptured, a process assisted by the goats, who have a liking for *biriish* and mesquite; indeed, a goat will eat anything. It is one of the environ-mental menaces of the Horn of Africa. In the day, when Hamid was absent and the steel-and-mesh gates at the entrance to the compound were left open, they would come into it in twos and threes to intensi-fy their programme of environmental degradation until either Ian or

I chased them out with much waving of arms and cursing.

There were other uninvited guests. Donkeys were frequent intruders, wandering up the driveway past the car and, unseen, round the back of Ian's tukl. In truth they did no harm, but out of habit we drove them out too; not difficult, for they are surprisingly timorous and a war-whoop or two would send them cantering, shocked, little spurts of dust shooting from their hooves as they clattered on the baked-earth surface of the drive.

They were less stubborn than the sheep that came in one day, looking for good grazing. Sheep do not roam freely in Sudan; this one must have detached itself from its flock on the way through town, either while being taken to market or driven across the Atbara River from Abuda in search of richer pastures. I found it chomping happily near Hamid's bed one clear blue afternoon in winter, and it was quite placid until I tried to shoo it out. Then it rebelled. A stupid, trusting creature with shaggy brown coat and long ears and tail; as I tried to push its rump it stood its ground, and I felt rather a fool, shoving as hard as I could while it turned and looked at me, distressed, betrayal and reproach in its big, liquid, dark-brown eyes.

We did have one pet I would have been pleased to see the back of. Bernadette the turkey liked to crap in the shower. And when not harassing the six or seven chickens who also lived in the Showak compound, she would pick and peck her way towards the *rakuba*, a wide canopy of woven rush that provided shade; there, she would find an iron chair that was occupied by a human being and peck at any flesh that was exposed through the gaps between the slats of the upright. Often after I returned from work at 2.30 I would slump into one of the white-painted seats with a glass of tea, only to feel Bernadette's beak upon my buttocks.

I suggested to Ian, my compound-mate, that she be dispatched at Christmas, some weeks hence. American friends suggested that Thanksgiving would be more appropriate. Ian agreed that she should go at Christmas, however, betraying a promise to the previous occupant of my *tukl* that she be spared.

"Whatever you do," he had said to me during a brief meeting in Khartoum before his departure, "make sure that Ian doesn't murder Bernadette for the pot at Christmas. I know he's thinking of it."

I promised solemnly that I would protect Bernadette with my life. That was before she started pecking my backside through the seat-back; and I realized, too, that her toilet-habits were incompatible with my own.

"The Sudanese," said Ian loftily, "always wear flip-flops in the shower. Anyway, you should make sure that the door is kept closed, then she couldn't do it."

When darkness fell, Bernadette always retreated to the top of a six-foot-high wall of woven rush that bordered the chicken-run. She perched on top and went peacefully to sleep; the chickens flew one by one to join her and I watched them crouch, untroubled, the electric light outside the latrine shining through their feathers so that they seemed incandescent in the hot, velvet night. By now Hamid, the *gafir*, or guard, would have arrived, and said his prayers for sundown; a series of mutters were delivered sotto voce towards Mecca as he knelt on the ground, having completed his ritual washing. His sword hung on the wall of my *tukl*, ready to repel invaders. When he had fnished I sometimes brought him tea, strong and sweet, served in a glass, without milk; then he settled down on the *anquarayb*, a bed of string woven in a fine pattern across a wooden frame, cool in the heat as it let the breeze, such as it was, blow against your skin through the gaps in its skein.

*** *** ***

IAN HAD not appeared in the least put out by the descent, unannounced, from Khartoum of a stranger to share his compound, which for a while had been solely his. A complex, capable man of about my age, he was helping to run the water team, a division of the COR workshop which maintained pump-engines in the refugee settlements, and he travelled widely through the region fighting the effects of age, dust and neglect.

Ian had himself only been in Showak for nine months or so, but had integrated himself into the life of the place to a far greater extent than most foreigners in Showak could or would. He spoke some Arabic, and later came to write it as well. From him, I learned a lot about the place I had come to live in. He started by impressing upon me the difference in cultures. "These guys squat to pee," he told me. "I'd noticed," I replied, somewhat stiffly. But he was a mine of information on how to cope with the town, where to buy food, everyday words and phrases, and, crucially, manners. Taking me to eat once, he explained the need to wash one's hands vigorously and publicly before sitting down in a restaurant, the sort of thing I might not quickly have noticed. Then, concerned that I might feel lectured, he added: "You don't mind me telling you all this cultural stuff, do you?" On the contrary, I was very grateful.

Although two more volunteers, Simon and Wayne, would join us in the coming months, Ian and I were the only occupants for now. But we were hardly alone. For a start, there was Hamid. Quite a few compounds, and all with foreigners, had a *gafir*. Although violent crime was extremely rare within the town itself, burglary was not, perhaps sometimes motivated by desperation. It was a good idea to have a guard, and Hamid kept out all unwanted visitors, admitting no-one unless they could give some good reason why they were there at night.

Hamid was a pastoralist. His herds were wherever good grazing was available, sometimes many tens of kilometres away; and sometimes he would go there, being replaced for a week or two by his son, Ahmed. Ahmed was not so bright as his father, and although not lax, was not really so conscientious. Grizzled old Hamid himself was a pro. At one stage Ian and he had a bet that Ian could not remove his sword, undetected, while Hamid lay sleeping. Gafirs were not supposed to sleep. They were supposed to patrol the perimeter fence, but I never saw any *gafir* do anything other than sleep at night, lying peacefully on his *anquarayb*. Ian had picked up some intestinal bug; it didn't seem to bother him much, but he was often up at night, and on his way he would sneak over to where Hamid's sword hung beside the aluminium container in which he kept milk and porridge. As Ian's hand approached the tasselled sheath, Hamid would open one eye (perhaps it was not worth the effort of opening both) and mutter, 'I can see you...' Ian would then stomp off towards the pit-latrine to perform the real business of the night.

Besides Hamid, we had neighbours. When the first VSOs had come to Showak, years before the Emergency, they had built the compound in open country a kilometre or two from the souk, reasoning that that would give them more peace on Friday, the Moslem Sabbath. But Showak, unfettered by planning constraints, had come out to meet them, and new compounds had clustered around them like antibodies. Now, the next-door compound was the home of Kafi, a Hausa.

Hausas are of course associated with West, not East, Africa, but for centuries they had travelled through Sudan on their way to and from the Haj, the pilgrimage to Mecca. A minority, unable to face the long journey back across Darfur and Chad to Nigeria, stopped and

Beiram Eid: The neighbours come to visit

put down roots. They spoke Arabic in public, but retained Hausa for
their own use. They did many useful jobs, from some of which they
had latterly been displaced by Eritrean refugees. Those still in their
hands included manning river-crossings and boats, and making the
alloy pots and pans that everyone uses in the region; this last was done
by a large Hausa community at Garb-el-Gash, on the outskirts of
Kassala. Their status was uncertain. The first Hausas had arrived several hundred years ago, the last in the 1940s; but they were not automatically given Sudanese passports if they asked for them. I do not
know that they were unpopular, however; I got the impression that
they were well-tolerated.

Kafi neither made pots and pans, nor guided men through fords.
He appeared to have been some kind of healer or traditional medical
practitioner. He always struck me as jovial enough, although I didn't
know him well. I do not know how many wives Kafi had (a Moslem
may of course have four), but I do know that he had 17 children, the
oldest of which was in her late teens and had six toes on one foot.
Occasionally she and the younger members of the family would spill
over into our compound to chat, drink tea, listen and dance to Zairean

music on our portable tape recorders or otherwise make harmless nuisances of themselves. On the feast days that marked the end of Ramadan, and the Beiram Eid 40 days later, it was the custom to lay out a plate of sweets or *taradas* (25-piastre notes) for the local children, who would come round unescorted, in their best clothes, to be greeted and given them. They were always rather shy, like young carol-singers at Christmas; and of course that was the nearest equivalent, although in Showak they simply dressed their best instead of singing carols. They were always polite. Kafi's children were the best turned-out of all, and I took a picture of them wearing immaculately-pressed 'fifties-style children's dresses, ears hung with bright baubles, and carrying neat plastic handbags in bright, attractive colours that reflected the glare of the July sun (it was Beiram Eid, 1989). They stayed for a while that day, to dance to the Zairean tapes we played them after they rejected Michael Jackson, put on at their request.

They liked to party. All Kafi's household did, and music and dancing could be heard through the hedge on any Thursday night; as a Moslem household they eschewed alcohol, but that did nothing to damp their natural gaiety. Sometimes the women would ullulate loudly, a habit that scared me when I first arrived. While Ian was away wrestling with a Lister diesel in some distant settlement, my quiet hour with Beethoven and a book would often be interrupted by the fierce whoops of the women next door.

*** *** ***

IF MIRIAM was not in the compound, then one of her children would be. Ian and I paid her S.60 a month each to do our washing-up, washing and ironing. Later, when Wayne and Simon arrived, they paid her the same amount. A princely £20 a month to support a family. "We're exploiting her," Ian would say in one mood; then, in another, he would remember that his own boss paid less than half that to the woman who looked after his own household. Probably Miriam did better than most in that situation, but there was no doubt that she was desperately poor.

She was about 27, and lived in a *tukl* across the yard behind our compound with her children, Ahmed, Awadea and Noora, aged nine, eight and six; a new baby arrived in February 1988. Despite this, her husband divorced her. I only met him once; rather older, and very quiet. They joined us for tea one evening, but he said little. Not long afterwards, he decided she must go.

I doubt if it made much difference to Miriam. He already spent most of his time in the city of Gedaref, 60 kilometres away, with the other of his two wives. In Islam, a man may divorce at will, provided he has witnesses; a woman has little say in the matter. But he is not supposed to acquire a further wife if he cannot already meet his obligations to those he has, and must treat them all equally. Neither does he rid himself of this obligation on divorce. Miriam went to the Shari'a court in Gedaref and took her husband to the cleaners, much to our delight.

But Miriam's life was hard, and the coming of a new child made it no easier. I suppose we should not really have been surprised that she made Ahmed, Awadea and Noora do some the work. And in truth, the children were far from unhappy; the harder they worked, the more polite and cheerful they seemed to be. Attractive, disciplined and clever, they scrubbed, washed, ironed and laughed. But they were very shy, especially Noora, who would talk to you but quietly, her hands cupped next to your ear.

If Ian asked her, Miriam would bring us a *jebenah*. This was a flask, round at the base and long in the neck, in which coffee was made; the beans were ground and then put in with water at the flask's base; the *jebenah* was placed on the *kanoon*, the frame of angle-iron supporting glowing charcoal on which all cooking was done. As it boiled and brewed, the coffee was passed in and out of the flask, often into a jug fashioned from a dried-milk tin. A little cinammon or ginger might be added, and it was then decanted into tiny handleless cups called *funjals* which, disappointingly, tended to be made in China. Into the base of the *funjal* the server had already put a large amount of coarse brown sugar, usually about half the cup; the coffee was drunk very strong and sweet and was topped up as you drank, so that none of the sweetness was lost. Normally, a *jebenah* would fill three *funjals*. Three cups was the normal amount that a polite guest will drink in the Arab world. It was wonderful coffee, especially when accompanied by a strong rough Nyala cigarette that had been smuggled across the border from Ethiopia; and the coffee's richness stayed at the back of the mouth for hours afterwards. The ability to make a good *jebenah* was held in high regard, and it was important that a guest should enjoy it. Once, Ian drank coffee at the house of an acquaintance and made the mistake, when asked, of saying that he should have preferred a touch less cinammon. He never heard the last of it, being asked thereafter whether the *jebenah* was satisfactory every time he called. But I never had one I didn't enjoy, and Miriam's were flawless.

Miriam was not really Sudanese at all, being from the Beni Amer tribe, pastoralists who wandered up and down the border. If anything they were probably Eritrean, but like many such Eritrean tribes they were Moslem, speak Arabic (albeit in their own dialect) and had always had close links with the people of Sudan. Miriam was, in fact, a refugee, but I don't know to what extent she saw herself as one. In any case, she lived in the town, and her children went to Sudanese schools. Interestingly, her husband's family did live in the nearby refugee settlement of Abuda. But, like many in that particular settlement, they were well-to-do; Ian told me they had much livestock, including camels.

Of all the children, I suppose I knew Ahmed the best, perhaps because he was the oldest and easiest to communicate with despite still painful shyness. One day, as the rains were beginning during my first summer, I went round the corner of the chicken-run to go to the latrine and saw Ahmed, immobile, crouching on the ground and apparently staring into space. What was odder yet was that Ian and Simon and Wayne were also squatting on their haunches and looking in the same direction.

I moved forward, but Wayne motioned me to stop. Without really knowing why, I crouched on my haunches beside them. Then Ahmed, smiling slightly, scattered breadcrumbs on the ground some way in front of us, stepped back, and waited. We all waited.

First one or two, then several birds descended. They were the size of a large sparrow, with handsome yellow breasts that set off their grey feathers. They pecked at the crumbs for a minute or two before Ahmed jerked his hand, and I saw that he was holding the end of a fine wire. The wire ran out across the ground between the bread-crumbs and in several places had been carefully looped, so that when Ahmed pulled it with the right amount of force the loops closed up and caught one of the birds around the leg. Like a fisherman, Ahmed reeled it towards him. He neatly broke the bird's wings and it was laid, disabled, on the ground behind another, also unable to fly. It looked cruel, but I doubt if Ahmed thought of it that way; almost certainly they were destined for the pot.

That was in July 1988. The rains were gathering strength, and within a month the whole of Eastern Sudan was in the grip of a malaria epidemic that would kill ten thousand before it was done. It took little Ahmed without much warning; as soon as he felt unwell, Miriam took him to the local hospital. They discharged him the next morning, saying he would be fine. He sickened further the following day and returned to the hospital, where he died in the night.

I was away in Khartoum, buying print, and did not discover what had happened until I returned after a long absence, in October. Miriam had little to say about it, but looked older. I gave her a photograph I had taken of Ahmed with the birds he had trapped, and she seemed pleased. But she never mentioned Ahmed again. Later I heard that there had been another, much older, child that had died a few years earlier. Child mortality in Sudan is high, and I suppose she saw nothing unusual in her loss.

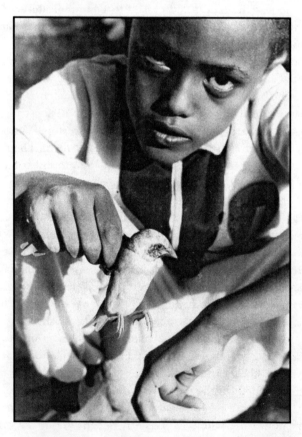

"...a photograph of Ahmed with the birds he had trapped"

*** *** ***

I HAD my own problems with malaria. One night in Khartoum, a few days after my arrival, I had enjoyed an illicit drinking session on Ethiopian cognac with friends on the roof of their flat; during the evening I was badly bitten on the forearms, but thought little of it at the time. I got malaria, and sometimes wonder if being exposed at that early stage caused the bouts I had later, for most Europeans didn't suffer that badly.

The disease struck on my third day in Showak. I awoke at 5.30, feeling slightly unwell; half an hour later I felt suddenly sick and rushed for the latrine, but failed to get there in time and threw up all over the floor of my *tukl* instead. The suddenness of it shocked me. I took the emergency dose of six chloroquine tablets, then went to bed again and slept for 12 hours. When I woke up again, I felt much better. But it would be about 10 days before I really felt normal.

The attack left me weak; I also felt rather isolated. And hungry. I had hardly had time to get into the rhythm of shopping for food as it is done in Sudan, and anyway the souk was about a mile away; too far to walk after malaria in a temperature of 110 deg F in the shade (and there was no shade on the way to the souk). I wasn't yet confident enough to ride the motorbikes we had in the compound, and they were notoriously unreliable anyway.

Not without sympathy, Ian, who rarely cooked, took me to the souk in the evening in the white Toyota pick-up truck that he used for work. This had an instrument panel like a Jumbo jet's, and a large pair of *dik-dik* (oryx) horns lashed to the grille. This journey to the souk in the evenings became a pattern. At six Hamid would arrive - a little earlier if he planned to water the trees; then he would say his prayers. When he was done, we would wedge back the gates and set off, the last light dying in the sky, our faces bathed in the surreal glow of the instrument panel, which included a turn-and-bank indicator with a neat little graphic of a car tilting alarmingly. We would bump and sway at 15-20 miles per hour past the concrete blocks of the new compound and onto the football field where the children of the district had just finished their afternoon game; then enter a long, narrow dust road, just wide enough for two cars to pass, although if a souk-truck came the other way you quickly ran the wheels up the verge.

The road was flanked by walls the height of a man. Behind them, low, square houses of one storey were surrounded by a *hosh*, or yard.

Therein the *gafir* of each household, prayers done, was settling down to a night's sleep untroubled by the thought of the burglars who certainly might come. A short way down was one house flying a red flag from a pole; for months I thought it a mark of allegiance (there was a mature Marxist party in Sudan). Later I found out that it was simply the flag of a Khartoum football-team, Merikh.

Just over halfway to the souk, we arrived at Beshir's. A Pepsi at Beshir's shop was part of the evening ritual. Everyone drank Pepsi in Sudan if they could afford it, Coca-Cola having pulled out after a row about the repatriation of profits.

Beshir's shop was typical of the Sudanese store, a narrow shopfront across the width of the building, entirely spanned by the counter; and covered during the day by lurid zinc shutters that stuck out into the street and deflected the sun. On the counter stood plastic bowls of dried, flaked fruit, in a series of muted colours; sugar; and salt. An ancient set of brass scales stood beside them, and each purchase was carefully measured with a series of weights-kilo, half-kilo and *rottl*, which was about a kilo. The commodity requested would be poured off the measuring-tray and down a funnel of newspaper which, shaped like a cone, would be neatly closed off at the top so as to make an easy-to-carry vessel. Beshir himself, slim and young - not more than 25 - and usually smiling, with a thin pencil moustache and white *djellabiya*, would be laughing and joshing as he rolled up the newspaper. Sudan imported cast-off newspapers for wrapping goods. One day, one might have one's sugar or karkadee wrapped in the *South China Morning Post*; the next, in the *Straits Times*. Dutch, Danish and Indonesian newspapers were also common. Beshir would lay down the newspaper, ready to be rolled; and while he stacked his brass weights on the scales, one could read the television schedules for Copenhagen, or the racing programme for Nairobi or Hong Kong while standing in front of a tiny shop in a small town less than 100 miles from the mountains that rise out of the Middle Eastern plain to the fabled lands of the Queen of Sheba.

'*Peps - itneen, talata*' (two, three); another of the young men from Ian's workshop would arrive - "*arbaa, khamsa*" (four, five). And Beshir would hold out a bottle by its neck, the glass glistening with condensation from the refrigerator, so that Ian or I could lay a hand on it, test its coldness, and nod our approval, rather as one swills a little wine in the glass after it is uncorked at table.

"No *Peps*," Beshir would say gloomily if the electricity had been off, and he thought the Pepsi wasn't cool enough to sell. That often happened that autumn and winter, and we would instead load our pockets with *bazooka* -cheap chewing-gum from God knew where - and slope off to the souk, feeling vaguely cheated. But more often, everyone saw each other at Beshir's; a familiar face would appear, ambling slowly into the pool of light cast by the fluorescent strip across the top of the shop; or a small motorcycle would sweep into the glow, its rider sitting well back, djellabiya streaming in the wind; or litle knots of schoolgirls in pajama-suits and headscarves. Now and then women would float by in their *toabs*, the younger ones drawing our wistful glances.

*** *** ***

AFTER the aperitif, it was time for dinner.

The approach to the souk was through a side-street that was completely dark at night. The souk itself, about half a kilometre long and 100 metres wide, burst upon you as you rounded the corner from blackness to see row upon row of fluorescent lights across the tops of shops, restaurants and soft-drinks bars. At seven it was always busy. There were many shops like Beshir's; there was an ironmonger or two selling nuts and bolts and Bulgarian lightbulbs, and a cycle-shop, outside which were rows of small, heavy, old-fashioned Flying Pigeon bikes from China. These had recently supplanted the even older-styled bikes from India, and the people of Sudan were becoming acquainted with cable brakes and with pedals that flew off in the street. The soft-drinks bars sold Pepsi or its rival, Stim - the latter being cola, orange squash, or sweetened, sterilised milk. They also sold *basta*, which was thick sweet heavy pastry not unlike baklava in the Levant. Or you could have grapefruit juice, made in blenders and dispensed from great alloy pots made by the Hausas at Garb el-Gash. Or if one felt wealthy, there was *manga* - mango-juice.

In the centre of the souk were rows of four-wheel-drive vehicles; old Land-Rovers belonging to local businessmen, new ones from aid agencies, new Land-Cruisers driven by personnel from the UN High Commissioner for Refugees (UNHCR) and Government officials, and ancient ones belonging to the local traders who flogged them up from Gedaref in the early morning, laden with vegetables and fruit. Sometimes there were souk-trucks, though these usually parked in an impressive phalanx behind the meat-market. There were pale blue

Mercedes lorries with the UNHCR crest; they carried food supplies to the refugee settlements in the region. And there were donkeys, waiting; not so much patient as apathetic.

In front of the soft-drinks bars stood the men of the town, out to meet their friends and talk. Women scurried between the groups of men, laden with heavy bags of shopping, bags of coarse fibre that for some reason often bore the mark of a Romanian cement-factory. Here and there a European drifted along in slacks and sandals, looking for cigarettes. And the fluorescent lamps lit the whole souk in a series of shadows and electric glows so that when you walked towards a restaurant and a large group of men came towards you, the fluorescence shone through their white cotton *djellabiyas*, shilhouetting the body and the baggy *sirwals* beneath; and these ghosts walked in clouds of fine dust that filled the air and also caught the light, like snow.

Beside the cars in the centre of the souk there crouched or squatted women with trays of nuts or *taamiya*, small hard balls of fried ful-beans that were salty and sharp on the tongue; and curious, plasticky envelopes of field-beans that one squeezed so that the seeds shot out into your mouth, bitter but full of calcium. They never looked at you as they did business, these women, and I suppose that for them there was little point in the ritual courtesies of buying and selling. People do not, out of habit, say please and thankyou in Sudan; but shopkeepers and waiters quite enjoyed the foreign way of doing so, finding it attractive rather than eccentric. But the women in this and other souks that crouched over their trays of peanuts always looked exhausted and resigned; it was a job for the very poorest.

We might, on arrival in the souk, decide on a takeaway, and go to one of the many *ful*-stands.

Ful-beans, also much eaten elsewhere in the Arab world, resemble kidney-beans and taste similar when eaten on their own, but are a little more bitter. They were cooked for hours, and kept warm in large vats that reached a man's waist and were shaped like milk-churns. One asked for however many ladlefuls of *ful* one wanted, and that number was placed in your plastic bowl. Then *sim-sim* - sesame-oil - was poured on them, and they were crushed with the end of a coke-bottle. That, for many people, was all that was eaten, once a day; nothing else. The cost was about 20 pence for two.

In later months, when food ran short, that was sometimes all that was available at any price. In November 1987, however, few people ate *ful* on its own unless they really were quite poor. In our case, it was always a luxury *ful*. The beans and the sesame-oil went into the bowl, and were given a preliminary crushing with the base of the coke-bottle, which was grasped by the neck and worked round and round. Then a salad of grated green vegetable and chopped fresh tomatoes would be scattered on the surface, followed by *jibna*, the fierce local cheese that couldn't be taken on its own, but lent spice to many things. This, too, would be grated vigorously and then powdered all over the *ful*.

If money was not too short, one would ask for an egg. Hard-boiled, it would be peeled on the spot and then grated with equal enthusiasm. Finally a little cumin would be sprinkled over the surface, and then the bottle would be grasped by its neck again and pummelled hard into the bowl until everything was reduced almost to a purée. Two loaves of round, flat Showak bread would then be slapped on top.

It was a poor thing, this bread. The wheat with which it was made was usually infested with weevils, and tasted of them. It didn't taste too bad if eaten fresh and hot, but if Gedaref bread, soft and oblong, was available, that was better. If, as was sometimes later the case, there was no bread around, then *ful* would not be served. This was because,

Awadea and her baby sister

45

as in all Arab countries, you ate with your right hand, not a knife and fork. Bread is used a scoop, and the two eaten together. This was a good source of carbohydrates, while the beans themselves provided protein, so all in all it was a pretty healthy meal.

Unless you'd brought your own bowl with you, the *ful* was poured into a thin plastic bag. It was advisable to use two or three *kiis*, as these bags were called, unless one wanted steaming hot *ful* pouring down into one's crotch on the way home in the car. The *kiis* were sold by small boys who darted around the souk and were onto you with cries of *kiis! kiis!* as soon as you reached the ful-stand.

Before pouring the goo into the *kiis* you might have added, not only salt, but a large amount of red pepper, the latter being known as *shatta*. The name was appropriate, as that was pretty much what happened if you took it to excess. The Sudanese used lots. Ethiopians of all nationalities used lots more. It was an essential source of vitamin A, and shortage of it was what had caused the Tigrayans to suffer from poor night vision on their terrible journey across the mountains two years previously.

Lots of *shatta* in one's meal was a source of macho pride, so shared meals could result in much sweat and a burning throat. For this, we got our revenge at an Eid barbecue some months later. It was Beiram Eid, 40 days after the end of Ramadan, and we had slaughtered a sheep in the compound. Set out with the char-grilled meat were little saucers of what we innocently called *shatta inglese*. "Be careful," we warned the 15 or so mechanics from the workshop who were our guests, with their brothers and fathers, that evening. "*Shatta inglese* is very hot." They didn't believe us, until they tasted Colman's Mustard.

I liked *ful* a lot, but it could get monotonous, and if we had the money we would go for a sit-down dinner. The Green Valley restaurant, the largest and most fashionable of several in the souk, was a brick building with a shack-like frontage; there was an inside room but we generally ate in the enclosure in front, in the open, where we could watch the world go by and where Ian's many friends could see and join us. The Green Valley was known to Europeans as Al Green's, as all but the a and l of Valley had disappeared from the English version of the sign tacked to the wall.

Al Green's did do *ful*, but not particularly well; you didn't go there for that. Instead we would treat ourselves to a half-chicken (very small, scrawny, but with taste) or *kostaleti*, little cutlets of lamb that were dipped in a secret sauce, different everywhere, and deep-fried.

These were excellent. Better still, money permitting, was *chaya*, small lumps of meat braised on stones heated directly by charcoal. Everywhere I saw *chaya* prepared, it was done by a man working on his own, outside the main restaurant. You paid him separately; he had no direct connection with the restaurant. *Chaya* was in fact only sporadically available at Al Green's, because the *chaya*-man was in and out of prison all the time.

The tables were unsteady, flat tin devices. They were shoved together, so that you would often find yourself eating with several other people. "*Fadl*," you would then say. This is a word that has no direct translation in English; it means go on, help yourself, have some of mine. Two people in a doorway will politely *fadl* each other (after you). In a restaurant, it means, share our food; and I don't think I ever sat at a table with a strange Sudanese, even in Khartoum, without hearing this word that the English do not have. At the time, I connected it in my mind with religion, and to be sure generosity is an important part of Islam; but I think it was also good manners. Often, in the Green Valley, our *ful*-bowl would be replenished by the contents of someone else's, which would then be tossed aside; and they would share some of our *chaya*. It was automatic and pleasant.

I was often ill in Sudan but not usually with stomach-trouble. Customers washed their hands very thoroughly before entering the restaurant, using taps mounted on an old oil-drum and the coarse purple soap provided. In the restaurant, they ate strictly with their right hands (though you could use both hands to break bread). Probably the men who prepared the food were just as scrupulous. My first sight of the restaurant's interior horrified me; the kitchen looked especially dingy. But there was a view that dirt was quite harmless unless it got into your food, and my stomach seemed to agree.

*** *** ***

AFTER a week in Showak I had seen only the inside of our compound, the souk, and the inside, briefly, of the other compound where volunteers lived. Malaria was mainly responsible for this. But late one afternoon Ian said he would drive me to the river in the Government pick-up.

Two miles from us, on the other side of the town centre, the river went under various names; on the world atlas it is called the River Atbara, but I often heard the name Settit mentioned. It rose in

Ethiopia and wound its way across Eastern Sudan to join the Nile at the city of Atbara itself, many hundreds of miles away to the north of Khartoum.

We left the compound at a quarter to five. The afternoon was softening, and the sky was turning a darker blue. The boys still played on the football field. Beshir hadn't opened yet. People were just beginning to stir after the afternoon sleep. The sun, starting to slant, slowly turned the dust surface of the road from light grey to brown, and the grubby bricks of the *hosh* walls took on a new life. We rattled and bumped past the tree at the entrance to the souk, where men sometimes sold fish - Nile carp, or tilapia; and turned right through a similar street, instead of going left into the souk itself. The street narrowed, then opened out into a wasteland, after which the houses gave way to huts. We picked our way between them, the track very narrow now, and the flanks of the Land-Cruiser almost scratching the mesquite hedges; and then started to go down a steep hill with switchbacks and troughs in which four-wheel-drive was needed. The huts gave way to poorer ones, and finally to hovels of cardboard, some with a slab of corrugated iron to deflect the sun. There were one or two goats; men and women lay on *anquaraybs* in front of the hovels; and then they, too, were gone and we were heading down yet more steeply, towards a wide, flat valley in which the blue ribbon of the Atbara glittered in the distance. Beyond it, the bank rose just as steeply towards the refugee camp of Abuda, which was over the horizon; the road twisted its way up through a cleft. Then it continued some hours' drive to the Ethiopian frontier at Humdeit. Of dirt, deeply rutted, and just wide enough to accommodate a Bedford truck, this track is shown on the Michelin map of north-east Africa as an international highway. It is.

On our own side was a beach of packed mud, perfectly flat, and we bounced down to this and levelled out towards the water's edge. The river was falling, for it was winter, and the rains were well over. It was only 400 yards wide, and one could wade across if one knew one's way. In the shallows near the beach stood two souk-trucks and a pair of small Hilux pickups; the royal blue of the truck cabs gleamed richly in the lowering sun as boys, stripped to the waist, moved around them with rags to remove the dust of the day. Meanwhile the drivers of the Hiluxes were disconnecting their fanbelts, ready to plunge across the river to Abuda.

It was a ford, but when I saw a truck go across from our side, I noticed that it did not go direct; instead, it zigzagged, guided by two men in long shorts and, for some reason, woollen skull-caps, who took a few *gineih* from the driver for providing this service. This was just one of the odd jobs that the Hausas did; and it was best to trust them, for at least one UNHCR official attempted to cross without their guidance and dumped his Land-Cruiser nose-first in an enormous underwater pothole. It took a couple of camels to haul him out.

On the bank some yards down I saw, to my surprise, an old-fashioned boat of some 40-50 feet, complete with a separate wheelhouse. It was high and dry. I commented to Ian that this was a bit like having the *Queen Mary* to take you across the Thames but he replied that this was not so; when the wet season began across the border in Eritrea, even that big boat would have to cross with care. And when the river was really flowing strongly, it wouldn't be able to cross at all.

For now, however, the river flowed gently. Behind us, where the dunes came down to the beach, there were patches of bright green; these were irrigated by single-cylinder Lister diesels whose chugging could just be heard in the stillness of the evening. These patches were the work of men who had found employment building the trunk road when it was forced through from Gedaref to Kassala in 1979; they had sunk their earnings into a plot by the river and a Lister to make their vegetables grow. It was a good business.

The sky had now deepened further in colour, and the water with it. From the east bank came a man on a camel. The camel stepped cautiously into the water; behind it, it dragged an enormous clump of brushwood, like several bushes. It was for heat and fuel, but later I learned that illicit liquor also crossed the border in these branches. On the camel was a man of, probably, the Hadendowa border tribe, carrying a whip; he knew the way and needed no Hausa to guide him. The camel's legs broke the surface of the water and sent little droplets into the light; the current, such as it was, tugged at the dun fur, and the water rose in rounded crests around the legs. The beast seemed to take a thousand years to reach us, but was unworried about this, as was its rider. His face was impassive, his whip unused in his hand. He greeted the truck-cleaners quietly as the camel stepped onto the bank, and then he passed us, the camel rolling to port and starboard with a pitch that must have been as familiar to the Disciples as it was to us. We could see man and camel for 10 or 15 minutes afterwards, slowly climbing the winding track to the town.

One afternoon, months later, I was sitting in one of the cushioned garden chairs, outside the kitchen. Wayne was with me, and we were leaning back gazing at the sky. Its colour, during the day, was bleached to so pale a blue that it was almost white but now, at about five, it had become vibrantly blue and had a transparent air to it, as if you could look straight through to Heaven.

There were snowy egrets in the town, nesting in the neem-trees in the souk. Every now and then something would startle them and they would scatter into the sky above the Green Valley, wheeling and darting. But today, there were eight or nine of them flying in neat formation, line-abreast, then wheeling around so that the line formed a shallow half-oval, then straightening the front of the formation only, so that they were like a flying question-mark. They held this shape, and soared higher and higher; we could see them clearly for perhaps a quarter of an hour, and because we knew they were there we could track them for longer, higher and higher, clean white birds against a sky as blue and translucent as layered lacquer. To the end of my life, I will always look forward to that time on a summer's day when the afternoon mellows, and the sky comes slowly to life between full day and sunset.

Chapter Three

December 1987: *Oliver Twist and Ethiopia*

At length my strength returmed, and it was time to start my job and get to grips with the Sudanese way of work.

Once, when the Arabic teacher, Abdel Moneim, was trying to explain to me what I would find in Sudan, he described an incident before independence, in the Law Department in Khartoum. A British administrator had read details of a case in which the appellant was, in his view, being importunate. He scrawled across the margin: "This reminds me of the case of Oliver Twist!" Some hours later, his Sudanese assistant was found searching the files for the case of Oliver Twist, which he assumed must demonstrate a precedent in law.

Now the boot was on the other foot, with foreigners as bewildered by the Sudanese administration as the Sudanese had ever been by theirs. Over the next two years I was to be offered numerous reasons why my wages were late, or there was no diesoline, or we could not obtain advance expenses to travel to Khartoum before Ramadan, or we could not obtain advance expenses to travel to Khartoum after Ramadan, or there was no money to pay my wages. Sudanese colleagues would insist that this was the result of three centuries of corrupt and lazy Turco-Egyptian administration over which the British had presided only briefly. Moneim himself argued that the British had promoted people who would get the job done without asking too many questions - that is to say, efficient, perhaps honest, but lacking in imagination; and that this legacy had come down to modern Sudan. Personally, I thought it was just the heat.

Richard Dowden, Africa correspondent of *The Independent*, once addressed the subject in an engaging piece called *On Carrot Soup in the Bath*. (The title referred to the water filtration in Khartoum's Grand Hotel.) Bureaucracy in Sudan, he explained, was as lousy as everywhere else in Africa, but it did at least come with charm. I will endorse this. Even as the official sat behind his desk explaining (quite sincerely) that something could not be done until there was a Z in the month but would then be no problem, he would be knocking his palm against the spring-loaded, chrome-plated bell that adorns every official desk in the nation, summoning a secretary who would enter, *toab* swirling gracefully in any breeze there might be, with your glass of hot sweet tea spiced with cinammon.

I am sure that my first year in Showak and, particularly, Khartoum shortened my life by decades; during my second year, however, I reacted by sitting around chatting with friends in the office (I could speak some Arabic by then, which helped) and then found that my travel permits/diesoline requisition/signed invoice appeared when I least expected them. In the early months, I had wondered whether the Sudanese derived some amusement from torturing Europeans in this way. Later, I realised that they were very rarely malicious about anything (although Europeans, behind closed doors, were frequently malicious about them); and that they probably found European impatience puzzling.

More often than not, one's interminable waits in offices were occasioned by the need for a *warriga*. A *warriga* was any official piece of paper. To obtain a travel permit, a foreigner or a refugee had to collect two or three from local officials or employers, and take these round to be stamped by several different officers at the city police station, 60 kilometres away; at a certain stage these documents had to have a revenue stamp affixed, and a whole cottage industry had grown up to supply these stamps outside Gedaref police station, which demanded these but did not supply them. Boys at these stands also supplied tissues, cigarettes and tea to sustain the hopeful traveller.

Neither were travel permits the only *warriga* one needed. Requisitions for diesoline at the Commissioner for Refugees (COR) office for which I worked had to be signed by the General Project Manager, the chief driver, the head of administration, the head of the workshop and I think the head of the Commodity Logistics Unit as well. All were quite reasonable men, but were hardly likely to be in one place at the same time. Thus it was not uncommon to rejoice in getting a *warriga* signed, only to find that all that had been achieved was to get permission for it to be signed by someone else. Usually, we got four out of five to find that the fifth was out to lunch or had gone to visit relatives at Darfur or Port Sudan. Sometimes, I got other people to do the chasing of signatures for me, reasoning that since they knew the language and the officials better, they would be able to do it more quickly. If anything, this was worse. One would spend hours wondering if the warriga in question had been forgotten. I think the Water Team had the worst problem with this. Many a time they would receive an urgent message that the pump engine was broken in some far-off refugee camp, leaving 10,000 people without water; they would then hasten to put hoist and tools on the back of the Toyota, and fill in the forms for fuel, only to spend two days waiting for the signature of some wretched functionary who had probably gone to visit his family.

Physically, at least, the Sudanese office was uncluttered. There would be a bare floor, thick walls to keep out the heat, and a high ceiling. There might be a tin cupboard, and there would be plain steel desks, the drawers of which never seemed to run smoothly. There was a plain steel-frame chair with a plastic wove body on seat and back, and around the edges of the offices (always the edges, with geometrical precision) there would be steel-framed easy chairs; low, comfortable, with thick cushions. There would be as many chairs as could be placed with their backs against the wall. In any office, there might be several people sitting, chatting, drinking tea, reading the paper or, towards midday, simply slumped over with sweat pouring down their cheeks, comatose.

There was rarely, if ever, any paper on the desks. This puzzled me at first; until, always untidy, I left a few papers on my own. Paper in Sudan was always foolscap, and unbelievably light. It tore easily. Worse, a slight breeze was enough to send it floating into the centre of the room, and picking it up was felt to be undignified; I never saw any Sudanese official do it himself. Even on still days, the electricity in Showak cut in and out so often that I kept leaving work on my steel desk while it was off, and then coming back in to find that the fan had re-started and documents were scattered all over the room like confetti.

There was little else on the desks. There might be the stainless-steel clockwork bell for summoning the messenger, as they called the office-boy. In Khartoum there might be a telephone as well, but there was no line to Showak (we were linked to the camps, and to Khartoum and Gedaref, by VHF).

In any case, the telephone was of limited use, as many numbers were unobtainable. It was often easier to ring London from Khartoum than it was to get Omdurman. After the catastrophic flood of 1988, many more lines ceased to function altogether, so that it was common to ask someone for their number and be told gravely that the 'phone hadn't worked "since before the flood". Even before that, a worker in VSO's London headquarters had dialled the number of the field director's private home in Khartoum, only to be told by the international operator in Sudan that it was unobtainable. Why? she asked. "Well, all numbers beginning with seven are unobtainable, of course," replied the operator.

"Of course," replied the worker, and rang off, feeling rather foolish.

*** *** ***

OUR OWN office had been built in the early 1970s when it was first decided to administer the refugee-settlement programme centrally from the town. By the time I arrived in late 1987, to join the fledgling public relations department run by a refugee journalist, Berhane Woldegabriel, the office had grown. Built in an L shape around a dusty yard adjoining the main souk, it was a two-storey concrete block with six offices on each wing, and numerous outhouses and ancillary buildings. These included a cool conference-room that was not without elegance.

From these offices 40 or 50 civil servants, detached from every major department in the Government to deal with the refugee crisis, oversaw the settlement of about a third of a million Ethiopians, Eritreans and Tigrayans. They were the cream of the civil service, all hand-picked, and were probably the best people in Sudan that I could have been given the chance to work with. It was some time before I saw past the frustrations of everyday working life to realise this.

Across the way from my own office was that of Suleiman Osman, supervisor of water services, and Ian's boss; a strong man intellectually, prone to sharpness, but also capable of great kindness. Next door to him was the head of construction, El Hadi, who was older, with courtly manners and genuine charm. Across the yard Ibrahim Omer, 30 years with the Gezira Development Board, had arrived to oversee the setting-up of a community development unit. Above me was a friendly south Sudanese, Dr Alex, who had spoke Italian, English and some French and German, Arabic and presumably the Dinka language as well. He was trying, against the odds, to co-ordinate the work of the 50 or so voluntary agencies known as NGOs, or non-governmental organizations, a quarrelsome maelstrom of Sudanese, Ethiopian, English, French, Dutch and American aid workers. He brought great tact to a difficult job. Dinkas are usually at least six foot tall; Dr Alex was about five foot and knew that grace was more useful than aggression.

There were many more of them. Dr Omer Mekki, head of medical services, was concise with a dry wit. Mohammed Tom, head of the workshop and deputy general project manager, was kind and unbureaucratic. Hamed El Haj was seeking to bring refugee enterprises within the Sudanese cooperatives movement, and drove me hundreds of miles to see his projects, which included recycling of molasses and fish-farming. Zahra Mirghani was the head of nutrition. She was responsible for ensuring that COR knew exactly how much the 234,000 refugees in the settlements were getting to eat, whether it was enough, and whether it was the right stuff. This was a difficult job, of which more later. She was, I think, a devout Muslim, and I remember she wore a headband which resembled that of the Moslem Sisters. Sudanese Islam was not completely monolithic with regard to women, and although Zahra was unusual in being a woman in senior management, she was not alone.

Showak from the office roof, complete with traditional tukls, mud-brick hosh walls and zinc or corrugated-iron doors

We all worked for one man. The General Project Manager was responsible for a quarter of a million refugees; all those, in fact, who were in settlements in the region, rather than in the towns. In most respects he also controlled life in Showak.

Hassen Mohammed Osman was old by Sudanese standards; he was in his sixties, although I thought he looked younger. He had gone to the University of Khartoum in the days of British rule and then, I think, studied in England.

Ian had warned me from the beginning that he was an absolute monarch and that I should not cross him. "What he says goes," he said darkly. "This isn't England. One word from him and he can have you out of the country in 48 hours. The guys here are terrified of him." I was not reassured by early meetings with him; although polite, he was extremely brusque. He had many fewer words than the average Sudanese and tended to bark rather than talk, an impression strengthened by the way he had adapted the English language for extreme brevity.

For eight years, until his removal by the then-new Beshir regime in 1989, Hassen Osman struggled with the problem of settling growing numbers of refugees in regions that could barely support their own people. In 1984-85, he had to face the events that followed the famines in Ethiopia and Sudan, when some 20,000 people a month fled across the nearby border. But he had retained considerable humanity and commitment to liberal values in the treatment of refugees. In retrospect, I am very pleased to have worked for him.

Hassen's strong personality was indispensable, for he was a key player in a refugee crisis that was becoming very hard for Sudan. By the time I arrived in there, it was in an almost unique position among refugee-hosting countries. It had the largest refugee population in Africa, a continent bedevilled by such movements. Globally, only Pakistan was host to a greater number. By 1987, refugees accounted for 1 in 20 of Sudan's population. To put that into perspective, one should imagine that between 1962 and 1987 Britain had accepted between two and three million completely destitute refugees of a race, creed and language different to the majority population.

In 1987, an official estimate by the United Nations High Commissioner for Refugees (UNHCR), disputed by Sudan, put the number of refugees in the country at 974,000. Of these, 677,000 were reckoned to be Amharic/Tigrayan/Eritrean with a sprinkling of ethnic groups from elsewhere in Ethiopia, such as Oromos. Probably it is these other groups that UNHCR underestimated, as many were self-settled, and no-one knew where they all were; they may have been nearer a million all told. On top of this there were 95,000 from Chad (down from 120,000 a couple of years earlier), and a further 5,000 in the south, from Zaire. The latter had been in Sudan many years. There had also, until recently, been 200,000 people from Uganda, but Sudan's Commissioner for Refugees and UNHCR were repatriating them; with increasing stability in Uganda and a worsening war in south Sudan, they were better off going home. None of these figures included several hundred thousand (maybe a million) displaced Sudanese citizens from the south, who had fled to Khartoum; as these were nationals, they were not the business of COR or UNHCR, but they were effectively refugees nonetheless.

It also has to be said that Sudan's own civil war had sent 350,000 Sudanese into southern Ethiopia, so it was a two-way trade. That was the rough figure in 1989, although things would later have changed.

Of the 677,000 Ethiopian refugees acknowledged by UNHCR to be in Sudan, about 400,000 were Eritrean; the remainder were Tigrayan or Amharic. (The Tigrayans had led many of their own people back to Tigray the previous year.) Some understanding of the relationship between these groups is necessary to understand why Sudan was faced with a refugee problem; they were not all there because of famine. Were that the case, a simpler answer would have been found eventually. Once again, however, what follows is a thumbnail sketch; more detailed information can be found elsewhere.

The Amharas were then still the dominant race in Ethiopia, as they were under Haile Selassie; he was a Shoan Amhara himself. Yet they only accounted for about a fifth of the population. Eritreans have a distinct culture of their own, and a different language, Tigrigna. A related dialect is spoken by Tigrayans. Eritrea is the northern part of Ethiopia through which, crucially, there is access to the sea.

Eritreans are a diverse bunch, as they themselves freely acknowledge. They came mostly from the Arabian Peninsula in the first century AD; Christians long before the Europeans, they sometimes seemed more European than African. But not all Eritreans speak Tigrigna. A large minority are lowland pastoralists, living in the mountains near the Sudanese border, rather than the higher ones further east. They often speak Arabic and are Moslem (Miriam was an example). Across these two distinct cultures there was a total of nine distinct linguistic sub-groups.

The Eritrean liberation movements seemed keenly aware of this diversity; the Amharas, by contrast, forced others to learn Amharic. A man from the Oromo people in Western Ethiopia once told me that he had been flummoxed by this when he first went to school. "I thought, these are wild animals speaking," he said. "This has nothing to do with us."

Why was Eritrea under Ethiopian rule, anyway? Historically it had been once, but not all the time. In any case, in the late 19th century Italy, like Germany a newly-unified state, was keen to join the scramble for Africa. One of the few areas not dominated by the British or the French was Ethiopia, which Italy invaded in 1894. They took Eritrea and advanced into Tigray, but here they werere heavily defeated by the Ethiopian Emperor Menelik I at the battle of Adowa. However, they retreated back into Eritrea, which they kept. Thus Eritrea and Tigray developed diferently, from Ethiopia, rather as Bohemia and Slovakia did, being dominated by Austria and Hungary respectively.

Meanwhile the Italians had still not forgotten the humiliation of Adowa. In 1935 they reinvaded Ethiopia. Ethiopian resistance was spirited and not ineffective, but Menelik I had not faced poison gas and aircraft. Ethiopia was occupied. Despite an impassioned plea by Haile Selassie from the podium of the League of Nations in Geneva, the rest of the world confined itself to sympathy.

A few years later, Italy's entry into a larger war found its armies in Ethiopia next door to the British in Sudan. Italy invaded, taking the city of Kassala and a strip of Eastern Sudan. It then made a major misjudgement. The terrain was difficult in the wet season, there were no real roads, there was little fresh water, and they lacked confidence in their ability to oppose a sustained British counterattack. So they stayed put in Kassala. In fact, the British commander in Khartoum, General Platt, possessed no forces of any substance; everything available had gone north to fight in the desert campaign. Undaunted, he sent what few troops he had on long journeys through the country, telling them to kick up as much dust as possible in order to mislead Italian reconnaissance.

It worked, and when in 1941 Platt was able to wrest a few extra troops out of Middle East command, he decided to 'have a go'. In the first lasting British land victory of the war, a combined British and Ethiopian force pushed their way north from south Sudan towards Addis. Meanwhile, British and Indian troops pushed the Italians in the north back into Eritrea as far as Keren, where two crack Italian Alpine regiments, ably assisted by loyal local troops, made a determined stand. After one of the least-known and bloodiest battles in the African war they were dislodged, and the British swept on down to the sea at Massawa. According to Richard Dimbleby, who followed the campaign all the way from Kassala and described it wonderfully in his book *The Frontiers are Green*, the Italian commander went down to the quay to symbolically snap his sword across his knee. It refused to break, bending instead. In a fit of petulant disgust the Italian, to Dimbleby's glee, threw it into the water.

The British mopped up the Italians from the rest of Ethiopia and brought Haile Selassie back from exile in Khartoum, but they kept their troops in Eritrea. They were not sure what to do with it. Haile Selassie argued that it was part of Ethiopia; but the British were not sure that the Eritreans wished it to be. So they stayed on while the United Nations tried to sort out some sort of settlement. In 1952, the United Nations finally decided that Eritrea would be federated (not united) with Ethiopia for 10 years, after which a plebiscite would be held. The British seem to have had some doubts as to whether the Ethiopians would really discharge their obligations under this settlement, but decided not to question it, and withdrew.

The plebiscite was indeed held in 1962, but the result - a predictable vote for unity - was rejected at once by the Eritreans, who started to fight. They would fight for nearly 30 years.

*** *** ***

HAILE SELASSIE was deposed in 1974. In 1975 power passed to an army officer, Mengistu Haile Mariam. Shortly afterwards the deposed emperor himself died in circumstances still unclear, apparently by the hand of Mengistu personally.

It was a significant accession with two immediate major consequences. First of all, Ethiopia had always been supplied with matériel by the United States, while the Eritreans were underwritten by the Soviet Union - which also maintained good relations with Nimeiri in Sudan. Now Mengistu adopted socialism and turned to the Soviets for economic help and arms. It was received and within two years the Eritreans, who had been quite close to victory, faced defeat.

Secondly, Tigray also now rose in rebellion. It did not ask for independence; distrustful of its powerful neighbours, the Eritreans, and knowing that it could face territorial disputes with them, it opted instead for federation within Ethiopia: home rule. This was refused, and a second civil war began in parallel with the first. Meanwhile, Mengistu embarked upon a programme of calculated terror, the *fetasha*.

By 1987, however, huge tracts of Eritrea had already been liberated from Ethiopian rule, and these had hospitals, schools and orphanages, while the need for basic light-industrial goods such as drugs and sanitary towels was met with portable plants that could be moved swiftly across the mountains and set up underground in the event of an air attack. By the late 1980s, Eritrea had developed one of the few indigenous pharmaceutical industries in Africa, and it was completely mobile.

When I left Sudan in August 1989, the Eritrean army was dug in above Keren, where the Italian and British armies had faced each other nearly half a century before. The Ethiopian army, consisting mainly of impressed 'men' of 14-15 years of age, staged occasional forays against them, but were always repulsed. Further south, the Tigrayans - also busy organising mobile schools and hospitals and, in their case, even road-building - had set up a convoy system in and out of Sudan, fed by a spectacular transport depot in the East of Sudan (everyone knew where). They too had advanced, and were barely 200 miles from Addis Ababa. All of this had been achieved using captured weapons and, in the case of the Eritreans, what was left over from Russian aid 14 years earlier.

But there was still a war, and there were still refugees. Almost from the beginning in 1962, they had crossed the border into Sudan. But at that stage they caused few problems. Most were Moslems from the border tribes; some had relatives in Sudan; and in any case, the Sudanese interpretation of Islam would not have allowed it to refuse shelter to people in trouble, even if they had been *habbishers* (their name for Ethiopian Christians, vaguely perjorative). At that stage, few were.

It was not until 1967 that the Sudanese felt they should establish a formal structure for dealing with refugees, in the shape of the Commissioner for Refugees (COR); the Commissioner was an individual appointed by the State, but the name was also used for the administrative system he represented. However, it was another two or three years before the Sudanese decided to seek the assistance of the United Nations High Commissioner for Refugees (UNHCR); again, s/he is a person but the term is also applied to the body of which they are the head, so to speak.

There had never been any question of Sudan refusing to accept refugees. Apart from the tradition they have of hospitality-strong even by Moslem standards-the country is a signatory to the international conventions governing the status of refugees. These include the 1951 Geneva refugee convention, its 1967 protocol, and the Organization of African Unity agreement which is, if anything, even more liberal. Sudan did sign a reservation to the clause in the 1951 convention which permits free movement within the country of those to whom asylum has been granted. However, this only asks the host nation to permit such movement to the extent that any alien is entitled to it, and in the case of Sudan there was a system of internal travel permits for all non-nationals.

Sudan's overall attitude to refugees was decent. In 1974 it passed a liberal Asylum Act of its own, and this was still in force in 1987. It granted refugees equal rights to employment in all fields unrelated to national security, and provided for the granting of asylum to unaccompanied children. Best of all, it sanctioned the mass granting of asylum. (But not of citizenship; Eritreans who had actually been born in Sudan were not entitled to hold Sudanese passports. It must be said that, by and large, they did not want them. On several occasions Eritreans in their twenties spoke to me with sparkling eyes about 'going home', only to admit later that they had never been there.)

Eventually, however, the stress of increasing refugee movement across the border was bound to put this tolerance to the test. In 1985, the famine tipped no less than 400,000 people off the mountains of Tigray and on to the Sudanese plains below; they arrived in a country in which refugees were a painful issue already. Although they had been entering Sudan for 20 years, they had been a serious issue for about 10.

This was not simply a result of increasing numbers. When Haile Selassie fell in 1974 and the war in Tigray began, followed by Mengistu's terror in 1977/78, the composition of the refugee population changed. Formerly pastoralists or farmers, they were now often doctors, mechanics, students, teachers, university lecturers, dissident officials and airline pilots. In 1986, the University of Khartoum conducted research in Kassala to find out what proportion of refugees came from a farming background, and found that it had declined from 28% a few years earlier to just 2.4% (this was in a city). All these new refugees were competing for jobs with the local population.

They also competed for access to social services. This can be shown with reference to medical care. In 1984, Kassala had a doctor to every 16,000 patients. (In Britain, a GP's list at that time could be as small as 1,200, and would not normally be over 3,000.) A survey two years earlier had found that, of 100,000 outpatients attending Kassala hospital, half were refugees. And this was before the 1984/85 Emergency. Add on similar observations for jobs, transport, schools, accommodation (a very sore point) and water, and then consider the fact that the refugees were not really supposed to be in cities anyway; and it can be seen why, by 1987, the Sudanese were becoming disturbed.

The worst problems probably occurred in Gedaref, the business capital of Sudan's agricultural east. The best picture I ever had of what was happening to urban Sudan, and the way in which refugees were worsening its problems, was given to me by Pierre de Kock, a Dutchman who ran the Dutch Universities Gedaref Area Project (DUGAP).

In Gedaref, Pierre actually was DUGAP although, in the autumn of each year, a small group of four or five students would come from The Netherlands to join him for two or three months. What Pierre was trying to do was to devise ways of updating the city's infrastructure in co-operation with the city government. Late in 1988 I persuaded him to write a paper about this for the forthcoming VSO conference in Wad Medani, and he later kindly allowed me to use it in the magazine I was by then publishing from Showak.

The Sudanese population in 1986, wrote Pierre, was 22.5 million, including 1.129 million refugees. Overall population growth was 2.9% a year, giving a projected population in 2000 of 32 million. (In fact, it did reach around 40 million in 2008.) In the meantime, although about 80% of Sudanese were still rural, a combination of drought, the continuing growth of mechanized farming that cut employment opportunities in the countryside, and the development of large-scale farming schemes, still being implemented in 1989, had boosted the growth in urban population to about 10% a year. And the cities had no infrastructure.

Gedaref, he explained, had had a population of 18,000 in 1957. By 1987 it was 200,000; by the end of the century it would be 300,000. (This could have been way out; some sources suggested that there were already that many people in the city.)

Until about 1960, Pierre reported, infrastructure and services had just about kept pace with the growth in population. But they had long ceased to do so by 1988. Pierre mentioned matters such as traffic congestion, lack of space for businesses in the souk, and waste disposal, and was planning a system of donkey carts for carting rubbish away. (He also suggested that people be fined for crapping in the street. "Defecation in the town centre," he rasped, "should be an offence." I think he was on to a loser there.)

There was a further problem, and this Pierre mentioned only briefly in the paper, although he was well aware of it. This was water. The shortage in the city was chronic. Late in 1988, when we published the first issue of *Showak Magazine*, we included an article by colleague, Berhane Woldegabriel, about the pumping station at Showak. Built in 1970 to serve Gedaref, it was designed for a city of 100,000. By 1988 the population had doubled or trebled and the pipeline had silted, so that the 22 centrifugal or submersible pumps installed by the Italians were of little help.

"With total demand in Gedaref estimated now at 15,000 cu .m. daily, the station struggles to pump 10,000 cu.m. through the 20in. wide, 70km. pipe...[since 1970] the silt sediment by the side of the muddy River Atbara [has been] rising by an average of 30cm a year, piling up nine meters," wrote Berhane.

Berhane might have added, but didn't, that the disinfection and chlorination machinery had broken down years earlier and had been supplanted by a bucket of chlorine with a hole drilled in the bottom. This bucket was suspended in a strategic position and was meant to debug the water for a city of 300,000 people. Later that autumn, an American engineer working for UNHCR, Bill Hitz, took a sample from the river near the intake grates and found 105 different species of *E.coli*. (To add an especially perverse dimension, at the time Berhane wrote this article, the river had burst its banks and the pumping station was mostly under water. He gleefully headed the article: *Designed to drown?*).

Gedaref, then, was a mess. Sharing this mess, and not entirely welcome, were up to 35,000 refugees; some put it as low as 15,000, but that is still 5%. At the Eid that marked the end of Ramadan in 1988, violence broke out between refugees and nationals in the city, but in the event there was only one serious injury. This was fortunate. During Ramadan in 1980, five Sudanese - some of whom are thought to have been policemen - had gone into the mainly Amhara refugee settlement at Tawawa, five kilometres outside the city, for an after-noon of drinking and perhaps whoring. The latter was an industry in which Tawawa excelled, and that itself was a bone of contention. When the five Sudanese had finished, they refused to pay their bill. A scuffle ensued, and a rumour spread across the city that one of them had been killed. He hadn't, but by the end of the vioence that fol-lowed, five other Sudanese and 30 refugees had indeed lost their lives.

Gedaref was not the only place where there were large numbers of self-settled, often jobless, refugees. The Sudanese felt that the situa-tion had become intolerable. They reacted by instituting *kashas*. A *kasha* was really an operation in which prostitutes were rounded up, but the name was also used to refer to mass detention of unautho-rized urban refugees. Unfortunately, all sorts of people got swept up in the net, and dumped in remote enclosures for two or three days at a time before being carted off to some remote reception-centre.

I had some sympathy for the frustrations of the Sudanese, but felt just as much for the urban refugees who were supposedly causing the trouble. One day I was sitting drinking coffee at a stall in Gedaref, having come down from Showak with Ian to visit volunteers who lived there (and Pierre, who lived nearby). As we enjoyed a *jebenah* and cigarettes in the bustling souk, I saw a small man with strange, almost reddish hair go by, slowly, one broken flip-flop dragging off his heel. He was certainly a refugee - he did not look Sudanese at all - and wore tattered slacks and a striped shirt so worn that it was transparent. Bent forward, he was clearly ill; and his features contradicted each other as to his age, often a revealing sign. Probably he was about 30. He moved slowly through the dust past the meat-souk, where the stands were piled high with beef greying in the sun; it was the beginning of 1988, and food was still plentiful for those who did have the money.

I have seen people just as desperate in the cardboard cities at Waterloo, and even along the Strand. But there was something in the man's appearance, and manner, that fixed a certain image of the urban refugee in my mind. To be sure, some were wealthy and competitive, and they did take jobs off nationals - helped by education, skills and a work-ethic that were often superior. Nonetheless I could never quite consider the self-settled refugee as the predator that many Sudanese, by then, felt him to be.

*** *** ***

UNCONTROLLED urban settlement was not the only problem that Sudan had in coping with refugees. The other was that, quite simply, it was broke. In 1988, the government claimed that exports were paying for about 53% of imports, and did not see why it should bear the financial burden of refugees on its own. It was, it argued, an international problem. In about 1980 the country started a diplomatic offensive that was to bring benefits not only to itself, but to other nations on the continent that had played host to large refugee populations.

The point that Sudan's officials started to drive home in conference after conference overseas was that the care of refugees was an international responsibility as a matter of principle, and that there was no reason why a country so affected should cope on its own. Sudan, they said, was prepared to deal with the problem, but as it was doing so on behalf of the rest of the world, would the rest of the world like to pay for it? Twenty years on against the backdrop of the Darfur conflict, this seems a little ironic; but the argument was not a bad one, and by 1987, the diplomatic effort was bearing fruit. The first big success was under the Third Lomé Convention, under which aid to refugee-affected areas (as opposed to refugees alone) was to be given by the EEC. When the first tranche of this money was allocated under article 204 of Lomé III, Sudan jumped in quick and got 26% of it - something in excess of US$16m.

Sudan had also been arguing with the United Nations High Comissioner for Refugees (UNHCR). The latter funds the refugee settlement projects in Sudan, and has an office in Showak to supervise the work of COR, which implements the policy. But UNHCR had been maintaining that spontaneously-settled refugees away from the settlements were not its responsibility.

I like to think that I played some part in this argument, having been asked by Hassen to prepare a paper on National Assistance to Refugees, which I later found he had taken to the 1988 Executive Committee meeting of UNHCR that October. There, UNHCR had agreed that the 1988 grant of US$2.5m. for projects in refugee-affected areas would be repeated in 1989. I joked that Hassen should have put me on a percentage. But US$2.5m. was tiny in relation to the problems; the same applied even to the EEC's much more substantial package.

UNHCR did have an argument, however. It was already spending 15-20 times that US$2.5m. on the refugee settlements programme, which although run by COR was funded by Geneva. In the meantime, other African states such as Malawi were making increasing demands on its resources. Unlike Sudan, UNHCR was not broke; but it was severely strapped for cash.

However, the fate of Sudan's 677,000 spontaneously-settled refugees was not decided in Showak. COR's division in the town was concerned with the 234,000 in the settlements programme.

Sudan could claim some success in this field. In the south, where Ugandans had been settled into similar 'refugee towns' in the 1970s, some agricultural settlements had been so productive that they had started supplying food surpluses to nationals before the end of the programme. None of this had been painless; plenty of mistakes had been made, and they are described in detail in Barbara Harrell-Bond's book, *Imposing Aid*. But it was not a bad precedent to follow; and after all, there was nothing else to be done.

In fact, the programme had begun in the east very early, before it really took root in the south; but from the late 1970s onwards, it acclerated. Potable water was brought to semi-arid sites by sinking boreholes, sometimes several hundred meters deep; maintaining these was the job of Suleiman Osman and his staff. Row after row of *tukls* were thrown up, offices established, VHF sets brought out and wired up to car batteries. A souk would be built. Some of these settlements were extremely basic; many of the 30-odd that had been established by 1987 were also very remote.

Early in my time in Showak, I produced (from the research of others, particularly one colleague, Semere Tesfai) the *Showak Handbook*, a descriptive inventory of the settlements project. I have picked one at random: Dehema. I never went there, but can imagine what it looked like, with informal clusters of *tukls* in mesquite compounds, and perhaps two concrete buildings in its centre, far out in the middle of the great eastern Sudanese plain.

According to the *Handbook*, Dehema was one of the very first settlements, being established in 1969. It was agricultural (some are designated as wage-earning), and in 1987 had 2,995 inhabitants in 599 households (we extrapolated this last figure from an average). It was unusual in one respect; everybody was from one ethnic group, in this case the Beni Amer border tribe to which Miriam belonged. There were 600 head of livestock, and 900 feddans of allocated farmland, of which all but 450 were being worked. (Where possible, 5-10 feddans were allocated per family; a feddan is about an acre.) Dura (wheat) and sesame were grown, which means that it must have been in the belt that had about 650mm rainfall a year; a more typical average was 450mm. There were four Massey-Ferguson tractors, all of which would have been about 15 years old; it was not clear if they were working.

Rainfall apart, the water supply looks poor. There is no mention of any borehole, just a *hafir* (a raised earth reservoir, perhaps the size of a swimming pool) that was shared with a nearby Sudanese village. It was fed from the Rahad river; in this respect they were lucky, for some settlements were supplied from the Rahad irrigation canal, which was notoriously filthy.

There was a clinic, run by an indigenous Volag (voluntary agency, also known as NGO), the Islamic Relief Association. The clinic will have been basic, treated outpatients only, and will have had one paramedic. There was also a mother-and-baby clinic, which may or may not have been based there; it was run by another indigenous Volag, the Sudan Council of Churches.

The settlement was certainly isolated. The asphalt road was 115 kilometres away at its nearest point (but in the rains, five would have been too much, anyway). The railway was 50 kilometres away, but it was not efficient; I saw one train on it in two years. Finally, there seems to have been a COR workshop of some kind, a bakery, and a blacksmith; there was also a flour-mill run by the International Labour Organization (ILO).

Dehema was, as I have said, picked at random. It was not entirely typical; most settlements were a little larger, and would have been more diverse ethnically. It was also well-established. Most settlements were no more than six or seven years old. And a number were very much bigger; for example the notorious Tawawa wage-earning settlement mentioned earlier. It was just outside Gedaref; few of its inhabitants had jobs, nobody had land, there were loads of prostitutes, much drink, and much crime. Tawawa had a registered population of 12,672 in 1987, but when I went there I was told that the real population was closer to 25,000. There were also the vast reception centres such as Safawa, Wad Sherife and the Shagarabs, where refugees went when they crossed the border; and where they sometimes mouldered for two years or more.

In all, 234,000 refugees were known to be living in the settlements administered from Showak, and a number more in the smaller network administered by COR from Wad Medani.

This was the sprawling empire that Hassen Mohammed Osman

controlled from his simple office in Showak, which had no telephone within 60Km.; just an unreliable VHF, and a nearby tarmac road that didn't go anywhere near most of the settlements. The dirt roads that did, became impassable after a few days of rain. It was a fragile life-support system.

Chapter Four

December 1987: *Working and drinking*

IN THE first week of December 1987, while Hassen grappled with the threat of a further refugee influx, I faced a flux of a different kind, perhaps from doubtful eggs from Beshir's shop. Or perhaps it was a hunk of the local weevil bread, plastered with a weird substance that claimed to be strawberry jam. In any case, I had come to know the pit latrine in the compound all too well.

The office toilets were best avoided. There were several, but the clean ones were kept locked, and the keys were kept by the administration section, which kept losing them. The alternative was a pair of truly evil holes in the ground round the back of the office. Once every couple of months these were filled with lime, but this just seemed to make things worse; I could never go in without gagging, and the thought of them makes me queasy even now.

But getting used to foreign habits is all part of travel. Toilet paper is not used in Sudan; as is normal in Muslim countries, they use water and the left hand - hence the cultural taboo on eating, or touching your face, with it. The toilet bowl in the hotel we had stayed at in Khartoum on had a thin metal pipe that curving out below your rear, a painted iron handwheel set into the white tiles of the bathroom wall, a little to the right of the bowl itself. It was rather stiff, but persistence was rewarded with a slim jet of water that squirted up at an alarming angle that made one glad the water pressure in Khartoum was not all it might be.

The standard facility as used in local homes was the proverbial brick outhouse, often built into the compound wall. In it there was a hole in the ground covered (sometimes) by a plank of wood and, in de luxe installations, a tap. A variation was the semi-detached double cubicle, devised by a Government department and much beloved of relief organizations (sorry). In our own compound, we learned to cover the hole carefully after one of the compound cats fell down it. It was fished out, but ran away before it could be given a bath. After dark, the arrival of malarial mosquitoes, divisions of cockroaches that crawl out of the hole, scorpions with a sting for your tail and, for some reason, hedgehogs discouraged one from lingering.

Sometimes, the hole was found atop a four- or five-foot plinth. On the other side was the street, and from zinc doors the waste can be removed straight into the cart when the time came. This was a logical arrangement but a bit alarming, as upon entry it rather resembled an Aztec temple in miniature.

When a pit latrine reached the end of its life - an event that tended to be obvious - it could be concreted over; or, if space was lacking in which to dig another, it was be dug out from the side. With this in mind, it was wise to leave a brick out of the lining at the time of construction so that moisture could drain away. Emptying a latrine on which this precaution has been neglected could be unpleasant.

Still, on this ocasion, my stomach trouble sorted itself out after 10 days or so - as did the malaria, for the time being; and, one morning in early December, I left for work feeling at peace with the world. By this time, with Ian's help, I had mastered the the 125cc trail bike. That morning, it started unusually easily. I sat on it just outside the compound, the engine idling quietly, and looked to my right at the hills across the river, beyond which lay Abuda refugee settlement. These low hills were the only feature in the dead-flat landscape. It was quite cool at that time of the morning; so much so that the Sudanese made their way to the office in parkas, unable to stand the temperature of just 75°F in the hour after dawn.

I felt extremely cheerful. This is a smashing country, I told myself, and I am going to do a good job here if I can.

*** *** ***

BERHANE had been a journalist on the English-language Government magazine *Sudanow*. Some years earlier, he had heavily criticised what he saw as corruption and inefficiency in COR. Later, Hassen had persuaded him to come to Showak and start up a public relations unit, on the basis, I suppose, that if you intended to run a corruption-free administration, you should have a man known to be honest as its public face.

The plan now was to start a quarterly magazine for the settlement administration. The problem was that no-one had agreed to fund it. Before I left Britain I had been told that Band Aid had made such a commitment, but they later said that they knew nothing about it. Eventually, I submitted a formal proposal to their Executive

Committee in London, and it was turned down; quite reasonably, I think, as it was technically a Government propaganda sheet.

Eventually, Hassen decided to push it through in the annual budget that was negotiated with UNHCR. But as late as March of the following year, they too knew nothing about it; a fact that I only discovered by accident when drinking with the Dane who compiled the budget at UNHCR. To make matters worse, the budget itself was long delayed by disputes about various items, of which the magazine was just one. We did finally get enough money from UNHCR to print the first issue, and I think Hassen raided the research budget to pay for the second. In retrospect, I wonder if Berhane could have attended to all this before I arrived, or perhaps VSO should have double-checked that someone had done so.

In any case, when I started work, there was no question of doing the magazine just yet. In the meantime, Berhane was gathering information for a book that would describe the workings of the administration, and list the assets that the individual settlements had; this was the document to which I referred earlier. It was a good idea, and the research had already been done by the administration staff and collated by a refugee, Semere. He had also written some of the descriptive material, in very good English. Berhane now gave me remarkable freedom to decide exactly how all this would be presented (I decided on a paperback-book format). I thus learned, while working on this material, a lot about how the settlements worked (in theory) right from the beginning.

But I was still finding life claustrophobic. And when Frank invited me to travel with him to a refugee camp, I accepted at once.

Frank was then a volunteer. He would shortly move across to join the EEC project being set up in Showak, helping to implement the first stages of the Lomé III aid to refugee-affected areas. For the moment, however, he was based at the vocational training school across the river in Abuda. This was one of the oldest and best-fed of the refugee settlements; and the school itself seems to have been a success, conceived by COR, funded by UNHCR and run by VSO instructors with refugee assistance. Its new premises, built under the supervision of VSO volunteers, had just been opened. One day just after Christmas, I made my first visit there and found a quadrangle with neat, square white buildings on three sides, including large teaching rooms where groups of 15-20 refugees learned bricklaying and other building trades. One thing I noticed at once was that it was clean. It is hard to keep anything clean in a country where there is so much dust. There were then two VSOs there; Frank, and Hughie, who lived in the other volunteer's compound too. A third, Trevor, had just left. There had been others over the years, and there were volunteers at the school virtually until the end of VSO involvement in Sudan.

But Frank wasn't going to Abuda on the day he invited me to join him. He had been asked for an opinion on damaged school buildings at Shagarab. Shagarab was not a refugee settlement; it was a reception centre, a refugee camp in the real sense, albeit of hastily built *tukls* rather than tents. The total population of the Shagarab sites, grouped together at the head of the Girba reservoir about 40Km. from the Eritrean frontier, was about 45,000. Most had arrived fairly recently. They would generally be moved on to permanent settlements in about 18 months to two years.

"Come along," said Frank. "You must be getting pretty pissed off sitting around here." He had been friendly from the beginning. He was well-liked by both the Sudanese and the Europeans. Having started off as a carpenter and then instructor in England, he was now in his late twenties, and just revealing a flair for administration that would make him an asset to the EEC.

So, just after breakfast two days before Christmas, we rumbled out of Showak in the Abuda school's ancient Land-Rover pickup, our bottoms burning on the thin plastic cushions. Frank and I sat in the cab beside Suleiman Driver, who drove the school's vehicles, sharing the task with the villainous individual who had picked me up from the bus-station. Suleiman was more traditional, wearing a *djellabiya*; there was a headcloth wrapped round his brow. He was perhaps 40 - age is deceptive in Sudan - and tall. In the pick-up behind us, sandwiched between a large wardrobe and a box of tools, rode Suleiman's Mate. I don't remember his name.

We travelled for an hour and a half on the tarmac road, crossing the glazed earth; there was not a feature in sight save for the odd railway building (the single track ran parallel to the road for much of the way). We were going towards Kassala, but we didn't go as far as the city. Instead we left the main road 50 kilometres short of it and swung to the right, into the town of Khashm el-Girba. Our first port of call was to be the compound of Christian Outreach, a church charity run by volunteers from Britain.

Khashm el-Girba was a strange town. It was a population centre in the rich dura-growing area of Sudan, but not as big as Kassala or

Gedaref. But it did have about twice as many people as Showak, where there were about 15,000. So it was quite big, but it had three apparent functions besides acting as a centre for agriculture. First of all, it was a garrison town, strategically placed near the huge dam at the end of the lake on the Atbara River; this lake, created by the hydro scheme itself, is so large that it may be seen on world atlases. The hydro scheme had been built with the help of the Italians, and they were still involved in its running. The combination of this, and the Italian influences on refugees from nearby Eritrea, made it the only place where I was greeted with the word *Salute*.

The Army, which guarded the hydro scheme closely, was much in evidence. While being shown a clinic for children run by Christian Outreach, we saw a huge Magirus lorry in olive drab draw up and disgorge a load of troops in the street outside. They were southerners, with very African features, and were very smartly turned out. Someone once told me that the southern regiments were all stationed in the north while the northern regiments got on with fighting southerners in the south. I am not sure how fair this was, but I did notice that most of the troops I saw were of southern appearance.

Girba's second function was the refugee industry. Some of the largest reception centres and settlements were clustered round it.

The third function of Khashm el-Girba must have been religion, to judge from the number of mosques I noticed when we arrived. But then, I had been in the frontier-town atmosphere of Showak for five weeks; so perhaps it was their colours that struck me. The towers, minarets, were painted in candy shades, their tips pointed and weird; they grouped themselves on the near horizon like tropical plants in some glasshouse at Kew. I knew that, after dark, they would be ablaze with light, the lines of bulbs around the towers like necklaces, almost like funfair towers in Britain. There was nothing remotely depressing about a Sudanese mosque, certainly in the towns; neither was there, to a westerner, any gravitas. They revealed a love of crypto-modern gewgaws, preferably ones that could be plugged into a wall-socket. But I liked them for their lack of pretension. Unlike many Europeans (and southern Christians), I never found Islam in Sudan oppressive.

As we drove through the town centre, leaving the souk behind and crossing an open area ringed by anarchic groups of huts and mud-brick houses, the fairground mosques piercing the pale-blue sky in front of us, we passed a small, square one-storey building. There were bars across the full-depth windows, and the white arm of a man in a *djellabiya* hung through them.

"That's the nick," said Frank. He lit another cigarette. Frank and I smoked cigarettes constantly when we were together, often harsh Ethiopian Nyalas.

I said the gaol looked a bit basic.

"Horrible." He blew an acrid cloud of smoke past Suleiman and out of the driver's window. "If they don't have families, they risk starvation. They don't feed them in the same way we do, you know. And you see that stain across the bottom of the wall? They have to go in their cells, I suppose."

Probably they did. I looked back at it as we bounced away over the deep, dry ruts towards the Christian Outreach compound.

*** *** ***

AS WE entered Girba, we had crossed the first leg of the irrigation canal that runs north-west from the lake. It was wide and deep, and its banks were ablaze with the most luxuriant vegetation I had seen anywhere, a treat for the eyes after the featurelessness of the plains. In three or four seconds we were across the canal, and the grey-brown dust returned; but I was thinking of the fact that people sometimes swam in the canal and also in the great reservoir although, it was said, there were tiny fish there that nibbled your nipples.

"Come and swim here. You're welcome. Honestly. Any time," said a friendly English nurse with reddish hair. You could sit on the rocks just offshore in the canal, she explained, and dive in and climb out at will; it was quite private, and a mercy on a hot day. She showed us around her beautifully-painted white *tukl* in the Christian Outreach compound. The *tukl* was clean and neat inside, with a huge double bed that took up most of the space. A mosquito-net floated ethereally above it.

But we didn't stay in the Outreach compound long. Twenty minutes later we rumbled onto the parapet of the dam, where a machine-gun emlacement watched the area from the top of one of the towers. There were many fortifications around Girba, and I was carrying a camera, which aroused great suspicion at the checkpoint on the dam itself. Eventually we were waved on. "You must have a guilty face," said Frank. "I've never had any trouble there before."

I made myself as comfortable as possible on the thin, sweat-soaked plastic cushions as we left the lake. The enormous sheet of blue-grey water slid away behind, and we hit the plain - which would have made the average desert seem a riot of incident.

The 45,000 inhabitants of Shagarab reception centre lived about 20 miles from Girba, linked to it by a track across the plain; this track was quite impassable two days out of three in the wet season. Provisioning Shagarab was notoriously difficult. On the third of those three days, a lorry might struggle through, churning the earth into ruts that set hard when the ground dries out in October; for the next eight months, it is an easy journey but a very bumpy ride. Suleiman's technique was impressive; he forced the Land-Rover faster and faster until it took off between ruts, floating from crest to crest. (It never worked so well in a Toyota; I think it must have had something to do with the Land-Rover's colonial breeding.) Yet there was a constant swaying, so that the thigh and stomach muscles were kept tense, trying to keep the body steady; long journeys were never relaxing in Sudan.

There was little vegetation, and certainly no sign of the savannah that had covered the area 25 or 30 years previously. Here and there there would be a lonely clump of mesquite. A camel or two wandered past, and every now and then a souk-truck or Bedford-based bus would thunder towards us, bound for the checkpoint on the dam. There, every last grain in the sacks they carried would be examined for illicit cigarettes or gin. Twice after leaving the dam, we slowed briefly in front of makeshift shelters where armed soldiers stood, indolently watching the road; normally they just waved us on, anxious not to expose themselves to the broiling sunlight.

Halfway from Girba to Shagarab, a small shape caught my eye some yards off the track. It was a light tank; I could not tell whether it was British or Italian, but its camouflage paint was still quite clear, as were the two slits through which the crew could look ahead of them. It was a reminder that migrations of men in arms are not new in Africa.

*** *** ***

SHAGARAB, at first, I dismissed as a mirage of the type that I had seen on the Medani road, where what appeared to be rows of trees or rocks had stretched across the horizon, only to vanish as you approached. But Shagarab did not vanish, although I am sure that both UNHCR and the Sudan Government would have been happy

Refugee children in Shagrab reception centre

for it to do so.

The row of low *tukls*, all identical, and all of straw rather than brick, unfinished by the donkey dirt that seals them in the villages, ran from far left to far right like a huge army holding the line across the plain. We drew closer. A small blue metal sign urged all visitors to report at once to the camp authorities; underneath, the message was repeated in Arabic. "That says, *khawajas* [foreigners] go to hell. Infidels keep out," said Frank. He was joking.

I seem to have been left nonplussed by my encounter with one of the larger refugee-camps in Africa. One thing that stood out was that there were very few people about. Admittedly it was mid-afternoon, when people in Africa do sleep, but this place of 45,000 people was completely still. And it all looked the same; the miles of broken-down *tukls* without compounds, packed together so that they must have been a dreadful fire-risk (and there were fires in the camps and settlements, in Hawata for instance, that devastated large areas of settlements and killed many livestock). Probably no-one stirred because there was no point. Later in the afternoon, visiting the compound of an Irish Volag in the camp, we did see a group of Eritrean teenagers playing football. But that was the only sign of movement.

Apart, that is, from Teclemariam, the man that Frank had come to see. He was a kind-looking man of about 30 with a very high forehead and a slight stoop, and he was telling Frank why the schools were falling down. The schools were, in fact, just raised slabs of concrete covered by straw canopies supported by steel rods. It is said that all a good teacher needs are four walls, a roof and a blackboard; in Africa they can manage with just the roof. Herein lay the problem. The rods had been sunk into the base while the concrete was still wet, and the mixture had then hardened around them. During the wet season, water had seeped into the tiny gap between the poles and the concrete, and corroded the steel. Somehow, they would have to be extracted and the rooves re-supported. "It's the same everywhere here," muttered Frank. "They just won't learn." I reflected that the Airey homes built in Britain at the end of the last war were being rebuilt at huge cost for exactly the same reason.

We left the silence and dilapidation of Shagarab at about five. I was not to return for 18 months; when I did, in May 1989, the place made a much better impression on me. This was thanks to Christian Outreach, who were presenting graduation certificates to eight or nine refugee women who had completed a vocational training course Outreach had organized in handicrafts. The women were so painfully shy that they could barely stand up to accept the congratulations of the senior woman official who had come from Showak to preside over the ceremony. But everyone seemed to be happy, and to enjoy the breakfast that was held afterwards. Despite it being a cool, overcast day early in the wet season, it seemed a cheerful enough place. But on that earlier afternoon in December 1987 the only sign of life in most of the tukls was the yellow plastic *abrique* that stood at every door.

We rumbled off again. But it was cooler now, and the descending sun slanted across the plain, casting an orange veil across the brown earth, picking out every contour, however slight; and the sky darkened from bleached, watery blue-white to the deeper afternoon colour, so that one felt less exposed on the vast plain below. In the country outside Shagarab, people stirred. On the edge of the lake was a small Sudanese village; sheep wandered, goats picked about, and the odd herd of 30 or so livestock was driven across the void by small boys with dark faces and white *djellabiyas*, wielding long sticks that they waved, shouting, at the fleeces in front of them. Men with faces like leather moved timelessly on huge camels. We drifted quickly across the corrugals, fearful of missing the six o'clock curfew on the dam; nothing could move across it after that time, and it would be cold when the sun went down. Probably we would have returned to Shagarab, but we just made it. At a quarter to six we crossed the checkpoint and skirted the shore of the lake near Girba town. In the shadows was a field of rushes, the water between the blades set ablaze by the setting sun; this descended towards the horizon so quickly that you could track its movement, and without hurting your eyes, for the veil of dust over the landscape reduced it to a soft, perfectly round disc of living colour. First its tip, then its lower half disappeared below the ground, and then the last rays shilhouetted a snowy egret that stood on one leg in the rushes, the white of its feathers just visible against the last of the day.

*** *** ***

WE HEARD gunfire from Khashm el-Girba souk at eight. For an hour or so, the noise had been building up outside the Christian Outreach compound, which was about a mile from the souk itself. When one of the Outreach volunteers returned from an expedition there, she told us that it had been quite a scene; rifles had been loosed off, and a tank run between the ramshackle shops.

They had been celebrating the news that the Sudanese army had retaken Kurmuk. Kurmuk was a Sudanese town on the Ethiopian frontier, recently taken by the SPLA after fighting about 100 miles south of Ed Damazin. Roughly 400 miles from where we sat; not far by Sudanese standards.

The celebration was not simply that of a military victory. Five weeks earlier, lying sweating and malarial in my tukl, I had heard about the original battle from the BBC. It seemed that Kurmuk had been softened up for the SPLA by Ethiopian artillery, and the Sudanese had quite properly regarded this as an act of aggression. I later heard, however, that far from fighting tooth and nail to recover the town, the Sudanese Army had simply walked in when the SPLA, knowing that it couldn't hold the town forever, walked out.

The noises in the souk were unnerving, but no-one else seemed particularly concerned. Frank was worried, it was true; but not because the locals were recreating the Somme in the souk. Frank was worried because he had arranged to meet an attractive redheaded American aid worker with long red hair in Showak, and was afraid he would be late. We had turned down a kind offer to stay the night at the behest of Suleiman and Suleiman's Mate, both of whom wanted to get home that evening. However, it would have been churlish to refuse supper. So Frank sat and fretted and thought of the wrath of the redhead while our Christian Outreach hosts dished up a pleasant meal in the compound, and the air got colder as the day drew to a close.

It was indeed cold after the heat of the day. We set off at eight-thirty, by which time a chill wind was blowing; and, as there was room only for three abreast in the cab, Suleiman's Mate stood in the pickup behind and wrapped himself in a *chamma* - an Ethiopian wrap of very soft cotton. As we accelerated away from the junction with the main road, he remained standing, the *chamma* flowing behind him, staring forward across the cab roof like a spare horseman of the apocalypse.

In my office the next day, I heard aggressive chanting from out-side; and, I think, a gunshot or two. I looked out to see two soldiers leading a group of 10 or 12 schoolchildren in dusty white *djellabiyas* along the road behind the office, fists clenched in the air. Customers at the shop opposite, which was a carbon-copy of Beshir's, stood between the purple zinc shutters drinking Pepsi. I cannot remember that they looked impressed.

"Victory parade for Kurmuk," I told Ian when I got back to the compound at half-past two.

"They ought to be ashamed of themselves, using schoolkids like

An Eritrean woman helps run a craft fair organized by
Christian Outreach in Shagarab reception centre

that," he grumbled.

It had been an incongruous sight in the town full of Land-Cruisers with the badges of European and American relief agencies stamped on their doors. There was an essential oddness about Showak; because of the refugee assistance operation since 1985, a lot of the Europeans in Sudan were here. But most of them lived a mile outside the town, near the main Kassala highway, in a sheltered compound erected for the UNHCR personnel.

Such places must once have abounded all over Africa. Later, when I read V.S. Naipaul's *In a Free State*, I was struck by the similarity in spirit between his fictional compound, and this one. A perimeter wire encircled it, patrolled by two or three *gafirs*. Within were 10 or 15 pre-fabricated bungalows not unlike those erected in Britain after the war. These were the Begus homes, Swedish creations that were in fact the outside walls of packing cases; during a crisis they would be shipped to a relief centre, and when they had been unpacked the panels would be re-erected as a bungalow - complete with everything the international staff member might need. Everything meant everything, from a smart European-style flush toilet to a cooker to towels right down to the toilet paper. Even the furniture came in the packing-case. There was a certain twisted logic behind all this; economy of movement, combining the functions of providing oral rehydration solution, sorghum, oil, medicine, and what have you in a crate, and providing accommodation for foreign relief workers. Yet the end result was bleak and weirdly suburban. The inhabitants frequently grumbled about the close, back-biting artifical atmosphere in this compound, but with one exception I don't think any of them ever moved into a Sudanese house in the town. Apart from the VSO volunteers, and the Americans of the Lalmba charity, who had a more sensible arrangement next to the clinic they ran, there were no more than three European-occupied homes in the whole of Showak.

Bill didn't move out of the compound. But he had his doubts about it, and came to see us often. Bill was the UNHCR water supervisor; his job was to ensure that Suleiman Osman spent UNHCR's money properly, a task fraught with misunderstandings. He was very tall, and well-built, with a mass of curly jet-black hair. He was partly Amerindian and came from Arizona. Bill was unfailingly generous, with his time as well as with the little luxuries that come with being a diplomat. He had gone into the Marines at 18 and found himself in Vietnam; straight afterwards he had become an overseas volunteer, doing 12 years with the Peace Corps and with the United Nations volunteers before taking the Showak post as his first paid job in development. His commitment to overseas aid was complete, but he never said that himself.

We watched many videos in his Begus bungalow, often fortified by food cooked by his half-Vietnamese, half-Yemeni wife, Rapna; her hospitality, too, was never-ending. In their strange bungalow on the Sudanese plain I saw *Casablanca* for the first time, along with *Charlie Chan*, *Robocop* and much else besides. "But we thought you guys lived in huts and shat in holes in the ground," people said when I returned to Britain. "We did," I replied.

Bill was not the only person in the compound to offer hospitality to the British volunteers. (I remember an extremely drunk darts match with two Danes with particular affection.) But he was unusual; by and large, these people kept themselves to themselves, and sometimes fought amongst themselves as well. Later, when an energetic Englishman, Robert Ashe, took over, things improved somewhat.

So too did the relationship between the UNHCR personnel and their Sudanese colleagues, which could be strained on occasion. Just how this occurred was demonstrated by an incident during my early weeks in Showak. Bill was then working under a senior water advisor, an Englishman. During this period, their senior counterpart in the COR office, Suleiman Osman, was on a course.

While he was away, his shoes were filled by a less experienced official. Many jobs that went wrong, and matters came to a head when he requested the following year's supply of chlorine for the settlement water systems. He put in, not for the 15 tons that was needed, but, if I remember correctly, 400 - enough, said the Englishman, to poison every Eritrean in the east of Sudan. "The suspension of matter in fluids is so complex that I hardly understand it myself," he growled. "This idiot hasn't got a clue." Many meetings took place but no compromise could be reached until Suleiman returned from abroad and resolved the situation.

Arguably, it should have been possible for Bill and the Englishman simply to advise the official that the amounts were excessive or, if he refused, go to Hassen Mohammed Osman and tell him that the man could not cope. It was not possible. The relationship between COR and the mostly European advisors at UNHCR was a delicate one, with pride, post-colonial *amour propre* and and the sovereignty issue all mixed together in one lethal cocktail. Neither could a Sudanese department have accepted advice from the UNHCR in such a way, thus admitting its own officers to be incompetent (which, in the main, they really were not) just as it was pushing its case for more assistance in the field of refugee settlement. Difficulties of this sort were compounded by complicated one-to-one relationships; I had more than a few arguments with Berhane himself. He had a powerful intellect (and a biting wit). But his lack of method and organisation could cause chaos. The problem was that to criticise it led to his wondering out loud whether I did not trust his judgement because he was African rather than European. This was crap and Berhane should have seen it as such, but it is hard to blame him when he could see the inhabitants of the UNHCR compound - not neccessarily better-qualified than himself - earning 15-20 times as much through better luck with their place of birth.

In any case, there were things that Berhane and I had to swallow together. One of those was the video.

*** *** ***

THE VIDEO was a sore point with me. It had cost S.32,000-about £3,500, which was enough to pay the salary of three very senior officials for a year. (Although VCRs were fairly common in Britain by then, the cameras themselves were still expensive, heavy and complex, and were very much rich men's toys.)

Why, I muttered in Berhane's direction, was COR paying money it hadn't got for something it didn't need and which would surely disintegrate within a year with the dust and the untrained handling to which it would be exposed?

"You have to understand," said Berhane, indicating the retreating back of a senior manager, "this man's brother has returned from working in Saudi and has brought this back, and they want to give him some money. Anyway, Hassen wants you to write a paper explaining why we need it."

"He *what?*"

"Well, he wants a paper from us giving our opinion on whether or not we should buy it for COR. Just say that we should. We will find proper uses for it, Mike, for sure."

Knowing that Berhane was unimpressed with people who bought toys for their own sake, I decided that he must have thought it politic for the future of our work. I got out the typewriter (itself Berhane's personal property; we needed one far more than we needed a video, and it would have been a quarter of the price) and got to work. I couldn't quite bring myself to recommend that we buy the video, but I said what a wonderful machine it was and added that if treated very, very gently, it might survive some months. Berhane decided that this was the best he was going to get from me, and stumped off to Hassen's office with the piece of flimsy foolscap dangling from his hand. A few days later the money was cleared and the video acquired. We found ourselves *in loco parentis* and locked the toy in a plywood cupboard in our office.

Berhane added a bit to the blurb on the Agriculture Department that I was writing for the *Showak Handbook*. "The department," he wrote blithely, "has recently acquired modern audio-visual teaching aids." He handed it back with a sardonic smile.

A few days later he appeared in our compound in the evening with the video and its assorted umbilical cords under his arm.

"There is a tea-party tomorrow-night," he told me.

"Eh?"

"A tea-party." Berhane rarely repeated things he thought self-evident. "So we have to learn how to operate this bloody thing, you and I."

We spent the next two hours assembling and disassembling the camera and practising operation and composition, and at the end we were both fairly proficient.

What the party was, I found out the next day. Piers Vigre, an English agriculturalist with UNHCR who had himself once been a volunteer, and a Dutch member of the same team were both to leave Showak, having each racked up three long years in Showak. It was a sad day on two counts. First of all, Piers (I hardly knew the other team member) was generous and entertaining. Second, they were the last remaining international staff to have served in the Emergency of 1984/85, and that probably meant something to the Sudanese; after all, they had seen plenty of foreigners come and go, and perhaps felt that these two understood them better.

At four the following afternoon Berhane and I, laden with equipment, walked slowly through the dust to the COR rest house. This was a large three-storey building with a courtyard and outhouses, set in a compound near our own; it dwarfed the other structures in the area and had a garden full of what almost looked like roses. It was for visiting dignitaries, but was also much used by the local officials as a club. As we approached, I saw two trucks parked by the perimeter wall, crowded with mechanics and drivers from the central workshop; they were not invited as such, but were welcome to watch, and were craning their necks to see over the wall and into the yard.

The next thing I noticed was the skirl of bagpipes. It was a bizarre surprise in a small town in Africa, but it seemed the piper was a good one.

Cautiously I entered the courtyard. Long tables had been set up in rows in front of the building, and laid with tablecloths so white they dazzled; at intervals of a yard or so were splendid sparkling stainless-steel teapots, and there were plates laden with biscuits, jelly and cake. Having been hungry for the previous three weeks, I found the sight almost too much to bear. At the tables sat officials of COR and UNHCR, the Sudanese with trousers even more smartly pressed than usual. Piers and Margriete had been allocated comfortable seats on a small raised platform; Hassen also sat there, wearing traditional Sudanese dress of *djellabiya* and turban in place of the slacks and shirt that he wore during the day. I did not recognise him at first and sat at first in one of the chairs reserved for the guests of honour, an embarrassing gaffe that fortunately was not held against me.

In the corner by the courtyard door, a large military band played-bagpipes, trombone, tuba and all, each brass instrument polished to perfection.

It was sad, Hassen said in his speech a little later, to lose such welcome guests after such happy years. But it was clear that he did not mean to let them go without saying a proper goodbye.

We made our video, Berhane and I, and it was pretty dreadful; it ended up locked in a drawer and I expect it is still there. Later in the evening a less restrained celebration took place on the roof of the UNHCR office, and Piers appeared in a Sudanese turban and *djellabiya* that Hassen had given him, carrying a magnificent Hadendowa sword from the same source. We all got progressively drunker.

*** *** ***

BOOZE WAS not a problem in Sudan at that time. It had been outlawed four years earlier and the legal supplies poured away, as I have said, for the enjoyment of the crocodiles. However, across the border in Eritrea there was the Melotti brewery and distillery founded by the Italians in 1939. This was busier than ever, despite the war raging around it. In 1987 camel-load after camel-load streamed across an unguardable border into Sudan, where the price rose depending on one's distance from the frontier. In Khartoum it was more expensive; the supplies had to run the gauntlet of the police roadblocks that dotted the main roads to the capital, so that it cost about S.120 for a bottle of Asmara or Baro's Ethiopian gin. A small premium was charged for Melotti, which was better. In Showak, we paid about S.90. Excellent and very strong Melotti beer in small bottles was sometimes around, and Melotti also made *zabeeb*, a strong ouzo. For the homesick there was Ethiopian cognac. I rather enjoyed that, but most Europeans thought it a cross between Tabasco sauce and industrial alcohol.

For highly-paid expatriates in Khartoum, who did not like Ethiopian spirits, there were supplies of Johnnie Walker and Red Label and the occasional crate of Carlsberg. These all dribbled through cracks in the diplomatic bag, along with the odd blue movie. Personally, I always thought that the Ethiopian distilleries did us well; the gin was went down well when mixed with *limuun*, strong lime juice that we made in the blender.

When cash was short (it usually was in our compound), we resorted to the local alternatives. The usual social drink for rural Sudanese, and for many others in the provinces, was a thick, heavy beer called *marissa*. This was probably rare in Khartoum. Brewed from dura, it was greenish and had bits floating in it that tended to distract you from the full, soft, slightly sweet flavour. It was often served in huts that were the equivalent of pubs, and Showak had a number of them in the red-light area on the main road from the COR offices to the central workshop. Clerks quite often congregated there in the hour or so after work finished at 2.30, going home to sleep it off in the hot afternoon period between *ghada* (lunch) and *asha'a* (supper), when no-one was expected to be awake anyway.

At least one guide-book on Sudan has praised *marissa* for its nutritional value, pointing out that farm-labourers sometimes drink it before starting work in the fields: "A nourishing way to begin the day," its says, with slightly smug approval. I don't know about nourishment, but it was deceptively strong. I got proof of this one afternoon when I returned on the motorbike just before three to find Wayne, Ian and Simon slumped and twisted on *anquaraybs* in the afternoon sun. They had collapsed on them, insensible, making no attempt whatsoever to drag them into the shade. Having finished work at one-thirty, as did all the manual and technical COR staff, they had gone to a *marissa*-hut at the back of the compound somewhere and each had several rough-alloy bowls of beverage; this had snuck up from behind and laid them out. They were just about able to move by suppertime.

Marissa was Sudanese, but the Ethiopians and Eritreans had an equivalent. This was *tej*. In the highlands of Ethiopia, it is brewed from honey, and at its best it is clear, sweet and potent. Lacking honey, the refugees in the settlements used to brew it from dates, but it was still enjoyable. Supplies reached us in one of two ways. Either someone would find a source of supply in Showak itself; rare, though it happened. Or, more often, a jerry would be taken to a camp by a volunteer or UNHCR official who was working there and replenished in the evening, during a sojourn in one of the *tej*-houses in a big refugee camp like Safawa. It would be brought back in five-gallon cans and held against a rainy day. On one such trip, someone did get a jerryful of original brew, made from honey; it was delightful.

Supplies were erratic. Bringing the stuff in from camps in the border area was chancy. Someone from UNHCR stashed two five-gallon cans in his Land-Cruiser before leaving one of the reception centres, but was stopped on the way by one of the police/army patrols that infested the frontier zone. He lost his *tej*; he also had his car taken apart in a search for other contraband.

"They can't do that," I told the victim. "You have diplomatic immunity."

"Yeah," he replied, "but *he* had a machine-gun."

If one fancied something a little harder, there was always *aragi*. This was the indigenous Sudanese spirit, distilled from dates. If you were lucky, that is; in May 1988 six people died in Port Sudan after drinking *aragi* that had been made from old rubber sandals. And the lead in the pipes of the backstreet distilleries must have been lethal. A cautious man would never have touched it (although, to be fair, he would never have touched *tej* or *marissa* either; both were notorious for spreading hepatitis). But *aragi* was at least cheap and plentiful. And it really was strong.

Sources varied. My favourite came from a house some way away; and once Ian took us to a compound of southern, African, people, where they sold us a gin-bottle-full, measured out in the usual Pepsi-bottle quantities. This then had a twist of paper put in the top to stop the fluid from slopping. I remember that African compound for the foul-tempered mongrel dog that guarded us, snarling, while a young woman filled the bottle. We crouched on the ground and gazed back, and it never quite had the nerve to spring.

Sometimes we mixed two gin-bottles'-worth of *aragi* with the juice of *karkadee* and *limuun* and made a pleasant punch - though this masked the strength of the alcohol, sometimes to very ill effect.

But although *aragi* was relatively cheap, it still cost a day's wages for a full gin-bottle. Towards the end it would cost much more, and from time to time crackdowns by the police made it much harder to obtain. If funds for Ethiopian gin were lacking, the answer was homebrew. I was no expert at this, but did my bit on a journey to Khartoum by begging a consignment of equipment off a departing expatriate and bringing it home to Showak, complete with a five-gallon jerry.

This nearly misfired. The expatriate had been making some foul brew of his own in the jerry; I brought it back across Khartoum from his flat in a taxi that I had hailed in Gamurihiya, but the top was clearly designed for brewing purposes, so I put it in a bag, along with the various bungs and tubes we would also need. I didn't realise that the jerry hadn't been properly washed, and the inside of the taxi smelled like a distillery.

In fact, I had had trouble finding a taxi that afternoon; when one did stop, the driver, pulling away, sniffed and glanced at the jerry and asked if it had contained *aragi*.

God forbid, I replied hastily. I had been using it for benzene.

Apparently satisfied, he drove on for 20 yards before seeing a police officer standing on the corner. To my horror, he pulled in and picked the officer up.

"My brother," he explained pleasantly. "Do you mind? I can give him a lift on to Omdurman after we have dropped you."

"No, of course not," I said, so relieved that I nearly offered to double the fare.

Another 20 yards or so later the police officer said to his brother, "Is that *aragi* I smell?"

"He says it's petrol," said the taxi-driver, a note of doubt creeping into his voice.

"Oh," replied the officer, and, after an interval, "Good."

I got the taxi to drop me some way from the rest-house, and scuttled.

We took the jerry back to Showak on the back of a pick-up, Berhane insisting that it pay its passage by carrying diesoline. Washing it a second time took longer. Shortly afterwards, Wayne brewed wine out of tea-leaves in it. The tea wine did the job but was awful, with a distinct tang of diesel fuel. I drank some, but felt foul the following morning.

But there was no need for tea wine in at the end of 1987. You could still get what you wanted if you could find the money. My last memory of that party at UNHCR was of Piers swinging the sword about on the roof before we all retired, tired but content, to our beds through the cold night air, the sound of bagpipes still ringing in my ears.

*** *** ***

JUST DOWN the road from our near-empty compound was the other VSO compound, newer, with square brick buildings; its bleak aspect was beginning to be softened by some well-watered neem trees that the occupants had planted when they moved in, two years previously. There were six volunteers in that compound, but one of them left not long after I arrived. I remember him well enough, though.

He was a former engineer on a transatlantic liner. He had helped to look after the plumbing on the ship, and I was intrigued to find out that he had been on board when I crossed the Atlantic on it aged 11. B. was scathing about some of the passengers; particularly wealthy women who came on winter cruises, and with whom a uniform did wonders for a man. One night he regaled us with the tale of a passenger who liked to be screwed against a palm-tree, preferably by a number of crewmen in succession. He surprised me by identifying her as a very famous Hollywood star who is dead now, but was then very much alive. I suppose it would be incautious to name her. "Funny, she was always dead cold when you done her," he mused, cradling a glass of *aragi*, of which he was rumoured to drink a bottle a day. "Some of the others were fine, but she made like she'd never seen you." And he lit a Life from the packet by his elbow. Lifes were cheap and horrible, and often referred to as Deaths; their name was changed from Life to Lite not long after.

How B. co-existed with John was beyond me. John, the oldest VSO in Showak, was 64 when I met him; but he was much the fittest of any of us, and an upright and rather old-fashioned man. He had started his working life flying as a navigator in Liberators and completed a number of operations over Italy. (He was not the only ex-flier among the volunteers in Sudan. Another VSO was still partially deaf

A refugee compound in Karkora settlement

after being shot down in his Spitfire while flying in the Royal Australian Air Force.)

After the war John had trained as an engineer, and rose to become chief engineer of a large North Country port - a job he resumed, after Sudan, on a contract basis. Like many such men, he missed the smell of oil. It was not a rare phenomenon in VSO; a successful engineer would retire at 60, having been behind a desk in management since 40, and decide that he should do some more fieldwork before turning to golf. John was an old Africa hand, having worked in Tanzania in the 'fifties, and I suppose it was natural that he would choose the VSO route back. There is a mass of such expertise around, men who are too old to be re-employed by commercial firms after retirement, but are still very fit, and would like to turn their skills to development work for two or three years before finally putting their feet up. Their lifelong experience not only helps them in their work; they also know how not to get sick. In John's case, I remember him being a bit unwell for one day, and that was all. John was a courteous and generous man whose work brought very direct benefit to people in the region. He was overseeing a drilling-rig, and was attached to the American division of SCF - the Save the Children Federation, which had hired the rig commercially in Khartoum in order to drill for water.

It was not easy work. John was long delayed at the outset while the hire of the rig was negotiated, and then while it was brought to Showak and made to work; even afterwards, it was not always reliable. I think that John felt increasing frustration towards the end of his stay. There were other problems. The SCF project aimed to benefit the inhabitants of Sudanese villages near the refugee-camps. COR had built up a massive infrastructure for the provision of potable water in camps, and this was open to criticism from the local population, as well as political groups like the National Islamic Front; it was argued, with some justice, that refugees were the targets of far more foreign aid than the local population, which was often poorer. So SCF had targeted several Sudanese villages to which John would take the rig in search of sweet water. One of these was just outside the sprawling Shagarab complex. I drove past it once; a poor and rather hopeless place of broken-down. *tukls*.

Drilling to sink a borehole in the region often meant going down 300 metres, and a ground-pump sunk to this level had best not go wrong, for extracting it from that depth was not easy. Sudan's Rural Water Corporation had earned some respect from expatriates for its ability to do this.

John's brief was that sinking the boreholes was to be a self-help project; the village sheikhs must give a prior undertaking that the villagers would help. Often they did, working with John through all the hours God sent. But sometimes they could not give a damn. Moreover, towards the end of John's posting, the constant delays caught up with him; the great rains of 1988 closed in, making the rig immovable. John knew that further work would now be impossible until long after his posting was over, and went home in disgust. But not before visiting 20 or 30 villages that had no water; and finding it for them, with a startling success rate.

John worked to geological surveys. He was an engineer. His secret weapon, however, was water-divining. This apparently very orthodox man had made the unorthodox work extremely well.

He used aluminium rods, which he bequeathed to his successor. But he used more than that. He had a pendulum. It would answer any question, yes or no; swung back and forth, it would continue or stop according to the reply. Would we hit basalt next? No. Would we hit mud next? Yes. John and his crew always knew what to expect before drilling began.

Seeing is believing, and by the time John left Sudan most people did accept that it worked. I know I did. One night, the electricity in Showak failed just as I was settling down for a good read. Exasperated, I braved the dogs and strolled down to the New Compound for company. For some reason long forgotten, only John was there. I found him in their little kitchen, clearing up by the light of a huge candle brought from England (the thin Chinese ones sold locally melted in the heat).

We chatted for a while. John told me that he had taken the pendulum out to see what time the light would come on again. This was uncharacteristic: "I try not to use it to answer trivial questions," he told me, looking almost embarrassed. He respected the power behind the pendulum and feared that if he misused it, it would no longer be at his disposal. "But I was reading a good book, too, and I thought, dammit, shall I go to bed or shan't I?

"Anyway, I asked it a series of yes-no questions, feeling rather guilty."

He had asked: Would the power come on again before 8.30? No. Before 9? No. Before 9.30? No. Before 10? The pendulum stopped.

"I confess I can't quite take it seriously myself," he mused, escorting me to the compound gate a little before 9. "Actually, I think I'll go to bed, after all...Goodnight, Mike. Thankyou for dropping by." John's manners being what they were, I think he would have said that even had I been the last person on earth that he had wanted to see.

In my own compound, I settled back in the easy chair with my personal stereo, and listened to the Beethoven violin concerto. Somewhere around the end of the second movement, the compound was flooded with light. Blinking, I looked at my watch. It was 9.35.

*** *** ***

JOHN sometimes expressed doubt about the wisdom of our presence. Were we simply pretending to help keep things under control, he asked, while the country slowly disintegrated? John's boss expressed more specific worries when I went to visit him one day late in 1988. He was sitting in his office, teaching one of his staff to use the computer. He came over to join me, and started to speak of his fears for the future.

In his early thirties, he was a Californian agriculturalist; he left SCF and Showak a month or so later to resume the farming life near his home town. A smallish, rotund and friendly man, he was an unlikely Cassandra. But he questioned the value of the whole settlement programme. Not only were refugees being allocated much less than half the absolute minimum acreage they needed for self-sufficiency, he told me; there were other ways in which the infrastructure could not cope. And was the soil going to last forever? It was already suffering. (Another American expressed doubts to me about drilling for boreholes in the region, saying that we were lowering the water-table too much, and that no-one had really worked out just how much we could safely take from it. Suleiman Osman denied this vigorously when I put it to him.)

Was the Californian right? Looking back, I think he was - to the extent that he pursued the argument. But he put forward no alternative plan, and I couldn't see one either. The Sudanese would not have dumped a quarter of a million people in the middle of a baked-earth plain unless the alternative was worse, or did not exist.

I didn't try to work it all out, anyway. To me, Showak in those early days was a collection of faces; Sudanese, Eritrean and Ethiopian, Danish, Thai and Japanese. Never mind why they were all there. I can still see many of them, in the light of a naked bulb in a compound at night, or the glow of the hurricane lamp when the electricity had failed; or standing in the souk, their features shadowed by the angle of the midday sun.

Chapter Five

January 1988: *Volunteers and visits*

On the first day of 1988 I awoke with a hangover and lay staring at the morning sunlight that had sought out the holes in my roof, making them twinkle in the gloomy interior of my hut. It was some time before I disentangled myself from my mosquito-net and rolled out of bed to face the shattering brightness of the day outside.

On the iron table below the *rakuba* was a note:

> *Hello Mike*
> *We are gone-as you see.*
> *thanks for the hospitality.*
> *have a good time here.*
> *bye bye Angeline*
> *Henny*
> *PS - we went to the bakery - here is some fresh bread*

There was no bread there; the cat had got it. But it was a nice thought.

Suddenly I felt very inadequate. Henny and Angeline, 12 hours in the town, and knowing not a word of the language, had made their way to the bakery and bought me some fresh bread that I had not bothered to find for myself. I stomped off to the shower to freshen up. Halfway there the thong of my left flip-flop detached itself from the sole, leaving the it flapping uselessly off my heel. F*** this country, I muttered, and limped off to soothe myself in the shower-water that, coming from an overhead oil-drum, still retained a little freshness from the night before.

Henny and Angeline had entered my life late the previous afternoon. Henny's craggy face and hippy locks had appeared around my door while, bored, as Ian was absent in Khartoum, I sat in my roughly-carved wooden chair reading Eric Newby's *On the shores of the Mediterranean*.

Henny explained in broken English that Theo, boyfriend of Elaine, the VSO physiotherapist in Gedaref, had told them to find Ian or Mike in Showak and they would be given somewhere to stay the night on their journey.

"Of course," I replied. "There's a spare *tukl*. It's a little dusty but we can clean it out. You're on your way to Kassala, I take it?"

"Is our next night stop, after Girba," said Henny.

"Then where are you going really?" I asked, puzzled. Gedaref to Kassala was about 200 Km, or three hours - hardly enough to justify two night stops.

"We are Dutchjes and we are travelling to China," Henny explained gravely.

I stepped outside. A tall, slim woman of about 30 stood in the yard; she had cropped blonde hair and a smoothly-contoured face, a contrast to Henny's crags and ravines. She was holding two smart, heavily-loaded bicycles, clearly European ones.

They had left Amsterdam on June 12 and had suffered amazingly few problems, riding through Germany, Austria, Yugoslavia, Bulgaria, Turkey, Syria and Jordan before hopping on a boat to Sinai and pedalling on down beside the Nile to Aswan. Taking the ferry down Lake Nasser, they had arrived at Wadi Halfa; there they had been forced onto a train for the first time by the sand surface of the 'road' that links Khartoum to the Egyptian frontier. They had just suffered their second delay; Angeline had been unwell for a week in Germany, and then in Gedaref all their documents had been stolen on Christmas afternoon. In the face of this disaster, they had done well to get underway again so soon. They would now undertake the long journey along the tarmac road to Port Sudan and would ship there for Yemen. They were unsure whether they would reach Beijing as visas for China were tricky, but they would try. In the meantime, Henny was 'phoning dispatches to a radio station in Amsterdam to earn money for the trip.

As we had no gas in the kitchen, I cooked them some rice in the other compound. Angeline was starving. I was embarrassed when she found some cheese in the refrigerator and wanted to eat it; someone had brought it, carefully wrapped, from Europe earlier in the year and was looking forward to it as a special treat. It could have caused quite a rift. Why didn't I just tell her to eat and be done with it?

We had a New Year party in the compound that night. It was a washout; few people came and even Bill and Rap didn't stay long, for a dust-storm was blowing and it was unbelievably cold. We drank some date wine brewed for the occasion by a European who did not himself turn up. (There was plenty left over, as it tasted foul; but it matured nicely during the next week or two, and Ian and I spent many happy nights in January playing Scrabble in a drunken stupor.)

We saw the New Year in, and then I was alone, although I sat up myself until two, trying to pick up the chimes of Big Ben at 12 GMT; then I would know that it was really New Year, I told myself. I could hear nothing from the BBC, however - a message in itself? I woke up in the blinding heat of the new day, hung over, depressed, and in some discomfort from a urinary-tract infection that I had had for several days. Henny and Angeline had gone, leaving a note, a memory and feelings of inadequacy. 1988 was in business.

*** *** ***

OF COURSE things improved when Ian returned a few days later, as I had known they would. In the meantime, in the office, Berhane was gearing up for the Khartoum Fair.

This international trade event had gone downhill with the economy, but was still quite an occasion. What Berhane was doing was collecting exhibits from the refugees for the Eastern Region pavilion. Thanks in part to him, it was to be much the best at the Fair.

One day two refugees from one of the settlements brought in a beautiful triptych in strip-cartoon form depicting the legend of Solomon and the Queen of Sheba. This traced the legend of the origin of the old rulers of Ethiopia through the ancient Kingdom of Axum, the seat of the Queen of Sheba. In 1988, Axum in Tigray was the target of air attack. But the triptych was a reminder of two millennia of civilisation in the Horn of Africa, its figures drafted and coloured in a stylised way that spoke at once of the region.

The refugees also brought with them elegant one-string viols from Eritrea. And there was more. One Friday morning I went to the office, working on the Sabbath to get access to the computer upstairs; the pride and joy of the administration department, it was a twin-drive Toshiba laptop with no hard disk, and was then the only computer operated by a Government department with responsibility for the lives of a quarter of a million people.

While I was getting the key to the office from the *gafir*, Hassen Osman appeared in the yard on foot. He greeted me politely, and then asked: "Have you seen all the items for the Khartoum Fair?"

"Some of them," I replied.

"I am going to see them now. Please feel free to come with me," he said. He led me to the conference-room, where the tables had been arranged in a circle. Behind them, Friday or no Friday, stood all the staff; on the tables were the exhibits. The viols were there and the trip-tych too, but so were myriads of *jebenah*-pots and *funjals*, the latter made locally for once and not in China; the sides of both were deco-rated with patterns of yellow and white, red and green, a riot of colour over the bare wooden tables of the conference-room. There was even a model of Abuda refugee-camp, complete with *tukls*, school, workshops and water-towers; even a little tractor in the livery of the Finnish Valmet company. It was impressive. Hassen strolled slowly around it, congratulating his staff and shaking their hands; they stood to attention as if it were a visit from royalty or a military inspec-tion.

A few weeks later, I was in Khartoum, and went to the Fair. It was held in a large modern exhibition-ground; it was an elegant complex, the stands and pavilions carefully arranged. But the collapse of the economy had bitten hard. Apart from the Bata shoe company and one or two sweet manufacturers, there was little in the way of locally-made hard goods; and there were fewer other countries exhibiting than there had been in previous years. When the fair was instituted in 1978, there had been 30 countries represented, according to the Government news magazine *Sudanow*. In 1988 there were 11. There were few imported consumer goods; only Yamaha and the Czechs had brought motorcycles. Only the American stand was really well-organised, and the British had not bothered at all. It was still a cheer-ful day out, but not an encouraging one for the Sudanese economy. It seemed that where there was no trade, the flag was loath to follow.

*** *** ***

TOWARDS the end of January Ian and I headed for Gedaref in the Land-Cruiser pick-up, by now shorn of its *dik-dik* horns (someone had nicked them). With us came Imat, Ian's Water Team driver, who promised he knew where to get *aragi* for us to take to Elaine, the Scottish physiotherapist; she was having a party. Imat found no *aragi* and went off, a flea in his ear, to drink *marissa* with friends. We went on to Elaine's to find the occupants sitting drinking in the hosh, their faces a ghostly presence in the dim cloud of light from an East German oil-lamp. The electricity was off again.

The electricity often was off in Gedaref. If it wasn't, the water was. Elaine and her housemate Trish, a radiographer from Lancashire, were out all day, the time when it was likely to be available. They caught it in buckets when they could.

Elaine and Trish never did have it easy. They had started by living in a straw *tukl*, both together in one room. Trish's equipment at Gedaref Hospital was old and one wondered about its radiological safety. Elaine did not have a department to work in at all to begin with. Worse, both were attached to the Hospital, built by the British in 1912 and spacious, but with no modern facilities at all. There had been a blood bank, but uncertain electricity meant that it had not been used for some years. Various wards had been added on, paid for by rich merchants in the city. But the hospital lacked a decent management infrastructure. It could also have done with better toilets. Later, the EEC started a project to assist infrastructure in refugee-affected areas, and Frank and Hughie tackled the hospital toilets; but when I saw them, they were a vision from Dante.

By the time I arrived in Sudan, Elaine had succeeded in opening a physiotherapy department at the hospital and had begged, stolen or borrowed bits of equipment. Despite constant politicking, she had managed to assemble some staff and was providing care to all those patients she had room to handle. Earlier in the month, I had visited the department with Frank, who was delivering a set of parallel bars he had built for Elaine's patients to exercise on. The place was bright and cheerful, and decorated with posters in Arabic that sought to raise awareness of disability. Everyone who came in looked happy to be there, staff and patients alike.

I always rather admired Elaine, but she needed no-one's approval and, a year later, would be embarrassed to find herself cast in the role of an angel. The cause of this was a magazine article. Some months later Nicholas Gordon, the editor of the *Mail on Sunday* colour magazine, *You*, arrived in Sudan for a flying visit. It was a brief journey (he was in and out of the country in 36 hours), but a sentimental one, for Nicholas himself was a former VSO volunteer in Sudan. He had worked as a teacher at Rufa'a, opposite Hasaheisa, in 1969-70 before starting his career in journalism.

He came to Showak with Ibrahim El-Bagir, VSO's Sudan field director, and Alastair Morrison, a likeable photographer who was doing much work for the magazine. The trio were late arriving in Showak and found that we had eaten the supper prepared for them, but sat down anyway and talked. Nicholas showed a lively interest in everyone's work that was not just professional; perhaps it recalled for him a time when people mattered more than layouts, schedules and getting just the right slant to all the articles.

Later that year I was to visit him in the *Mail* high-tech headquarters in Kensington, where the old Biba building had been taken over, gutted and transformed into a sort of yuppie paradise-on-earth. At the entrance, a portly journalist with a voice thickened by lunch bellowed across the hallway that he had forgotten his smart card, and would someone *please* let him through the electronic barrier? I ascended to the sixth floor in an extraordinary lift that took the form of a glass bubble, crawling up the side of an enormous atrium, the floor of which contained a collection of fountains that would not have disgraced the Alhambra.

In his eyrie, however, Nicholas Gordon seemed quite unaffected by the high style around him and gave me a courteous welcome. He showed me a pile of schoolbooks that he had gathered together and wanted to send to his old school in Rufa'a. (He had already sent some, but VSO, he said, seemed to have lost them.) And how, he demanded, was Elaine?

How was she? When last seen, she had been somewhat fed up about the article Nicholas had written about her.

Back in February, after an hour or so early in the morning in the offices and workshops of Showak, Nicholas, Ibrahim, Alastair and I had made for Gedaref in the car to see the legendary Elaine and the miracles she had wrought. We toured a ward where she was attempting to revive the punctured lung of a young man who had been stabbed in a street incident six months earlier. She worked on the man gently, a little embarrassed by the circle of journalist, photographer and assorted officials that had gathered around the bedside. As she worked, I interpreted for Nicholas in very bad Arabic as he asked one of the officials what had happened to the man, and how sick he was.

"I think this girl's going to be the main subject of the article," he whispered to Ibrahim in a low voice. At this point, Alastair took over and took her to a Land-Rover parked in the hospital yard, got her to climb on the cab and shot her against the sky, using bounce flash through a polarizing filter.

Before we left, Nicholas opened his wallet.

"Can I give you something towards the cost of running the department? Equipment, maybe?" he asked politely.

"Everything helps," she said truthfully, but her eyes stood out on stalks as he peeled off some hundreds of dollars in hard currency. I don't know whether it was *Mail* money or Nicholas's own, but I strongly suspect the latter. For some time afterwards, Nicholas wondered what had happened to the money. Elaine left two months later, having overstayed her term by some weeks, but a replacement arrived, and the money was spent quite properly; on equipment, I believe, rather than on a new extension as orignally planned. However, VSO seemed unable to tell him this.

That was later. Meanwhile, Nicholas went home and wrote his article, and I saw it in Khartoum some months later. Elaine had been presented as an angel of mercy, as she had rather feared she might be. But wasn't that the way a competent reporter would present such an individual? Albeit with a lack of saccharine - Nicholas was too good a journalist for that. Moreover, he had devoted some of the article to slagging off wealthy Gedarefenes for letting their hospital degenerate; although the city was poor, there were a surprising number of rich men in it, due to its role as a centre for mechanised agriculture. Someone once said that it had more dollar millionaires than Hollywood, although I doubt that. Nicholas was not being entirely fair to them as a few had paid for new wards to be added over the years, but in general I agreed with him.

I actually quite liked what he had written, but the incident exemplified the fact that nobody wanted to be regarded as unselfish or heroic. I think VSO did not really encourage recruits with such motives, probably rightly; confronted with the reality and compromises of development work, they might prove brittle. In fact, I think many male volunteers - particularly the technical ones at Showak - assiduously cultivated a hairy-arsed image.

*** *** ***

TWO DAYS later we loaded Elaine and her boyfriend into the Land-Cruiser and set off for Khartoum.

It was about ten when we left, having had a good breakfast at the Gedaref office of Help the Aged. Many offices were still breakfasting, and as we went past one yard or another, groups of men and women could be seen sitting around trestle tables in the shade of acacias, eating and chatting. It was not yet too hot; perhaps 90°F, quite comfortable in a country where humidity is so low.

Ian was going on holiday in Britain, and would spend a few days in Khartoum first. Elaine and Theo were off for a holiday elsewhere in Africa. I would spend a month or so in Khartoum doing a language course, which I had missed when I arrived three months earlier. We were all in a holiday mood.

I spent the first hour sitting in the cab with the two Sudanese drivers, later moving into the pickup at the back. There the four of us sat with our baggage, having covered it with rugs. The seven-hour journey in the open was not so grim as it might sound, for the slipstream kept us cool; however, the real problem was direct exposure to the sun, which affects the skin. A hat blows off at speed. And the wind can dehydrate you, slowly, without your noticing.

But I seem to have enjoyed it, watching the immense nothingness of Eastern Sudan slip by, the odd discarded fanbelt or tyre or complete wreck at the side of the road. We eased past old Bedford lorries piled up to twice their own height with sacks; on top of these sat eight or nine passengers. Near Wad Medani, Imat stopped to pick up a family going to Hasaheisa; I counted 13 adults and two small children in the back of the Toyota, but Imat, unconcerned, rattled on at a steady 100kph, radio blaring in the cab.

Slowly the landscape changed as we crossed the Nile at Medani and moved into the Gezira. Irrigated fields started to appear, palms by the river, a little greenness here and there and mud-brick villages beside the road; and I felt as if I were watching a film of my previous journey being run in reverse. Then the last checkpoint passed with much fumbling for documents, soldiers rifling through the cargos of the lorries stopped beside us. At about four we passed into the suburbs. Concrete blocks rose out of patches of bare baked earth, reinforcing-rods sticking out of the rooves, ready for another storey that would never come. Bit by bit, we came to the inner city and steered through Khartoum Three, the truck bouncing on the broken edges of tarmac, and made for Sharia Huriya, which would lead us across the Huriya Bridge and into Central Khartoum.

Below us, as we crossed the bridge, were the marshalling yards - eight or 10 tracks, of which one was free; the rest were crammed with decaying coaches that reminded me of 19th-century American stock as seen in films, with platforms forward and aft. Once, they had had grandeur; the great colonial express had steamed steadily from Port Sudan to Khartoum by way of Atbara, carrying Condominium officials on the last stages of their journeys from Britain. Dinner would have been served on white tablecloths between carriage walls of hardwood, polished, gleaming; polite waiters, compartments with big ceiling fans that turned night and day to ease the heat. But now the paint was gone, and many carriages were broken. Not a few were lived-in, children playing around the bogeys, washing hanging across the couplings from the eaves of one carriage to those of the next.

They said that the World Bank was going to Atbara to reorganize the railways. They said that there were a thousand drivers on the payroll, of which perhaps about 50 might have been on duty at any one time. They said all sorts of things about Sudan Railways; they were notorious, and much of the network had broken down completely. Buying a ticket was said to be a nightmare in itself, and the journey from Wadi Halfa to Khartoum was 55 hours; in a crammed carriage if you were lucky, on the roof if you were not. I think I saw about four trains actually moving while I was in Sudan. An Oxfam official I knew only ever saw one in the whole of her posting in the country. The trouble was that she saw it too late. She was driving across a level-crossing and was quite unaware of the train, as they were so scarce that no-one ever bothered to look before bumping across the narrow rails. The train hit the back of her Land-Rover and did surprisingly little damage, although naturally she was shaken. She never saw another train in Sudan until the day she left.

We had chosen a bad afternoon to enter Khartoum. Our route took us round by the National Stadium, where the two main clubs in the capital - Hillal and Merikh - were locked that day in combat; the streets were full of supporters who hung from cars and minibuses, waving flags, laughing, cheering, and blowing their car horns so often that my eardrums sang. They were smiling and friendly. This was not like a football crowd in England. The hysteria was real, but this was a day out, not a vent for aggression.

The Sudanese were mad about football. They were also rather good at it. Their teams have been consistently good performers in the Africa Cup, and Hillal once gave a good account of themselves against Liverpool. This had not been achieved by buying players from abroad for vast sums; Merikh did have a refugee from Ethiopia, but he was in Sudan before he was in Merikh. Players' salaries were far higher than an ordinary person's, it is true; but even a star would make what a bus conductor would in London. It was a fortune for Sudan, however.

The crowds were as good-tempered inside the stadium as they were outside it, as I discovered when I went with Pierre de Kock to see Hillal play a Zambian side in May. He, I, the Ethiopian supervisor of the VSO rest-house, Ngusi, and another English volunteer, Derek, went together; we were viewed with some suspicion by the police at the gate, perhaps because we were the only Europeans in the 30,000-strong crowd. They took us into a side-room and frisked us before allowing us to proceed. They didn't do it to anyone else; perhaps they had heard of the reputation of English supporters and were looking for alcohol. The match itself was played hard and well, a tough 90 minutes in thick air that, even at eight in the evening, was 110°F at that time of year. It was easy to see that Liverpool would not have found their hosts a pushover. A military band entertained the all-male crowd, which nibbled at nuts, cheered and barracked; squads of riot police armed with sub-machineguns guarded the perimeter of the pitch itself, but there was no hint of trouble. I could not have enjoyed a match like this so much in England at that time; it would not have been safe.

*** *** ***

THE TOYOTA eased its way through the crowds, taking an hour to travel the two miles from the Hurriya bridge to the VSO rest-house in Mogren. By now I was tired. When we arrived, there were 11 people chasing four beds. I spent the next few nights on the floor, but I didn't care.

Chapter Six

November 1987 and February 1988: *Khartoum*

But of course I had been to Khartoum before. In the hottest places, big planes come and go by night, so when I had first arrived in Sudan the previous November, the plane had arrived in Khartoum at about 3AM. We had stopped at Cairo, where the plane had virtually emptied. It was as if we were in a train stopping at the last station on the main line before taking the branch line into the depths of the country, where nobody goes, especially at night. The aircraft was a silent cathedral, a deserted cinema in the sky.

My first sight of Sudan was, I suppose, a pinprick of light in the vast darkness below us, about an hour after we left Cairo. I fondly imagined that it must be an Arab encampment in the desert. In fact it was probably the railhead town of Wadi Halfa, as a later flight in daylight showed that we followed Lake Nasser down to where it narrows back into the Nile, and we crossed the frontier over water.

An hour after that pinprick of light, I saw moonlight reflected in a great silver expanse of water below. It was the junction of the White and Blue Niles. We dipped a wing and circled the city, and slowly houses appeared, a network of square yards, shapes becoming defined, a roof here, a light there, finally a *gafir* sleeping on an *anquarayb* in one of the yards, oblivious to several hundred tons of plane screaming down above his head. Then we were down, ready to start the long journey through customs in a surprisingly modern arrivals terminal.

I travelled to Sudan with another new volunteer, who was bound for Dilling in Kordofan; a young banker from Dublin, he was expecting to administer a rural credit scheme for a British NGO. An ebullient man, he was well pleased with his skill at getting three times his baggage allowance onto the aircraft without surcharge. But he was to find that life in Africa had its ups and downs.

The introduction of rural credit schemes was a fundamentally good idea in Sudan, where peasant farmers were shackled by *shail*. This was a system whereby seeds are obtained with credit raised from the merchants, to whom much of the crop was pledged in return. In a good year, the peasant will get little benefit from an excellent harvest, as much of it goes straight into the merchants' sacks; in a bad year he will derive no compensation from the higher prices, for the same reason. So the idea was a good one, but the volunteer was to find that no preparation had been done; his boss was unsympathetic and seemed uninterested in him, and the civil war was creeping northward towards Dilling. He was even to have trouble getting there, making a 36-hour bus journey as far as the regional capital of El Obeid only to be told that his documents were not valid for the rest of the journey. He trekked back to Khartoum, changed his permit and cadged a SudanAir ticket back to El Obeid, finding his way thence to Dilling.

He never got the scheme underway. Later, a few people would say that he should have persisted. I was not so sure; perhaps he himself thought it might eventually be possible, but concluded that it was not worthwhile. In any case, rather than take a softer option - a ticket home to the job in Dublin that was being kept open for him - he spent a month or two working in the food distribution depot of the Irish aid agency Concern in Babanusa, on the edge of the war zone. With little to eat, he became ill. Eventually, he did find a soft billet in Khartoum, and sat out the remainder of his posting there; under the circumstances I cannot blame him. Moreover, even there he was still working hard. But after the coup of June 1989 this too turned sour, and he was later apparently asked to leave amid trumped-up charges involving arms-smuggling.

That night in November 1987, all this lay in the future. We were met by John Challoner, the then VSO Sudan Field Director, who drove us to a square concrete hotel with zinc doors; bare by western standards, it was clean and not unfriendly. How many poor sods, dreaming of saving the world, have found themselves lying at four in the morning, head spinning from flight and confusion, watching the fan turning slowly on the ceiling above, sweating in the unfamiliar heat? Actually the fan wasn't even turning that night. There was a power cut. I sweated, but it didn't bother my travelling companion. He was sound asleep, snoring peacefully in the bed next to mine.

*** *** ***

KHARTOUM had burst upon us like a blow on the head the moment we stepped out of the hotel early the next morning.

The impact of light in a desert land, upon one who had never seen it, was spectacular. It lit everything so brightly; the dust, the concrete, the broken black pipework and cables sticking out of the cracked pavements, the men in their startling white *djellabiyas* crouching by the side of the road drinking tea; traffic, donkeys pulling water-carts made out of old oil-drums lashed to worn-out lorry differentials, bright yellow taxis that were 20, even 30 years old; Ford Consul 375s and Hillman Minxes that honked and bucked their way round the souk-trucks that stood in the middle of the streets to discharge their loads or change wheels. The roads were tarmacked in the main thoroughfares, but they were badly broken, and where there was a pothole, it took the form of a savage little trench across the road, with jagged tarmac lips. As for the buildings, they all seemed to be of cheap, square concrete, discoloured, never white, never brown; just indifferent, with dingy doors set behind pillars of tiles or plaster. Between the two would be galleries where you could walk, but there was no pavement as such, and where there were gaps between buildings, pedestrians were forced to leap into the traffic and back again. Dogs slept, unperturbed, amid the chaos. My eyes hurt. The vinyl seat of John's pick-up scorched my flesh through the thin lightweight slacks. You have a simple choice, I told myself; take an interest, or consign yourself to two years of utter misery. So I took an interest, and slowly the city of Khartoum started to resolve itself into districts and faces, older buildings as well as cheap new ones, roundabouts here and there decorated with hibiscus, the odd dusty neem tree; and a few *hosh*, or yard, walls garlanded with bougainvillea that flowed across their parapets like a slow, fiery waterfall.

The city, I observed in an early letter home, seemed grim on first acquaintance, but every now and then one wandered into little squares, the walls of which were so garlanded... Did one? It must have been the heat. I was right the first time. Khartoum (although perhaps not Omdurman) was, at first sight, a toilet.

The simile comes easily. In 1943 Operation Torch took the writer John Steinbeck to North Africa and he commented that the whole of the Middle East smelled like the giant toilet it had been used as for four thousand years. This is unfair. It is actually the smell of the dust. But certainly this rank odour hung in the air in a big city like Khartoum or Gedaref or Kassala, and you could never quite get away from it, especially on thick, hot summer nights.

But there were oases in the capital. One such was the suburb of

Mogren, where VSO had its own office in a one-storey building surrounded by trees. Mogren means "the meeting of waters". It was here that the Blue Nile from Lake Tana in Ethiopia met the White Nile from Uganda; they came together in a great sweep of water several miles wide. Near here, the great flying boats of Imperial Airways swept down to refuel on their journey to the Cape, and it must have been a sight after hours above the desert; an inland sea. The riverbanks at Mogren were partially wooded, and you could walk across a short stretch of field from the ring road, beside rows of date-palms, watching oxen plough and small boys in dirty *djellabiyas* drive herds of goats just as they did in the countryside. And the earth just here was a rich dark brown. Richard Dowden of *The Independent* once wrote that he saw a goatherd guide the birth of kids yards from the Hilton Hotel in Mogren, and this does not surprise me. There was a timelessness about Mogren, despite its location in the inner city; even the pick-ups roaring down the dual carriageway beside the Blue Nile towards the heart of Khartoum often had livestock in the back, old-fashioned brown sheep with woolly coats and long ears, standing stupidly upright, ignorant of the knife that awaited them on the morrow.

Away from the river, Mogren was leafy, a place of trees and frangipani and quiet yards like VSO's own. Rich people lived there, and there was an embassy or two; that of Egypt dominated the entrance to the suburb and many times I walked past it in the night, dodging the dogs, and imagined the gastronomic delights being prepared within. And the river frontage was dominated by Friendship Hall, built for the congress of the Organization of African Unity in 1978; a splendid modern air-conditioned building with assembly halls, cinema and cafeteria, a total lunacy in a poor country, even when it was built. But I could not help liking the Sudanese for building it.

Follow the road from Mogren on the banks of the Blue Nile, towards the city centre, and you travelled back into another world. The bank was again lined with trees; opposite was Tutti Island, a place that belonged to those that were born there, and sold their houses to no-one who couldn't trace their ancestry back on that little patch of land. Ferries disgorged them on the beach from time to time, and shoals of white figures streamed up to the May Gardens, where a restaurant served well-prepared dishes of meat or of fish in batter, and the attractive young aristocrats of Khartoum came to meet their girlfriends. Romance pervaded the May Gardens; I even saw couples kissing in the darkness.

Walk on from the May Gardens, if you could stand the heat and the sand that makes walking slow, and you came to the Grand Hotel, where the British stayed in their heyday. The hotel was still elegant, with its terrace where a sugared *limuun* cost what the average Sudanese made in a fortnight. Still with its marbled colonnades, too; its cool, dark entrance hall with its whiff of fresh bread from the on-site bakery, and the classical bar where you could buy as many cigarettes as you wanted, even in times of shortage.

On from the Grand, and the Ministries began, overlooking the leafy corniche; the most spectacular of them all was a great red stone building, once the Sudan Club, where the British gathered, but now the Department of Protocol of the Foreign Office. Finally, a gateway appeared across the road; the presidential palace, two sentries in decorated frock coats and ornate headdresses guarding the entrance to the staircase on which the Mahdi's men did for Gordon a century before.

That was to your right; look to your left across the broad, grey-blue waters of the Blue Nile and you saw the enormous paddle-steamers, white behemoths with stern-wheels that slewed slowly through the murky waters of the Sudd as they had done for all the century, bearing the District Commissioner northwards from his lonely hell towards Khartoum, dinner, dancing and the train to Port Sudan, whence he would take ship for Suez and home on leave. A prospect to look forward to as one watched the wheel rip the surface of the White Nile and break it into a thousand fragments that caught the evening light as you smoked your pipe, watching the Nuer and Shilluk sleep peacefully on the decks below. But now the huge boats stayed where they were. The war had blocked the river-route south, and only the odd armed convoy staggered as far as Malakal in the early part of the year with ammunition and food for the besieged. It had been thus for five years.

To walk along Nile Avenue was a trip back in time, but the people of the city were too busy to make it with you. And if you opened your eyes a little wider, you saw the usual black pipes sticking out of the broken pavements, even here; and the groups of Southern teenagers with their flat, African faces, scratching along as best they could, selling cigarettes and washing cars.

*** *** ***

CONFUSION had greeted us at VSO that November. John spent an hour or so warning us of the manifold horrors that awaited us, then assured us that we would have a lovely time if we tried hard enough. (But he also kindly gave me a book on the history of the Sudanese media, which cannot have been easy to find.) He then went off to Showak with a visiting colleague from London, saying that the office manager, Fatih, would look after us for three days. Fatih, however, had other, pressing, concerns; but he was a nice man.

Of Western Sudanese descent - his family came, I think, from El Fasher, towards the Chadian border with Darfur - he was round, tall, cheerful, friendly and full of good ideas. Whatever was needed, he had an idea how to get it. One of his first tasks on my behalf was to give me a photography permit to fill in. When this was done, it would be taken to the Government office to be stamped. There was no charge for this. The paper is in front of me now, signed by me and dated November 3 1987. On the bottom is a list of conditions, mostly fairly standard, but a few of them rather odd, viz: "Slum areas, beggars and any other defaming subject are not to be photographed". It is countersigned Secretary Cinmatograph Board (sic). How one was supposed to decide what could not be photographed under this provision I do not know, but as most European journalists came expressly to film the things defined therein, it is a good thing it was rarely put to the test. But it is revealing. Sudan is a poor country, and the Sudanese were happy to acknowledge it. What galled them was the Western tendency to see only its poverty, and that I understood.

At any event, Fatih disappeared later that day and we were left in the hands of Hannah. Hannah was a fellow-volunteer who had been on a training course with me in England, and had herself been in Khartoum only a month. She was working as a public relations and liaison officer for the Institute of Traditional Medicine in south Khartoum. Small, wiry, with light, lively eyes and wavy brown hair, she later studied medicine in Britain. She was happy to see us that day in Khartoum, but perhaps not so happy to be lumbered with us. However, she had the good grace not to say so.

She took us for a walk that first evening through Khartoum to the Sudan Club, where British expatriates congregated in the afternoon and evening. The walk from the hotel in Sayeed Abdul Rahman Street to the Sudan Club, which was just off Gamurihiya, was a circuitous one; she took us through the souk.

We stepped out into the darkness, and I had - as I often would -

the sensation of putting on a warm velvet cloak that had dropped around me in gentle folds. It is not unpleasant; it is rather comfortable. We crossed the road outside, scraps of paper and rubbish showing light against the greyness, and walked along the side of the street in the thick, squishy dust, dodging the pavement slabs that, dislodged, lay between the bits of broken piping; and moved here and there into the shelter of a building, being careful not to step on any sleeping figure, be it man or dog. Down a side-street, eyes peeled for a taxi or bus reversing towards us; conscious all the time of the way light from any source, be it buildings, headlights or whatever, shone through the *djellabiyas* of the men and the *toabs* of the women and caught the dust particles in the air so that the world was strangely spectral. Through narrow streets past shops that sold essentials, past the spot where the tailors sat in long rows over their ancient, treadle-operated Singer sewing-machines, who could copy anything, and did. A favourite shirt would be duplicated and run up to perfection in whatever material you chose to bring them in just a day or two. A bolt of cotton cost about S.25 a metre - about £2; they could make a shirt from this, or from two metres would tailor those baggy, seamed trousers with great pockets and deep turn-ups that were so cool and smart in the heat.

The whirring of the Singers dropped behind us as we stepped into the souk area and found ourselves in the meat-market. As it was evening, the long covered shed that housed the market was deserted. We walked between cages and pitches that, in the morning, would be alive with men carving meat and poultry with knives.

What I remember most about the meat-market, that night and afterwards, was the smell; it really reeked, a horribly sweet miasma from weeks' worth of dried blood and waste. It made me retch; I could never go into it. In Showak, it was different. There, the meat market was a single stand with a counter raised quite high around its outer edge, where the butchers stood outwards, facing the customers. You went up to them, spotted a side of meat that you liked, and haggled with the butcher for a decent cut. You always watched to make sure that you got what you had requested. Far from being revolting, it was quite enjoyable, provided you weren't too squeamish about meat. But here in Khartoum, the meat-souk was a disgusting place. Hannah noticed our distaste, and shrugged. "This is where you come to get meat," she said. "You want to eat meat, it's up to you."

There was another shed, running parallel, where vegetables were sold. This was busier in the evening. In the mornings, it was very busy indeed, and the aisle between the sheds was packed with women and boys who sold the green and red peppers I used for cooking, off sacks on the ground; eggs, if there were any (they were usually all sold by 11 AM); and sometimes dried fish that looked to me so lamentable that I could never touch it. At the end of the sheds was an open space around which were the stalls of the established grocers, selling aubergines and great sun-ripened tomatoes grown in irrigated plots by the Nile near Merowe. There were carrots, too, unavailable except in Khartoum and one or two other big cities. There were beetroots. And there were potatoes; these were expensive, about S.10 a kilo, say 35p per pound, give or take an ounce or two. This was in a country where a well-to-do civil servant or professional man might earn only £2 a day. You did not use them to feed your family, but as a luxury served in small dishes, and this might accompany your breakfast if you were feeling rich. The same went for pasta, which was available but expensive; most was imported from Greece or Egypt or occasionally from Italy. There was a cheaper local variety used for making another small dish of very thin spaghetti sweetened with sugar. I never saw a Sudanese use either potatoes or pasta as a source of carbohydrates; always it was bread, which formed the bulk for every meal. They found our use of luxury foods as staples surprising.

On the other side of the open space were the fruit-stalls. These were attractive, raised above ground-level so that you looked up and across the merchandise at the vendor. The stalls held green oranges, small and sweet; guavas, tender, but with masses of pips that caught in my teeth; great bunches of bananas, green with the odd rogue yellow fruit standing out; and sometimes green grapefruit. Best of all, though costly even here, there were mangos; delightfully sweet and soft, but somehow disappointing because so little was flesh, the stones being enormous. A favourite, if messy, treat; sometimes I would cut them into strips and serve them with yoghurt and sugar. Although not unfriendly, the fruit-vendors never had quite the easy charm of the vegetable-vendors opposite. I think the fruiterers saw themselves as the aristocracy of the market.

In the centre of the open space were boys selling bags. Everything in Sudan seemed to be recycled; I have already described how the goods in Beshir's shop were wrapped in old newspapers imported by the shipload from abroad, so that your herbs and spices were decanted into a funnel made from the *Straits Times*. It was the same with the bags; normally they were rough linen ones with the mark, as in

Showak, of a Romanian cement concern. Or they were plastic. You paid; a a linen bag cost S2.50, not cheap-half the daily wage for some. They lasted well.

I liked the market, as I did in Showak. An expedition for vegetables was a friendly business, with the sellers - who were crowded together - shouting *"Khawaja! Khawaja!"* to try and interest you in their wares, pointing to piles of tomatoes or potatos with real enthusiasm. But I never heard them bid against each other on price; only on quality. If you liked what you saw, you bargained then, but the price never varied by more than 50 piastres between one vendor and another. After all, they had to sit beside each other day after day..

A curious feature of this bargaining - which was never very serious - was that, after finally conceding a *tarada*-a-kilo discount at the end of five minutes' verbal, a merchant would carefully measure out the agreed quantity-then, grinning, pick up your bag and tip in a few extra potatos or tomatoes on top of the ones he'd just measured out. The Sudanese, paradoxically, are good businessmen, but also hate to be thought of as mean, and are unable to restrain their generous impulses.

I often thanked God I was in Sudan and not in some country where the foreigner was a target for rip-offs. But even in those, perhaps, it's just a question of navigating the culture. One day towards the end of my time in Sudan, I was chatting with an acquaintance who worked in the air-conditioned, high-walled British Council fortress near Souk Two. He mentioned that he himself had been a VSO volunteer, in his case in Egypt. On his first outing to the souk in the small town south of Cairo where he had been working, he enquired at a stall the price of some aubergines.

"X pounds per kilo," he was told. Fine, he replied, I'll take a couple of kilos.

"No, no," said the stallholder, genuinely shocked. "You're supposed to *argue* with me. Listen, like this..."

*** *** ***

OUR WALK with Hannah, having taken us through the souk, continued past the crumbling Arak Hotel and into Gamurihiya, the Street of the Republic. This was Sudan's Oxford Street. It hardly looked it. Like every street in Khartoum, it was lined with crumbling concrete blocks from the 1960s. In the overhangs in front of them, traders set out their stalls - actually just mats spread out on the concrete. Men and boys sold items such as electrical plugs, shavers, batteries (lots of batteries), cigarettes from cardboard stands, cheap multivolt transformers from Hong Kong (always popular items - about S.50, but they rarely lasted long), screwdrivers, screws, and unidentifiable pieces of scrap and angle-iron. They crouched on their haunches day in, day out, and I suppose they made a living. Behind them were shops; often travel agents - Khartoum has many travel agents. Or shops selling stationery, or typewriter repair shops. At the posh, eastern, end of Gamurihiya there was a bookshop; there was the odd crafts shop, and in an arcade below the Sahara Hotel, many souvenir-shops selling small carved items of ivory, and jewellery, the value of which was hard to determine. Some of it may have been very good; the Rashaida women made superb items of gold that they sold direct in Kassala, the best place to go for it. There were other bits and pieces for the visitor. Incongruously, one of these shops displayed a letter acknowledging that some item or other had been presented as a gift to Edward Heath some years previously.

Gamurihiya was tatty. It was also seething with black-market currency traders, one or two of which were unpleasant. Usually, a polite "no thankyou" got them off your back, but some were more persistent, and I had a vicious argument with one who became too much of a pain.

There were two good reasons for not doing business, even with the good ones. The first was ethical. By offering three times the official exchange rate for pounds or dollars, they were undermining their own currency. (Foreign aid workers, their best customers, probably accounted for much of Sudan's foreign exchange.) As the country earned less than half its foreign-exchange requirements, this had to be wrong, but I am afraid that most of us were unscrupulous about this.

The second reason was that it was not safe. Standard procedure was to take you down a side-street to do the actual exchange; normally this was all right, as they were rarely thieves, but it could go wrong. More seriously, not all of them were ordinary decent criminals. Particularly around the Sudan Club, they could be members of the security staff in disguise. After the 1989 coup, these traders were cleared away, their fate unknown. I can not be sad for them. But the men who came for them also expelled the women from the souk - those harmless women who squatted beside the grocers' stalls, selling their little piles of green peppers and onions.

We followed Hannah through the posh part of Gamurihiya, stepping over the street-traders, until we came to a tatty side-street. We walked down this until we saw a gate of iron grillework set into the high white wall. Beside the wall was parked an unusual variety of vehicles, many of them Land-Rovers.

Through that gate was another world.

First there were flowers, growing on a trellis beside the well-tended path; a white building with an elegant verandah to the right; up the steps, a terrace where Europeans sat around tables with white cloths, quietly drinking Pepsi or *karkadee*, eating, talking, often in sports gear with squash-racquets on the floor beside them. This was the Sudan Club.

Every European who had passed through Khartoum for any length of time had been to the Sudan Club. Founded at the start of the century for British personnel, it was a survivor from the Condominium era. It was no longer in its original premises. Thomas Keneally's novel *To Asmara* described the place as an echo of the colonial past, with lawns and bars through which the old SPS administrators must have passed. But they never did. They had the huge sandstone building overlooking the Nile near the Grand Hotel, confiscated by Nimeiri in 1971. However, he gave them the choice of a lump sum or a lease elsewhere as compensation. Unwisely, perhaps, for it was now threatened with eviction again, the Club had chosen a lease on two adjoining white houses with gardens, in the very heart of the city. They had once been the property of a Greek merchant.

You couldn't get a sundowner here anymore. Alcohol was forbidden as firmly in the Club as anywhere else; it was not diplomatic territory. However, for some reason the booze stocks had not been removed, but placed under bond in the cellar. A rumour persisted that members had broken in on more than one occasion and drunk the odd bottle of Scotch on the terrace in open defiance, but I never saw it happen.

The bar now dispensed *karkadee* or *limuun* in litre jugs, Pepsi and cigarettes, and was manned most of the time by a soft-spoken, friendly young man from Shendi who spoke little English. The bar-room itself was almost always empty, people preferring to sit on the terrace outside. There were curious reminders of the past; a notice on a pillar warned members that sleeveless shirts and shorts were forbidden in the bar and dining-room after seven o' clock, while a cabinet in the corner held rows of cups for sporting achievement at cricket, tennis, or whatever over an 80-year period. Beside them stood a framed letter dated November 1964, thanking the committee and members "for your best wishes on the occasion of my 90th birthday"; it was signed Winston S. Churchill. He too, I suppose, left a little of his soul in this land.

There was a large, clean swimming pool in a raised enclosure above the lawn, and during stays in Khartoum I sometimes used this as the only place where I could get any exercise. There was a squash-court that I never used, and there were other facilities.

When I had gone to the VSO office for the first time that morning, a welcoming cheerful letter had awaited me from Liz, a community development worker who I had met in England; she had arrived with Hannah a month earlier, and had gone on to her job in El Obeid. "Hi Mike!" she wrote. "Welcome to Khartoum! I'm very glad you made it here - you must be fed up with all the delays - but now you're here forget the hassles and have a good time. I hope you're feeling positive... If you want a swim, go to the Sudan Club...It's a bit stuffy, but they have videos, snooker, a pool...colonialism...chocolate eclairs..."

Actually, it was not colonialism, so much as aspiration. Nicholas Gordon put it another way, telling me how 20 years earlier he had been to the old Club building by the Nile and found it full of lower-middle or middle-middle class people who would not have wielded much power at home, and who revelled in the chance to push the waiters around.

I once met a man in the bar who, for me, summed up the British Abroad (although this specimen was friendly). He was an official from the British Embassy, a curiously detached institution with whch most of us had little contact. Hot and sweaty after a good game of squash, he sat on a stool beneath the swamp cooler in the bar, enjoying a long cool *karkadee*, dressed in shorts and singlet, red thighs bursting out from beneath (it must have been before seven). His task, he told me, was to order certain administrative supplies for the building; he had been in Khartoum for two years of a three-year posting, and cheerfully confessed that he didn't know a word of Arabic. This was when I had been there about a year; my own Arabic was poor, but I could carry out basic work functions, do my shopping and certainly pass the time of day.

I remember another brief visitor, a girl of about 15, tall, blonde, a bit puppy-fattish, with large, erect breasts, big lips and a slightly surly expression. She was wearing a tight tee-shirt and the briefest of shorts, and perched on a stool, one sandal flapping off her heel. Her complexion glowed with youth; every time she moved, the breasts jiggled cheerfully under the thin layer of cotton, like two ferrets in a sack. The lad from Shendi averted his eyes. The members clustered eagerly around the bar for once. I suppose she was a change from the dusty aid-workers in from the provinces, who always dressed decorously so as not to offend Muslim sensibilities.

When I think of her, I think of another girl I saw at about the same time. I was in a midi-bus, one of those vans-with-seats that are the backbone of the public transport system outside the capital. I was waiting for it to leave Gedaref for Showak, a departure delayed by a shortage of diesel; the vehicle was crammed. It was mid-afternoon, the light was just beginning to soften, the sky just turning from its washed-out midday blue-white to the deeper hue it wore between teatime and sundown, when everything took on the form and colour that it had lacked in the fierceness of the day.

Some yards away, there stood or squatted a number of women, laden with large stainless-steel trays of nuts and seeds and other small items that people might buy to ease their journey. Some laid them on the ground; a few carried them on their heads, African-style. One such was a girl of around 12 or 13, her adult shape just forming; but her dress was still short, the hem high on the thighs, its green cotton stretched tight around her waist and her new breasts. She was quite tall; her face was half Arab and half African, indicating southern blood. Her eyes were slightly hooded; her lips, too, were full, and there was a bloom about her that brought to mind the teenager at the Club at once. When she looked briefly towards me I felt a sort of electric shock; felt, too, that she could look inside my head and understand everything that went on there, or at least, everything that was material to her. Then, slowly, the midi-bus pulled out across the broken tarmac and drainage-ditches towards the Kassala road, and she was gone forever. I wonder if she is still alive.

*** *** ***

THE SECOND day after we arrived in Sudan in November had been the Moulin - the Prophet's birthday. It was a public holiday and any agenda that VSO might have had for us was suspended.

Hannah came down again to take us out, the plan being to travel across the river to the house she lived in in the Morida suburb of

Omdurman, on the Blue Nile opposite the city centre. We went again through the network of side-streets opposite the hotel, this time in daylight, and came to the huge open space between the Arak Hotel and the Mosque El-Kebir. This was the central bus station; not the one for Showak, but the one for local traffic. The buses were mostly old East European or Indian-built ones, with a sprinkling of former American school buses, and quite a few second-hand Dutch vehicles still carrying Dutch advertisements and destination-boards for Amsterdam suburbs. During a working day, the place was chaotic. Streams of ancient single-decker buses poured in to load and discharge at the 10 or 15 bays, and passengers would fight their way on board with unbelievable ferocity.

We were lucky; it was quiet, as the day was a public holiday, and we went to the back and settled ourselves on the rearmost benches, our legs splayed round the dusty spare wheel that lay on the floor. One was not normally so lucky. On later occasions, taking a bus into the city centre from Mogren, I would have a job to cram aboard, as by the time they reached me they would have taken passengers on board from Morida, on the Omdurman side, all the way across the Omdurman Bridge. Even when the buses were frequent, it was common to have to wait for the fifth or sixth before one could board. Even then, it was sometimes necessary to hang on around the doorway, a hand on either side of the aperture, with passengers inside bearing outwards onto you, your arse flying in the air while you prayed that it would not make contact with a passing lamp-post. The boys who collected the tickets travelled that way as a matter of course; they looked very young, perhaps 12 or 13, although age was deceptive in Sudan and they were probably older than that. Perhaps they were selected for their agility, for they always seemed to be able to squeeze themselves back on after stops and then insinuate themselves through the aisle to collect the one-tarada or 50-piastre fare. They had little change; there were 10-piastre coins in circulation, but inflation was such that they were very rare. So they would issue credits to be used against the next ticket. Many passengers did not bother to keep these, regarding it as mean. If you had no change, you would simply pay the fares of the passengers on either side of you, and the next day someone would do the same for you. No-one ever tried to evade the fare.

When the bus into town arrived at Mosque El-Kebir, getting off was always difficult, as people were trying frantically to get on as soon as the doors came within range. I am surprised that my glasses survived two years in Sudan, so often were they knocked off my face in the struggle to get out of a crowded, decrepit bus while everyonr surged forward to take my place. No-one thought this rude. It was the local custom. Indeed, transport was so short that the struggle to get on a bus was taken to extreme lengths; I never saw anyone lose their temper, but I did see passengers leap through the rear windows of buses as they pulled out of the souk (the glass had often long disappeared). When this happened, others would lend a hand and pull the passenger in by his shoulders. The sight of a bus leaving with two or three pairs of legs waggling away out of the rear window was as comical as it was alarming. Fortunately, the authorities had forbidden people to travel on the rooves of the buses and this rule was observed, or I am sure that there would have been frequent fatalities.

But we were spared all this on the day of the Moulin, as I have said. We pulled out of the souk after about 10 minutes, crowded but not stifled, looking curiously at the Dutch advertising slogans and route maps on the walls above the windows. We made off down Sharia Jama'a towards the Omdurman Bridge, enjoying the breeze that came in through the glassless windows, and saw the zoo drift past; I never visited it, but was told that it was a sad place. The May Gardens with their excellent restaurant flashed by on the left as we gathered speed; and then we wheeled right onto the Omdurman Bridge.

This spectacular structure links Khartoum with Omdurman. The conurbation is known collectively as the Three Towns - Khartoum, Khartoum North and Omdurman. The spot where the bridge crosses to Omdurman was an attractive one. The long bridge was manned by police inspectors, but they did little until the hours of darkness. As you mounted the bridge the pleasure gardens of Mogren Family Park appeared, with their big wheel and other fairground rides, sticking out on a spit of land that supported the bridge for the first few hundred yards. Then you were over the flat-calm waters of the Blue Nile, the bus's wheels clinking and rumbling over the metal joints in the road. You could see left and right for miles, and the breeze across the water eased the mid-morning furnace. As the bus approached the north bank, one saw the great modern Parliament building, and the mosque beside it. The Parliament building was beautiful; a style best described as modern Islamic, with rows of lamp-stands descending the terrace to the water's edge. On the shore itself, I was intrigued to see a square kilometre or so of fertile land that was obviously in use. Later, I remarked to my Arabic teacher, Abdel Moneim, that I liked a capital in which you could watch oxen ploughing before Parliament. He replied that the land was seasonally flooded, and that that was the only reason it had not been built on. But I still remember it as something I admired about Khartoum, along with the goats that grazed in front of the Hilton.

Our route took us round the back of the Parliament building and the great mosque, then cut back to the right towards the Nile. We got off and walked back across wasteland towards Hannah's house, which she shared with a Sudanese staff member of VSO and the staff member's sister.

I was struck by the private nature of a house in Sudan; it was surrounded by a high wall, and the street outside was no-man's-land. The distinction between the general, which does not matter, and the personal, which does, is often much stronger outside Europe. Thus the Prophet's injunctions on personal hygiene may be strictly observed, and yet no-one troubles about the state of the place in a more general way. The streets around Hannah's home were typical; they were a mess, with the usual accumulation of discarded plastic bags, cartons, bits of peel and, alarmingly, used needles. Yet as soon as she opened the door of the *hosh*, we were in a different world. It had been smartly swept; there was not a bit of rubbish anywhere.

Like many Sudanese houses, it was of one storey and built around the courtyard in a rather rambling way. On the left was Hannah's room, with a patio outside that was covered over and fronted by two rather nice columns that looked as if they might have been insprired by the Parthenon. They sat well with the light-coloured stone. Inside, the ceiling was high, and supported fans that turned slowly on long shafts; it was dark, with zinc shutters that took the place of glass being firmly drawn shut to keep out the heat and dust of the day.

We sat on the patio in the shade, drinking *limuun* and eating fruit. I remember watching the doves that played on the wall, white between the light-brown stone and the deep blue of the afternoon sky; bit by bit the sunlight retreated up the wall towards them, the line of shadow moving with deceptive speed as the sun's hot rays left us in peace to enjoy the last brief hour of daylight, while Hannah made some *karkadee* in a jug, with lots of sugar. There was little sound in the *hosh*.

As darkness fell, Hannah announced that she would have to go soon to the bakery, or we wouldn't have any fresh bread. I went with her. We made our way through the unlit, unpaved streets, past the abandoned combine harvester (what was that doing in the middle of Omdurman?); across the stretch of waste-ground where the children played football in the afternoons; over a drainage-ditch and down an alleyway to where a gaggle of people, mostly women, waited in front of the closed shutters of a low mud-brick building. I remember that it was almost the only place where I ever saw the Sudanese form an orderly queue. The women reached out and smacked children who tried to push in front of us. If they were surprised to see two foreigners queueing for bread with them, they didn't show it.

The women were dressed in multicoloured, swirling toabs; they were mostly middle-aged, large, fat, rather fierce, many of them with tribal scars. A typical scar, that of the Sheguy from Northern Sudan, consisted of three vertical slashes down the cheek. There was nothing unusual about this, or about the scars on the wrists or temples that many people had from medical treatment given by the traditional practitioner in their villages.

At 6.15 the shutters opened, and a smell of new-baked bread flooded across us; immediately, everyone was pushing and shoving. Behind the counter, two or three men in dirty *djellabiyas* moved quickly, carrying long loaves very like French baguettes. I never did see bread like this away from Khartoum; every region had its shape, and this was the capital's. When we got to the counter, Hannah bought eight loaves for 15 piastres each. But they were too hot to touch, and when she tried to pick them up she was forced to drop them back on the counter.

"Perhaps you can make an apron of your dress and carry them that way," I suggested. Doubtfully she did so and I dropped the hot loaves into it, much to the amusement of the other customers, who laughed - not rudely - at the sight of the *khawajaya* marching off with eight long loaves bouncing in her makeshift apron. As we crossed the waste-ground, we started to eat the hot bread. I have never had bread like it since.

As we walked, laughing, munching, the moon lit our way. It had been rising since an hour or two before sunset, first pale silver against the light sky, then bigger and more distinct as the blue mellowed into night. Now the disc was yellow. Later we went down to the river; a breeze had come up, as it sometimes did after sundown, and the surface of the Blue Nile was covered with a million tiny ripples. The moon, ahead and a little above, cast an immense pathway of gold across the water towards us, so that it seemed one might walk down to the water's edge and along the beam to the Presidential Palace on the south bank. The moon shone through a canopy of date-palms and acacias, lighting, to our left, a series of low embrasures built by the Mahdist forces to defend the city against Kitchener in 1898. They were a monument now, but people lived there in lean-tos made of cardboard and corrugated iron; now and then, as we walked slowly across the packed earth, we would see a flash of white in the gloom as someone moved silently around them.

There was something ancient about this place and the mood of it

A Nile felucca under construction at Omdurman

held me, even after my companion and I had an argument with a taxi-driver who, after being given twice the normal fare, demanded yet more. (The Sudanese are less mean than almost anyone, but taxi-drivers can be an exception, as they can in any big city.) Without paying extra we walked away and settled into bed. Once again, my neighbour fell asleep at once, and I could hear his peaceful snores mingling with the squeak of the ceiling-fan above our heads. But I didn't sleep. I lay there and thought of a thousand things; of the white clubhouses with their green lawns and purple bougainvillea against a rich blue sky; of Dutch buses, displaced, rattling across a great steel bridge past oxen that ploughed dark earth in the heart of a city; of a vast yellow moon tipping liquid gold across a river between the date-palms, and the whiff of charcoal from the kanoon in Hannah's yard; of hot fresh bread and Doric pillars, of doves on a wall and *karkadee*. I will like it here, I told myself before I finally fell asleep, untroubled by the clangs and scrapes of zinc doors opening and closing and echoing through the bare corridors of the hotel. I am going to be happy here.

*** *** ***

NOT LONG afterwards, I had gone to Showak. Now, three months later, I was back for the language course VSO organized for all its new volunteers. The VSO rest-house was full, so I slept on cushions purloined from the sofa, while Ian crashed down on the cushionless springs and announced that he was quite comfortable. Ngusi, the caretaker of the rest-house and office, removed the odd beds he used as furniture in his room next door and they were put in the hosh, mosquito-nets being hung from bamboo poles lashed to the bedsteads.

Ngusi was an Oromo from Western Ethiopia; he had left in 1983 and scratched a living as best he could in Sudan until VSO gave him a live-in job. This kept him safe and not uncomfortable, although hardly rich. He was about 30, and anxious to begin a new life in Seattle, where he had relatives. He already had entry papers for the United States, and looked forward to seeing his brother, who was a pilot there; and to studying marine biology, which was what he had always wanted to do for a career. He was fluent and literate in both English and Arabic, although neither was his own language or script. His generosity and understanding with volunteers who straggled into the rest-house at all hours of the night were legendary, and if a volunteer was alone there, he would often suggest that they come to his room to watch football on television or to join him for a meal of zigani, a hot, spicy Ethiopian dish made with chicken, eggs and flat unleavened Ethiopian bread, and cooked by his girlfriend on the *kanoon* kept just outside his door.

Why hadn't he already gone to the States, I asked him? He explained that he was one of several thousand refugees who had been lucky enough to obtain third-country resettlement, but were being denied exit visas by the Sudan government. Every now and then he would stroll round to the United States Embassy opposite the Faisal Islamic Bank and ask the Americans there what was happening. He would be greeted with coffee and courtesy (more than he would have received at a British embassy, I suspect) and it would be explained to him that the Sudanese authorities were still being intransigent. Much

The first car in Sudan? An exhibit in the Khalifa's house

of the problem arose from the US decision to cut wheat shipments, which partially explained a dire bread shortage that began in 1988 and did not end in my time. The delicious bread that Hannah and I had bought in Morida would soon be a thing of the past, and suspension of exit visas was one way in which the Sudanese expressed their displeasure. However, the military government that took power in June 1989 scrapped the policy, and Ngusi got safely to the States after years of uncertainty.

When I had been back in Khartoum for five or six days, Ian flew to Britain on holiday. Ibrahim El-Bagir, the VSO field oficer for the Showak region, who had recently taken over from John as field director, drove Ian to the airport himself and I went with them; we left Ian outside the terminal building, shivering, sitting on his suitcase in the small hours of the morning in a biting February wind, the sword he had bought as a family gift lying across his knees.

The next day, my language course began. The Khartoum International Language School was a long way in two crowded buses. Neither was the tuition consistent; Abdel Moneim himself was very good, but had little time to teach. He was also ill, and had been rushed to hospital for an operation in early February. So we made do with his employees, some of whom were better than others. There were five of us, including Simon, a bricklayer from Coventry who was coming to live in Showak with us.

It was not an easy month; I had malaria again. It left me weak, and when it was still fairly bad I remember standing on Simon's balcony in his hotel, drugged up to my eyeballs with chloroquine and listening to

The Doors on his personal stereo and suddenly, just for a second, having the conviction that I could fly. Such notions are unfortunate when you are standing on a fourth-floor balcony, listening to Jim Morrison singing *The End*, volume turned up high.

The month had its lighter side, however. Although all but two of us had been in the country for some time by then, we were still technically newly-arrived volunteers, and were therefore treated to the odd excursion including a tour of Omdurman one Friday, which I enjoyed, and should have enjoyed more had I not had a low fever. It was organized for us by an official of the museum in Khartoum; this museum had been "temporarily" closed for some months and some people's opinion of the official was not high. Certainly he seemed a little odd, but he was friendly and helpful. He arranged a midi-bus for the afternoon and we rattled north across the Omdurman bridge, springs squeaking, bodywork swaying, making for the boatyard on the banks of the Nile.

This was where the traditional Nile feluccas were built. It was an area of shallow-sloping bank not far from Hannah's home in Morida. The area was littered with tools, logs and wood-shavings, and in several places the feluccas were supported on trestles, the hulls in various stages of completion. Two were already afloat, and were in the process of being rigged. There were no workmen there, as it was a Friday. I looked closely at the hulls; they had been put together without fasteners or nails, simply constructed with an eye to the way the wood would hang. They were quite impressive once launched, having a graceful shape, and somehow epitomised the Nile to Western eyes.

Down in the shallows, there were two souk-trucks being washed; they were surrounded as usual by the smaller Toyota Hiluxes, and by little shoals of riding-boys with rags, removing the grime of the week. The trucks reminded me of hippos at a lake's edge, bodies partly supported by the water, surrounded by birds. "They are not supposed to be doing that," said the official, frowning. "It is illegal." Yet they made an attractive sight, the brightly-decorated royal-blue lorries reflected in the still blue water, the boys calling to one another, enjoying their afternoon; probably it was as much a social occasion for them as much as anything else.

We moved on. Now we were bound through the quiet Friday streets of Omdurman for the Mahdi's tomb and the Khalifa's house.

The Mahdi's tomb dominated the Omdurman skyline, for there were few high buildings north of the river. It looked to us like a mosque, with a high gold dome that shone dully in the sunlight. Westerners were forbidden to enter, although I did later hear of a volunteer who was invited in by a family to which she had become close.

Instead we went to the Khalifa's house opposite. The Khalifa succeeded the Mahdi, who had died very shortly after taking Khartoum. The Khalifa gets a rough ride in Alan Moorehead's *The White Nile*; it is suggested that he was enormously fat and lay on his bed living the good life for much of the 13-year span of the Mahdist state, while his minions raked in taxes from a Khartoum populace that was oppressed as never before.

Sudanese people disputed this, and the Khalifa's house was actually quite austere (though I did notice the enormous bed). In the courtyard, a number of exhibits had been corralled; largely cobblers' and other craft machinery from the time of the Mahdiya. These items looked to me to have workmanship better than one saw in modern Sudan. And there was one item that gave me quite a start; it was what looked like an 1898 Daimler, the first car, it was explained, to enter the country. It looked in a good state of preservation, although the chain-drive was rusty and the paintwork long gone. I wonder if British motoring historians know that it is there.

But the real treat of the afternoon still lay ahead. We were going to see the dervishes.

Sudanese Islam is diverse; broadly speaking it is Sunni rather than Shia but is split into a hundred different sects. The number of mosques on the Khartoum skyline amazed us - but that they were not all used by the same people, there being so many subdivisions each with mosques of their own.

The dervishes of Omdurman revered a saint whose body had been washed up on the banks of the Nile in a good state of preservation long after his death. They honoured him by dancing and chanting themselves into a trance before a mausoleum on a patch of waste ground in the vast cemetery to the north of the city. We approached the mausoleum, where they danced an hour before sundown every Friday, to find that a crowd had already formed in front of the mausoleum, and were grouped around a circular area that the followers of the sect were keeping clear. It struck me at once that most of these people were simply there to watch, and that many were not Sudanese. On the eight-foot wall around the mausoleum, 10 or 15 people sat to get a better view, their legs dangling down towards where the dancers would be. Half of them were Westerners with cameras slung round their necks, and I have to confess that I had my own.

At about half-past four a lorry drew up some way away, and the dervishes climbed off and marched five abreast towards the clearing in the crowd, carrying great green banners decorated with verses from the Koran. Some also wore green robes; others were in green *djellabiyas*, incongruously sometimes with sunglasses. To the sound of rhythmic, rather sinister chanting from the loudspeakers wired up on the walls of the mausoleum, they started to pace hypnotically around

Dervishes arriving at the mausoleum, February 1988

the edge of the arena while the Western aid workers clicked busily away on the parapet of the wall above. Slowly the mood intensified. I found the whole thing puzzling as much as anything else; how on earth does one work oneself into a trance of religious adoration to feel closer to God while being watched by a crowd of a hundred or two, a third of them Western aid workers toting Nikons?

I ambled around the outside of the arena, looking at the refreshments being sold by the women who crouched on the ground a few feet away; vegetable samosas of some kind, sweets, bits and pieces of fruit. As I did so, a comotion broke out behind me. I turned to see what was happening, but I was too late; I heard later that a woman, overcome with religious feeling, had apparently launched herself into the arena and attempted to join the ceremony. She had been bundled out of the ring by the dancers, who were outraged that a woman should violate this male proceeding. One of them, it was said, had actually sat on her.

We left them to it, and bumped away between the tiny grave-markers across the vast sea of the dead that surrounded the mausoleum.

*** *** ***

KHARTOUM was a city of rumours. Every Middle Eastern capital is. But there was a special urgency about this, for Sudan was divided into two distinct halves; one a democratic state, the other a battlefield.

Two volunteers were stationed in Kadugli, on the border between the two halves. One of them, Mike Laing, had just gone there on a preparatory visit; he came back to Khartoum in December, not long after I arrived. He was attached to a UNICEF project, maintaining handpumps at wells in villages around the town. It was a confused situation, he told me; the Government still did control the countryside around Kadugli and he and his boss moved through it with surprising freedom, but during the wet season this control broke down, and there was fierce fighting only a few kilometres away. Dressing stations in the town were busy, and in the previous year (1986), foreigners had actually been evacuated from Kadugli for a fortnight in September as things were getting out of hand. Even at other times, one could still hardly feel normal when the UNICEF Twin Otter that served the project had to spiral straight down like an autumn leaf from 20,000 feet for fear of the Sam-7s in the surrounding countryside.

Mike Laing went back to Kadugli and stayed there until the spring of 1989, but by then things had got worse. They had long been uncertain. Mike Morris, the VSO field officer whose patch it was, had managed to get down to Kadugli by road in the autumn of 1987 to check up on the other volunteer. As was expected when travelling in Sudan, he reported straight to the police on arrival. The senior officer told him that his documents were in order, but told him to get out at once anyway.

"Can I stay to breakfast?" asked Mike, thinking that if he snuck out to a restaurant he could use the hour or so so gained to go and see the volunteer and ensure that he was safe.

At that moment the office door opened, and a servant appeared with the police chief's own breakfast.

"Of course. *Fadl.* Be my guest," said the chief, and Mike gritted his teeth, sat down and tucked in. In fact, the volunteer, blissfully unaware of the chaos around him, was out climbing a jebel.

But the situation in the south generally worsened during the following year. During 1988, some 200,000 people were murdered, died of starvation or stepped on land-mines. The Government had employed militias recruited from the Muslim border-tribes to try and keep order in the area, and the result was a massacre. Mike Laing himself told me of a village he had passed where 30 people had been summarily hung by such a tribe. The Mesiriyah, in particular, excelled themselves.

A landmark was the incident at Ed Duein, just outside the war zone, in 1987; refugees fleeing from the fighting were set upon by the militias and butchered in the railway station. Estimates of the number killed ranged from 125 to about 700. A year later, refugee-trains were arriving in Khartoum so packed that the dead and dying tumbled on to the platforms; in one train of 300, I was told, 30 had died in cattle-trucks.

Yet all through this, Sudan - at any rate, in the north - remained an oasis of free speech.

"We have complete press freedom here," I was told by John Young, a Canadian journalist working on the English-language daily the *Sudan Times*, "and we can print whatever the hell we like." Only once, he said, had a paper been closed down; that was when one of the Arabic dailies had libelled a Minister, suggesting that he had been giving information to another power and saying that they had tapes to prove it. When, after some days, they refused to stump up the tapes, the Government did lose its temper, and shut the paper down. But it was back on the streets again in three days. Occasionally, it was true, the Government resorted to underhand tactics such as rationing newsprint to the unruly; they could do this because the country was strapped for hard currency and all imports had to be approved.

The *Sudan Times* did not pull its punches, severely criticising the war in the south. It was edited by a southerner: Bona Malwal, a towering Dinka well-known outside Sudan for his writing and research, and a talented journalist. I met him twice. The first time he virtually ignored me, sitting behind his desk (which looked far too small for him) like a volcano about to erupt. The second time he was much friendlier, albeit brief. He must have known that the democratic inter-regnum in Sudan might end suddenly, and he was courageous to run the paper in the way that he did. Oddly, pure timing later saved him from detention and possibly much worse; when the 1989 coup did strike, he and a number of Sudanese intellectuals were in London, attending of all things a seminar on the future of their country.

The *Sudan Times* was not the only English-language daily. There was also a strongly anti-Government four-page sheet called the *Sudan Star*, printed on terrible paper, front page surmounted by a masthead that proclaimed: *The Paper for the Nation Without Fear.* There was much speculation as to who funded this (I later found out). Bringing up the rear in the English-language stakes was a well-written and beautifully-produced weekly broadsheet representing the active, well-organized Communist Party of Sudan. All these three were but adjuncts to a large and diverse Arabic daily press.

Neither was this freedom confined to newspapers. In 1988 Nigel Twose of the Panos Institute visited Sudan and commissioned a num-ber of distinguished Sudanese journalists, development specialists and academics, including Bona Malwal, to contribute to a book, *War Wounds*, an anthology assessing the effects of the war and the 1988 floods on Sudanese life. The contributors were very frank about the shambles perpetuated in Sudan by the failure to end the war; and yet it was written by Sudanese, in Sudan, and although published in London was freely available in Khartoum. I even had the freedom to review it myself in the magazine we were publishing in Showak. And we were, technically at least, a Government publication.

There were one or two areas where the press could not easily go, however. Anything to do with Sudan's relationship with its neighbours was sensitive, particularly with Ethiopia; I fell foul of this myself when I wanted to publish an item on the Eritreans' plans to provide education when the war in Ethiopia was over. Hassen firmly binned it.

The Canadian, John Young, encountered this in a different way. He cared deeply about conservation, and was appalled by the damage wrought on the country's wildlife by Saudi princes, who were said to hunt in Sudan with machine-guns mounted on Land-Rovers. You could, it seemed, write freely about a massacre of people. Oryx were another matter, so important was the relationship with Saudi Arabia; Sudan was dependent on the Saudis for oil supplies, and for remittances. Nearly a million Sudanese were thought to be working in Saudi Arabia and elsewhere in the Gulf, doing jobs for which the newly oil-rich states lacked sufficient skills. So the oryx were out of luck.

This irritated John Young, but the paper had other problems. In a country with little hard currency, little technical training and uncertain power supplies, producing a daily paper was a nightmare. One of the first things I noticed in the office was a dot-matrix printer operating with a sheet of carbon between the head and the paper, as ribbons were unobtainable. And when the *Sudan Times* failed to appear, it was usually because a power cut had stopped them using their computer typesetting equipment; even a brief cut was enough, for the air-conditioning would cut out too and then the room would have to be cooled down again before the equipment could be run.

This was not the only cross John had to bear. What was the production schedule? I asked.

"We aim to get the first pages typeset and laid out by three," he said, "when..." He turned round, flung open a double shutter in the wall behind him and leaped through it; he was now standing in the deserted art room, beside an empty layout table. "When these F*****G people turn up for work..."

*** *** ***

ON MARCH 1 Simon and I took passage in the Toyota Land-Cruiser that UNHCR ran as a shuttle-service between Khartoum and Showak. The language course was over; it was time to go home.

Joining us on the journey was a beautiful young American with rich red hair that flowed down to her waist; she was a reporter with the *Atlanta Constitution*. It was an early-morning start, and we were both fell to dozing, so that her head fell against my shoulder and her hair fell over it like a silky waterfall. Simon teased me about it unmercifully for months aftwards. In fact, she was a capable journalist called Deborah Scroggins who managed to travel deep into South Sudan and later published a well-regarded book, *Emma's War*. I spoke to her in Showak and was intrigued to find out that she had abandoned an academic career studying the achievements of the Vikings.

There were now four of us living in the compound: myself; Simon; Wayne, the mechanic from Manchester, who had transferred from elsewhere in Sudan; and Ian, who was still on leave in Britain. The first issue we had to face when we reopened the compound was

Bernadette. She had fallen into the water-tank. Ian had left instructions with Miriam's children to see that she had plenty of water, but they obviously hadn't done it, and the bird had drowned while trying to get a drink. In the tank, she had decomposed. I fished her pathetic remains out of the tank and buried her behind the kitchen; meanwhile Wayne and Simon set about draining and disinfecting the tank. While we were busy with this, some bastard sneaked into the compound and nicked Simon's wallet, taking his first month's salary and his passport. It was not a good start.

Chapter Seven

Spring 1988: *Religion and death*

Ian returned in March, just as the heat began to approach its zenith before the coming of the rains. One day in April, L., a driver with the Water Team, came into the compound to see him. L. was extremely tall, walked with a loose, slightly affected gait, enjoyed a drink and a whore and was stoned for most of the time I knew him, but today he had other things on his mind; it was Ramadan.

"I don't believe it," said Ian at supper that evening. "These bleeders are all fasting. Jesus, even bloody L.'s doing it. Anyway, he's invited us down for Ramadan *fatuur* tomorrow. Coming?"

Once a year (by the lunar calendar; it moves back a few days each time), Moslems maintain a fast from sunrise to sundown every day for a month. During the fast they touch neither water nor food in the daytime, and will not even smoke a cigarette. That year, Ramadan fell in April and May; these are the hottest months in Sudan, before the rains begin in earnest in June.

The fast was enjoined on Moslems by the Prophet, in order that they might understand the sufferings of the poor. There is no doubt that it does bring people closer together, and they included us, particularly if we made the effort to fast for a couple of days to see what it was like. I refrained from drinking water, eating or smoking in public, which seemed to be enough. However, there was water in the refrigerator in the office; as neither Berhane nor I were Moslems, we became a focus for fast-dodgers. These included the southerners who adhered to Western Christianity - usually Catholicism; and the Eritreans and Ethiopians, who had their own Orthodox faith. And there were the Moslem backsliders and dissidents; one very senior staff member, a Marxist, announced publicly that Ramadan was a load of superstitious twaddle and that he wanted nothing to do with it. Bit by bit the sinners started to beat a path to our door. Or to Hassen's; he was a practising Moslem, but kept iced water in his refrigerator as a courtesy to visitors.

The usual European reaction to Ramadan was that it was mad. I disagreed. On the first day of Ramadan, the English language service of the BBC broadcast the relevant *suras* from the Koran and I thought they made some kind of sense, particularly since they included a get-out clause for those who really couldn't face it. They might, it was written, give alms to the poor instead, since that was what it was all about anyway. Nonetheless, as the temperature rose and my colleagues began to look terrible in the 120°F of May, I began to wonder. And what would happen, I asked them, if they were working in the Arctic Circle, in the Land of the Midnight Sun? Would they fast 24 hours a day for a month? Eh? I never got a straight answer to that one.

Still, an invitation to Ramadan *fatuur*, or breakfast, at sundown was very kind, and we climbed onto the back of Ian's truck and went off to the part of Showak where L.'s family lived, in the sprawling mass of *tukls* on the other side of the souk.

Elaine, who was staying with us, was separated from us as soon as we arrived and taken off to the women's quarters. The rest of us knelt down around a tablecloth that was packed with nutritious foods-and drinks; *karkadee* and *limuun* to refresh us, but also rich dark beverages made from dura to restore us after a day of fasting. We waited until six, when the older men in L.'s family judged it correct to break the fast, and then ate. Everything was passed to us first, as we were the guests, even though we had not been fasting.

When the meal was mostly finished, the 15 or so men stood in two lines facing Mecca to pray. It was nearly dark, but the sky to the west was still pale aquamarine, and the Evening Star was the only one that could be clearly seen. Straight above us, the other stars were starting to become apparent in that strange way that they do; you can detect them when you do not look at them, but cannot find them when you try to do so directly. There was silence but for prayer; chanting - not mindless rhythm, but something more graceful. The men knelt, then stood; there was a breeze that caught their white and brown *djellabiyas* and made them quiver. I looked again for the stars, but could not see them; only when I turned towards the Evening Star, shining boldly on the horizon, could I sense their presence.

"So strange," wrote a friend, Jenny, to whom I had described all this, "to read about broiling heat and Moslem custom on a wet morning in London." I suppose it was. I had written her the next day, and must have mentioned the long line of men praying, stately, to Mecca; and she must have read the letter at her desk at *Fishing News* while the rain poured down on Farringdon Lane, outside her office window.

It was powerful stuff, this Islam, and yet it never affected our lives to the extent that people at home thought it did. If I wanted a drink

I could have one, albeit discreetly; I did cover my arms and legs in public, but it would have been madness not to in that sun. Women were more directly restricted; there were things they could not do. Yet the Sudanese women themselves were not veiled, unless they belonged to certain tribes. They did generally wear the *toab*, and were very restricted in their lifestyles, but they were not chattels, and they were proud.

They had a terrible cross to bear, though. Any westerner who visits Sudan must become aware of the custom of circumcision, which is performed on girls at the age of seven or eight. It is savage. In its most basic form, it is clitorectomy. Full Pharaonic circumcision involves the removal of the labia and the drawing tight of the aperture. It is often referred to today as female genital mutilation, which it is. About 85% of the women of Sudan are believed to undergo circumcision, and a large proportion of them are thought to undergo Pharaonic circumcision, although the latter was made illegal in 1947; this ruling, although not repealed after independence, was not enforced.

Besides restricting full enjoyment of sexual activity by the woman, circumcision has other concrete health consequences. Delivery requires a partial reversal of the operation; the mother will be stitched up again afterwards. This makes life complicated for Western midwives in Sudan, and a woman who had recently given birth once told Ian that she had had problems: "The *khawajaya* midwife isn't used to women like us," she explained, without censure. There are other distressing aspects to this; a woman may have permanent difficulty in passing water, and may suffer chronic infections, which she may well tolerate all her life. Too drastic a Pharaonic circumcision may also make intercourse difficult, and it is not unknown for a young man, desperate, to take a screwdriver to his bride on the wedding night.

Why persist with this? The older generation of women believe that their daughters will not marry if the work is not done. Midwives continue to perform the operation, often in unhygienic conditions, because it is their source of income; they don't have another. Men may believe that reducing the pleasure available to women through intercourse ensures fidelity. And they certainly believe that the tighter vagina gives more satisfaction to the male; they assume that intercourse with an uncircumcised woman must be unsatisfactoy.

This was not something in which foreigners could lightly get involved. It has always been a delicate matter, and change is best achieved within society itself. In Eritrea, where the EPLF was committed to social reform as well as fighting the war, there was said to be a trend away from genital mutilation. But elsewhere, the practice is entrenched in 30 countries in the northern half of Africa and affects about 85 million women. It is an ethical problem for foreigners; while they are best advised to leave the problem alone, it may be difficult for them to do so, especially if they are committed feminists.

But it should not be ascribed to Islam. I have sometimes heard it quoted it as evidence that Islam was an inferior way of life to our own, but there is little mention of the custom in the Koran. I understand that the Prophet is only known to have referred to the subject once; when asked by a woman whether she should be circumcised, she was told it was her decision. Even this, apparently, is in the equivalent of the apocrypha, not in the body of the Koran itself. Moreover, genital mutilation is hardly restricted to the Moslem parts of Africa.

In any case, our society has its own forms of violence by men against women.

*** *** ***

FATALISM is another charge made against Islam - the religion whose very name means 'submission'.

"We believe that all things are the will of God, and that we must accept them," said my colleague Yassin. We were sitting in his father's *hosh* in Gedaref a few months before I left Sudan; it was the first time that I had seen him for some weeks.

Yassin was one of nine children in the family. The second oldest, a son, had recently been in a bus that had been in a collision on the main road between Wad Medani and Hasaheisa. It had burned out; the escape door at the back had apparently jammed, and 44 people did not escape. Yassin's brother was one of the victims. He had been a successful and popular man in his 30s, working for the Sudanese branch of a large Western company in Khartoum. The incident had caused shock in Showak, where Yassin, who worked for the Administration, and his family were popular; they were highly educated, but Yassin in particular was committed to public service. He was one of the best people I met in Sudan, an excellent colleague and a kind friend.

When news of the accident reached Showak, it was time for *Fadat'h*, the giving of condolences. Abdel Jallil, the head of the com-

Schoolboys on morning parade in Abuda refugee settlement

modities distribution unit, would drive down to Gedaref that evening and take anyone who wished to come, so that we could express our regret to Yassin's father and family. About nine of us did so.

The procedure is simple. A number of others will also be there; you meet the head of the family, shake hands, then gesture with your palms upturned to signify the reading of verses from the Koran. Then tea is served, and you stay for a while.

The family was wealthy, and popular; there were an enormous number of people milling about the big house on the outskirts of Gedaref. We shook hands; verses were represented and then we took off our shoes and trooped into the room set aside for the afternoon, where the *khaddam* brought us tea and water. Yassin and his father looked quite broken.

The memory of Yassin's exhausted face stayed in my mind and a few weeks later, when business took me to Gedaref, I paused at the house and went in to see him. I found him much better. He talked freely about the accident. He also talked about a career-change he was going to make; his family planned to invest in light industry in Gedaref, employing local labour and bringing jobs and money to the region. He was clearly upset about his brother, and accepted it as the will of God; but there was nothing fatalistic about him, in the sense that a Westerner would understand of squatting on your haunches and giving up. Fatalism, to Yassin and other Moslems, meant not so much the acceptance of misfortune that was avoidable as dignity in the face of that that was not.

The fact remained that there sometimes seemed to be a curious lack of will to change things in Sudan, a strange acceptance of things as being unavoidable when they weren't. Still, in the spring of 1988 things lay ahead that would make a fatalist of anyone.

*** *** ***

CHRIS AND CLARE Rolfe had arrived in Showak while I was in Khartoum in February. They took the house immediately opposite our compound; it was a simple place, long and narrow, with a *hosh* fenced off by a *biriish* wall. It became a family home, as they had two children - Tommy, who was about three, and Louise, about half that age.

Chris and Clare had been sponsored by Ockenden Venture, a small British charity that concentrated on aid to refugees both in Britain, through aid to Vietnamese and other exiles, and outside it. They were to run the Community Development Unit it had set up with a consortium of contributors to work with Ethiopian refugees from a base in Showak. Chris and Clare were motivated by strong Quaker convictions, and had just spent three years in Somalia on community development and income-generation. They had been sufficiently pleased with the results to write, with a third party, a book called *It Can Be Done*; published by the Intermediate Technology Development Group in Britain, it was becoming a standard text. They became popular very quickly. In Sudan, the newcomer gets a warm enough welcome, but it is likely to be six months before s/he is really trusted. Chris and Clare appeared to win people's confidence much more quickly than that. Over the next few weeks, I got to know them.

At the beginning of April, we were all invited to a wedding. Yousuf, the computer operator at COR in Showak, was getting married; it was a genuine cause for celebration, as he was my age - 30 - and has wanted to marry for some time. The wedding was at Um

Shejerah (literally, 'mother of trees'), a prosperous farming village between Gedaref and Showak. We decided to go together. It took Chris and Clare an hour or two to bathe the kids and get ready, and then we climbed into their G-Wagen and joined the stream of Friday traffic towards the city. Children's drinks-bottles, nappies and other pieces of family junk flew around the car as Clare, in the back, fussed about and told the children to shut up as mothers do everywhere. Once there, she and the children went off to join the women while Chris and I joined the wedding-party with all the other staff from Showak, eating well. A *faki* arrived; Sunni Moslems have no priests, but there are learned men who know the Koran well. He gave a brief, cheerful oration at which everyone laughed; much tea was drunk; and I marshalled 25 or so people in the *hosh* for a wedding photograph. Yousuf himself stood at the front, looking like the cat that got the cream. Behind him were all his friends and workmates; Yassin is there, as is Chris, standing out as a tiny white blob in a sea of Sudanese men.

They had not been the only new people to arrive from England while I was in Khartoum. At the monthly coordination meetings of the voluntary agencies I sometimes found myself sitting next to Sally Rockett, who was working for the World University Service in Gedaref. She was an ex-VSO volunteer, although I didn't know that until later; she had been working in Nepal. I never knew her well, but we met a number of times.

It was getting hotter now; April passed into May, and on the second of the month a few blobs of rain fell in the early afternoon. I felt them as I rode home on my motorbike, and swept into the compound, throttle twitching, with an ironic cheer. "It's raining!" I yelled. "The rains!" Hastily we stacked the cushions for the garden seats in the kitchen.

But it wasn't really going to rain, not yet.

As the heat increased, Chris and Clare fretted about bureaucracy. Like all aid projects, they needed a formal agreement with COR; this was just a formality, since they were effectively working for it. But they needed a tripartite agreement signed by Ockenden Venture, COR and UNHCR, the latter being the funding body for most of COR's work. It seemed irrelevant, as UNHCR was not funding the Community Development Unit; Ockenden Venture was doing that, and COR was administering it. But bureaucracy had to be satisfied, and the delay in signing the agreement got longer and longer, while Chris and Clare itched to get their hands on the funds and step up their work.

They were not the only ones. Berhane and I had finished work on the *Showak Handbook*. I wanted it to be properly typeset and assembled as a neat paperback book that people working on the projects, or in the European aid agencies, would want to keep. Berhane had his doubts about this, but was prepared to try it if Hassen could be convinced. In the meantime, we still had no departmental budget. We bickered, lost and regained confidence in each other and generally managed to keep ourselves amused.

For Berhane, this was easier than it was for me. He had a role which was natural in a way; as an educated man and an experienced journalist and teacher, he was the father-confessor for refugees that had problems in the camps, and they would come to him and pour out their troubles. Knots of tired-looking Eritreans and Ethiopians would come into the office and he would sit there, apparently impassive, but actually listening hard.

Probably, in many cases, he did manage to help. In others, he must have passed the problem to Hassen Abdel Gadr, the legal advisor to COR, who was attached to the Gedaref office. Some of the cases that passed through the hands of Hassen Abdel Gadr and his colleagues at the UNHCR protection office made interesting listening. I heard, for example, of one case of an Eritrean refugee who had joined COR as a mechanic. Like many Eritreans, he proved better at it than his national workmates, and inevitably this caused resentment. Perhaps, in this case, the refugee was also boastful of his ability; if this was the case, he was unwise, because his workmates managed to frame him for a child sex murder. He was duly arrested and charged; but either Hassen Abdel Gadr or UNHCR got him off.

Hassen Abdel Gadr was a small, wiry and energetic man, who travelled from one camp to another exercising a protection function on behalf of COR. On the day that I met him in Gedaref, towards the end of my stay, he arrived at the office exhausted after having travelled for four hours on a lorry along dirt roads from Um Gargour, a small refugee settlement deep in the boondocks. And he was not young; I thought he was probably about 55.

One story that he told Berhane was so intriguing that Berhane decided to write it up for the magazine we meant to publish, and told me he thought such cases should be a regular feature in it; an idea I strongly supported. This one concerned Addisu, a 17-year-old newly-arrived from Ethiopia, who was arrested in Um Rakuba reception centre for stealing a transistor radio. He was also found to have 100 *birr* (Ethiopian currency) on him that he said he had brought across the border. The police did not believe this; and it turned out he had stolen it from the landlady of a pension in Um Rakuba camp.

It was 1983, and President Nimeiri had just introduced Islamic law, or Shari'a. The Eastern Region had been the first to apply it. Addisu confessed before the court that he had stolen the radio, having heard the testimony of four witnesses - as required under Islamic law - that he had done so. He was convicted and sentenced to right-arm amputation.

I said in an earlier chapter that this sentence was indeed carried out under Nimeiri. It was done under medical supervision (and the doctor in question got thrown out of the Royal College of Physicians for it), but it was no less barbarous for that. By the time I arrived, the Transitional Military Council that took over after the 1985 uprising had stopped amputations. They were suspended rather than abolished, but Sadiq al-Mahdi's government did not re-start them. (Flogging for drunkenness remained, however, and a man or woman found drunk in the souk was certainly lashed.)

In 1983, however, it looked as if Addisu, who was not even Sudanese, would lose his arm.

Hassen Abdel Gadr took the case to appeal. His case was an elegant one. Over a millennium before, he argued, one of the four Caliphs (successors to the Prophet), Omer ibn el-Khatab, had apparently pardoned starving slaves who stole fruit on the grounds that since they had no food, they could not have done anything else. Addisu, said Hassen Abdel Gadr, should be judged by the same criteria. He was penniless, spoke no Arabic and had no shelter or food. He might also have told the court that Addisu had probably fled the draft in Ethiopia, not wishing to be sent to the Eritrean front to fight a war which was not his own, and with which Sudanese themselves did not sympathise.

What the court did hear was that, all those centuries ago, Omer ibn el-Khatab had warned that the slaves must be fed, saying that if they were caught stealing again, their master's own hand would part company with its owner. The Gedaref court accepted this as precedent. Addisu got off.

*** *** ***

THE *haboobs*, dust-storms, were getting worse-a sign of impending rain. A storm is in fact preceded by a *haboob*. In the first week of May, the thermometer touched 47°C and every *haboob* was an occasion for hope. But still there was no rain. And the dust, which came so thick and fast that you could barely stand in it, came through cracks in my straw roof and settled evenly across the casette-player, letters from home, sheets, mosquito-net, books and typewriter; God knew how the latter kept working. Even when one was indoors, the dust coated the face and made it feel dry and cracked. Everybody became more and more irritable, both at home and at work; the more so because Ramadan was not yet over.

Berhane and I argued about whether to go to Khartoum and start printing the *Handbook* before Eid, the four-day holiday that marks the end of Ramadan. Berhane wanted to go early, because although we could only get one day's work done before the holiday began, we could then have a good time in the next few days. Berhane had many friends in Khartoum. I preferred to stay in Showak for Eid, so that I could spend a peaceful four days reading and writing in my hut, drink a little *aragi* in the evenings and watch videos at Bill's; he and Rap had just got a fresh load from the States, and I was suffering withdrawal symptoms from *Hill Street Blues*. Eventually Hassen himself settled the issue by saying that we couldn't spend the four-day holiday drawing Khartoum allowances for doing nothing. But he agreed that the *Handbook* should be properly printed, and released the funds for us to do it.

In the meantime, Chris and Clare had also made progress. They would sign their agreement with UNHCR in Khartoum any day now, Chris told me. One afternoon in the second week in May, they dropped in to visit. I was bent over the motorbike with Ian, who was teaching me how to dismantle the carburettor and remove most of Africa from the float chamber. It was another curious day; very sticky, very close, and there were clouds in the late afternoon sky, forming strange mountain ranges of grey and gunmetal, white and blue; even a hint, here and there, of green. We sat round the table, chatting. The air started to feel even thicker; but still it didn't rain.

A day or so later, an unfortunate incident occurred. A COR Land-Cruiser left Showak for Gedaref with four or five staff in it. After a few minutes, the driver asked the senior staff member next to him if he could be relieved at the wheel, as he felt unwell. The official refused. A moment later the driver suffered a massive heart attack.

The Toyota slewed across the path of a packed midi-bus heading for Kassala. They collided, and 13 people died. Several more were badly injured.

For some reason Clare found herself ferrying the victims to Gedaref in the G-Wagen. I later heard that its interior was badly bloodstained; as they were about to leave for Khartoum to sign the tripartite agreement, there was no time to clean it properly. The family left the following morning for Khartoum, having vaguely agreed to meet Berhane at the Acropole Hotel on Sunday, May 15. Had we left for Khartoum when we intended, I might well have gone to the Acropole with him.

There was still blood in the car when they left.

*** *** ***

BUT BERHANE never went to the Acropole on the 15th. We were delayed in Showak for several days after the Eid; I can't remember why.

There were no clouds in the sky on the morning of the 16th. It felt fairly clear and fresh, although extremely hot. Because it was still Eid I was at home, although it was Monday. I did not mind the heat. The night before, I had sat up by myself until one, enjoying the velvet cloak draped about my shoulders, the stillness, and the peace. One of the many cats that lived in the compound had had kittens several weeks previously, and had hidden them in a lair below the shed. Now they had reached the stage where they would go out alone at night, provided there was no-one around. Behind the kitchen there was a tapstand, and the four kittens were playing on it, striking the rubber hose that led from the tap with their tiny forepaws to see how it would bounce, making feeble little blows at each other and rolling on the ground. I stayed stock-still, and they seemed quite unaware of my presence. Eventually I stole away, hoping not to disturb them, and settled into bed. The electricity was on, and I left my fan running; in the gloom, I could just see the white mesh of the mosquito-net quivering gently in the airstream.

The next morning, I awoke about nine and made tea, then sat below the *rakuba*. Ian was there. So was Elaine, who had joined us for Eid while her boyfriend, Teo, was in the West of Sudan. He was due to pass through Khartoum that day, and might join us here in Showak later.

After an hour or so we heard the sound of a diesel engine in the drive and Bill came towards us in bright blue shorts and white T-shirt, both dazzling in the glaring sun.

"Sounds like five of your people got done over by a bomb last night," he said.

"Eh?"

"It was on the BBC. At the Acropole. They said something about an English family, all dead."

I stared. "Did they give names?"

"Nope."

He went not long afterwards.

"It's Chris and Clare," I said stupidly.

"Why should it be?" asked Elaine.

"An English family," I replied. "They were staying at the Acropole."

"That doesn't mean it's them. Why should it?" She looked annoyed. "Look, for all I know it could have been Teo."

The day wore on. Later someone heard on the radio that four of the five victims from England had been identified as Chris and Clare Rolfe and their two children; there were thought to be other casualties as well. There had been a parallel attack on the Sudan Club, but no-one knew of any casualties. I thought at once of Hannah, who was often there.

It was a clear day; there was little of the sultry, close feeling that had ruined the weather recently. The rains seemed farther away than ever.

*** *** ***

EID ENDED. In the middle of the following week, Berhane and I made for Khartoum with Adem, a squat, middle-aged driver from the workshop who was known as Adem Schita - Adem Monkey; a reference to his appearance, and to his strange, hissing laugh. We left late, as always, and then hung around for some hours in Gedaref trying to get a travel permit for me to enter the capital. Nothing I had said to Berhane that morning would convince him that permits were not issued from Gedaref police station after 12, and as he had an annual pass he had little experience of the place. To give him his due, he hurried as much as he could to get there for two, only to find that the police had indeed stopped issuing permits two hours earlier.

We eventually met two senior police officers in the courtyard of Gedaref police station after dark. There was a power cut; two armed policemen on guard were forced to stop watching their little black-and-white television, which had been showing a film of schoolchildren dancing. They sat instead by their *kanoon*, drinking tea. Then a Toyota Hilux swung into the yard, its headlights flashing off the weirdly jumbled shapes of the crashed cars that were dumped, by order, in the police yard after an accident; a ghostly display. The two men climbed out, their white *djellabiyas* shining strangely in the darkness, and wrote out a travel permit for me by the light of a torch. We set out for Khartoum then; it was eight. As 11 approached, we neared Wad Medani. Adem Schita, tired, swerved towards the edge of the road for the third time. We jabbed him awake and decided to stop at the COR rest house in Medani for the night.

We slept on the third-floor verandah, out of reach of the mosquitoes and cooled by a pleasant breeze. It was a good night's sleep, but a brief one; at 5.30, the sun just turning the sky to silver, we rolled out of bed and into the car for the final leg.

The car hummed through the Gezira. Adem seemed relaxed and cheerful; Berhane read a newspaper he had bought in Medani. I looked out of the window. Berhane turned.

"What are you thinking about?" he asked.

"This and that."

"England?"

"Sometimes."

I expected some cynical response, but he smiled. Sometimes I forgot that he was himself an exile of a decade and that, unlike me, he did not know when he would go home. I wondered what he thought of his own life, in quiet moments; of air attacks on his home town in Eritrea, perhaps, or his wife and children, who were in Frankfurt (he felt they were better off there than with him in Sudan). Only a trace of bitterness now and then revealed what he might think of the situation. More often he was penning an article, in imperfect but fluent, lively English, about some absurdity of refugee life in Sudan, or making people fall about at his mordant wit, which was an effective weapon in three languages. I knew him well, but hardly knew him at all.

He turned back to *Al-Ayyam*, holding the paper wide open and shielding us from the fierce morning light. I looked back at the countryside, the irrigated cotton-fields just starting to appear as we approached the capital in the bright sunshine; Adem was hunched, short-legged and long-armed, over the Toyota's wheel.

The sun rose higher and the morning freshness left the sky. Berhane ceased to read the paper. We both moved restlessly on the plastic seats, which trapped the moisture from our bodies and soaked our shirts. The first shacks and houses appeared; the rambling mess of Souk el-Shaabi passed by on our left. We came into Amharatt, the New Extension, where many of the embassies were, and the wealthy gave diplomatic parties; and well-to-do Europeans lived in flats in the breeze atop the high blocks, drinking their smuggled Ethiopian cognac away from prying eyes.

I remembered that the Institute of Traditional Medicine was near here. Even as the thought crossed my mind I saw Hannah standing on the broken pavement within a row of neem-trees, stock-still; she was holding a bicycle. Perhaps she had seen us.

"Adem, can we stop? I've seen a friend," I called.

He pulled the nearside wheels across the broken remnants of the kerb. I got out. Hannah made no move towards me, but stood and stared. I walked briskly over to her and spoke; she answered in a rather numb fashion, and her gaze seemed to pass over my shoulder.

I asked her if she was all right.

Yes, she said, not too bad.

That was good, I said; I had been afraid that she might have been in the Sudan Club on Sunday night, and I was relieved to see her.

Yes, she said, she had been there. She assured me she was all right, but she was clearly not; in fact the incident had happened only three or four days earlier. She told me what had happened in more detail much later, in London.

On the Sunday night Hannah had been, as usual, to Mass in the large, almost Italianate cathedral that overlooked the river. Set amid acacias and cooled by the wind off the Blue Nile, it is elegant but one suspects also an irritant to many Sudanese, for there is no mosque of comparable grandeur near the river, at least in the town centre.

Hannah had gone there with Father John Ashworth of the Diocese of Malakal. John was a missionary, although I found the term a little old-fashioned when applied to either him or his friends. Malakal is in the south and he had been forced for the time being to leave it, although he was to return briefly duiring the ceasefire of 1989. But he had remained in Sudan, the diocese having moved its operation lock, stock and barrel to the far north of Omdurman, where it helped to run educational and other projects with the southern Christian refugees in the area. He was stocky, bearded, droll and at first sight a most unpriestlike figure. In fact he once told me that he had first thought of entering the priesthood after chatting to two priests in a pub and being struck how normal they were. His knowledge of spoken and written Arabic was excellent.

I never saw him in his vestments; I never saw him don so much as a clerical collar but on Sundays he did, officiating from time to time in the great pile by the river. I do not know whether he did so on that Sunday evening, but he was there. When Mass finished at 7.30, not long after sundown, he and Hannah went off to the nearby Sudan Club for supper. Sunday is an ordinary working day in Sudan, and the Club was not crowded; only on Fridays was it packed.

They sat at a table on the inner end of the main verandah, next to the stairs that one would use for access from the gate. There are only two or three steps on them, and a diner sitting at that table would have his waist level with the head of someone walking in from the street. Halfway through the meal, at about ten past eight, they heard a very loud explosion; Hannah didn't remember that it came from any particular direction. She did not think at first of a bomb.

"I thought at first it was a very near exhaust," she said later. "If you remember, they fart like hell out there, don't they? I never did hear any sirens - do they have them out there? [They do.]

"Thirty seconds later - at most a minute, I'd just said what the hell was that - we heard gunshots. Then they came in. John said to get down."

He knew what gunfire sounded like, having been kidnapped by the SPLA and held hostage for several weeks in the early stages of the civil war. When he realised what was happening, he yelled "Move!" and dragged or led her into the bar. Hannah's recollection two and a half years later - which she said might be faulty - was that there were three gunmen and that they were firing towards the diners from the path that led in from the gate. I was later told that they threw a grenade that rolled under the tin table, exploded and flipped it upwards, shielding John and Hannah from the blast. Hannah said later that this "could be true - or could be absolute drivel", but a UNICEF official later showed me the remains of the table behind the bar-building at the Club. Escapes from the effect of blast can be quite bizarre, and it could have happened.

"I took off my shoes and left them on the floor of the bar. They had bullet-holes in them afterwards... Or actually I think that they'd thrown one of those bullet-filled Russian grenades and it'd exploded against the pillar, shattering the concrete and sending out shards.

"Then we went into the space at the back, where the staff were. People tried to persuade me into the cellar, but I wouldn't go. I was afraid we'd be trapped.

"After about 10 minutes [the firing had stopped quite quickly], we wondered if the police or someone would come for us.

"Nobody came. Nobody came at all."

They never did come, and Hannah left the Club with John. The following day a friend did come to find her, concerned because one of the English victims at the Acropole had still not been identified, and she was afraid it might be Hannah.

Hannah was reluctant to talk about the experience afterwards as she felt that she had not suffered much; after all, she hadn't been hurt, although seven had been killed (all at the Acropole). An eighth, who was seriously injured, was the only person badly hurt at the nearby Sudan Club. They must have been poor shots. The victim, a southerner, was a friend of the doorman. He collected five bullets in his chest, but he recovered.

Although the police never went to the Club, they picked up some of the men more or less immediately. Five men were eventually imprisoned. According to Hannah the police claimed the three gunmen had performed both attacks, but that sounds unlikely. The initial explosion she and John had heard had been the bomb at the Acropole, about half a mile away. She was fairly certain that the gap between the explosion and the Club attack was too short for the same men to have performed both. A fourth man must therefore have thrown the bomb in the hotel, as it was not set off by a timer device but lobbed into the dining room from the staircase above, packed in a valise or suitcase.

Seven people died at the hotel. They were Chris, Clare, Tommy, Louise, a waiter, an Englishwoman who was not identified until later, and a senior officer in the engineering corps of the Sudanese army. I was told later that this last victim had gone to the hotel to meet a newly-arrived European aid worker who was going to work in the officer's home town. According to the account I heard, he wished to make the aid worker feel welcome, and tell him something about the town; he paid a high price for his kindness.

The mystery woman was later identified as Sally Rocket, from

Budleigh Salterton in Devon, the former VSO volunteer who was working for the World University Service in Gedaref; the one I had sat next to at the monthly coordination meetings. She should not even have been there. She was going to Cairo to spend a short holiday and should have left earlier in the day, but her SudanAir flight had been delayed by 24 hours.

Exactly who backed the attackers was not clear. They seem to have been Palestinians associated with the Abu Nidal movement, and had entered Khartoum some months earlier, using a legitimate business as cover while they prepared for the attack. The business had been started using some tens of thousands of dollars'-worth of hard currency, the movement of which must surely have been noticed by the Sudanese authorities; but there were plenty of legitimate Levantine ventures in the capital, and perhaps they thought it was not unusual.

Why Khartoum? Security in the city was notoriously lax, and indeed the Khartoum Hilton had been the venue for the assassination of an Iraqi opposition leader in January (ironically, Hannah had arrived there a quarter of an hour later and found herself virtually stepping over the body). Security was stepped up considerably after May 15, with bag inspections at all hotels; the police also provided armed guards at the door of the Sudan Club.

There were a number of unanswered questions, including the non-appearance of the police at the Club despite their equally strange rapid arrest of suspects afterwards. Things took an odder twist later.

The terrorists were locked up in Kober Gaol, and rumours spread that the prisoners had been mistreated and sodomised there, but it is impossible to be sure of such a thing. In any case, Sudan was left with the problem of what to do with them. In Islam, the penalty for murder is death. However, the beheading of the terrorists could have exposed Sudan to terrorist reprisals, and for months the Sadiq government seemed to be dragging its heels on the prisoners' fate. Although a trial took place, nothing had been settled when the democratic constitution was overthrown 13 months later.

The military regime that succeeded it decided, late in 1989, that under the provisions of the Islamic penal code, the relatives of the dead were entitled to decide over the death penalty. The Rolfe family in the Home Counties, and the Rocketts in the West Country, were asked if they required the beheading of terrorists thousands of miles away in Khartoum. They said no, the Rolfes taking the view that, as a Quaker, Chris would not have sanctioned such a penalty for any rea-

Collecting water from the borehole in Karkora camp, 1988 or 1989

son. There things stood for some months more until on January 7 1991 the Sudanese released the five prisoners, saying that under Islamic law they might pay blood money instead. One of them apparently announced that he would resume his career in terrorism until Palestine was free.

These incidents left most of the Europeans I knew oddly unmoved. The Sudanese, by contast, were extremely upset. The Commissioner for Refugees, Hassen Attiyah, issued a statement expressing his shock and regret. "Chris and Clare were kind and friendly colleagues, and we will miss them both professionally and personally," it said.

In Showak, Hassen Mohamed Osman produced a statement of his own, condemning the murder in the strongest terms. Of his feelings there was no doubt. Early on the morning of May 17, two days after the murders, when I was still in Showak over Eid, I had been awakened by Ian hammering on the door of my *tukl*.

"What," I grunted, looking at my watch. It was not yet seven, and we were still on holiday.

"Hassen Osman's here to see you," he said.

"Stop taking the piss."

"I'm not," he insisted, aggrieved.

I found Hassen sitting in one of the garden seats outside the kitchen, dressed in his off-duty gear - a dazzling white *djellabiya* and headcloth. He rose politely to greet me and apologised for waking me so early in the morning (it was not early by Sudanese standards, only by ours). He had urgent business in Gedaref, he explained, and it would not wait until later in the day. Would I please rough out an obituary for Chris and Clare and their children and forward it to the *Sudan Times* via the UNHCR telex link to Khartoum? I fetched a pad and paper and together we composed the obituary. I read it back to him. He nodded and stood.

"Thankyou. I will see you after Eid," he said. He looked exhausted. He went slowly to the gate, where his Eritrean driver was waiting with the G-Wagen.

*** *** ***

WHAT Hassen's urgent business was in Gedaref, I found out later. Trouble was always possible in that city. In 1980, serious violence between refugees and nationals at the end of Ramadan had left five Sudanese and 30 refugees dead; I described this earlier. Now, similar incidents had been reported. The situation had been tense for some time and on May 16 matters had come to a head, prompted on one side by Moslem religious feeling at the close of the Ramadan fast, and on the other, if anything, by the denial of medical treatment to refugees at the public hospital. Early reports suggested a number of deaths, but this proved pessimistic. However, several refugees had been badly injured, and it was alleged that police officers had forced Ethiopian Christians to recite the *Shehada* (the Moslem affirmation of faith) at gunpoint.

Denial of medical treatment was certainly a sore point with refugees, and could have serious consequences, as the treatment of a young refugee from Um Gargour was to show at the end of that month. According to the *Showak Handbook* I was then working on in Khartoum, Um Gargour, a refugee settlement about 100km from Gedaref, was an agricultural one with a population of just under 8,000. It had been there since 1976. The ethnic groups in the camp were mainly Beni Amer, Baria and Bilen, suggesting an established and largely Moslem population; indeed there are two mosques mentioned, one of them described as a permanent structure (although this probably just meant corrugated iron).

There was one small outpatient clinic, owned by COR itself but run by the American Save the Children Federation. In addition, the Sudan Council of Churches ran a maternity clinic with a microscope, refrigerator and 20 beds. It was probably staffed by a Traditional Birth Attendant, or TBA. Water came from a borehole, pumped up by three Lister diesels. There was a bakery, a flour-mill, a bicycle repair-shop and, oddly, what is described as a cheese factory. It was isolated; there was a COR VHF set, the nearest point on the asphalt road was 31 kilometres away and the railway, for what it was worth, 25 kilometres. I never went to Um Gargour, although Ian had sometimes been down to maintain the Lister diesels. I can imagine it well enough; a cross between Karkora, which I did know, and a less prosperous version of Abuda, the relatively wealthy settlement just across the river from Showak. With the exception of the odd teacher or official, no-one in Um Gargour would have lived in anything resembling a European building. Rather, they would have had straw *goateas*, round round huts about 15ft in diameter, with conical rooves. These provide effective shelter when in good condition, and after 12 years the people of Um Gargour had probably built proper compounds, with *rakubas* for shade.

One day in late May, Sooraya Husein Hadgai, a 16-year-old refugee of the Eritrean Baria ethnic group, ate what Berhane reported to be hair-dye tablets. God knows what these were, and Berhane, whose story it was, did not enlarge. Sooraya was upset because she had become pregnant, and expected a thrashing from her mother. Taken to Gedaref Hospital by the police, she was admitted with severe breathing difficulties.

The doctors at Gedaref were at that time refusing to treat refugee patients. Their argument was that refugees numbered 35,000 in Gedaref, about 10% of the population, but were occupying 40% of the beds. International conventions lay down that a host nation should treat refugees as well as, but not necessarily better than, their own nationals in all matters including health care. Berhane believed that the doctors were thinking of this when they approached UNHCR and suggested that the treatment of refugee patients was its problem too, and that it should provide a generator for the hospital. This was needed; as I have said, the blood bank had been out of action for some years due to the irregularity of the power supply. UNHCR agreed to provide the generator.

But the generator did not turn up. The doctors seemed to have believed that this was deliberate; God knows why, for international procurement systems were notoriously slow. Moreover, goods routed through Port Sudan could be delayed for months. I once heard of a car being stuck there for nearly two years awaiting customs clearance. So while it may have been UNHCR's fault, there was no reason to suppose so.

What exacerbated the situation in the eyes of the doctors, apart from the growing decline in the economy and the rising pressure on the hospital, was the fact that it was the dry season; the water level at Girba was low, and power cuts were frequent. Certainly in Showak we had three days a week without power, and in Gedaref things were usually much worse. Late that spring their patience snapped, and they announced that they would treat no more refugees until there was a suitable response from the international community to the problems that the refugees were causing the hospital.

Sooraya Hussein Hadgai was nevertheless admitted, Berhane said because she physically resembled a Dinka; and Dinkas are Sudanese. A tracheotomy was performed and a breathing-tube inserted, and she was put on an intravenous drip. At this point, one of the doctors realised that she was not Dinka but Baria; and Sooraya was kicked out of the hospital. In fact, Berhane suggested in his original article in the *Sudan Times* that they whipped out the breathing tube as well, but they did not do that.

The police suggested that Sooraya be taken to the refugee clinic run by the International Rescue Committee (IRC) at Tawawa, the sprawling refugee-camp on the outskirts of Gedaref. She arrived there on the evening of May 30. But IRC discharged her too. It was later said that they had done it to put pressure on the Gedaref doctors; after all, IRC and other relief organizations never hesitated to treat host nationals, and must have found the ban the other way offensive. IRC denied this, however, saying later that they simply lacked the equipment to keep Sooraya's airways clear. They told the family to take her to Kassala, and offered to transport them there.

But Kassala is three hours' drive from Gedaref, even at night; so the family again approached the police, who told them to try Gedaref hospital again. A judge apparently suggested the military hospital in the city. But the latter also refused to admit her.

Now the family did make for Kassala, in the car of the project manager (senior Sudanese COR official) from Um Gargour. Sooraya was still alive when they arrived at Kassala hospital, over 200 kilometres away. This time she was admitted. But the hospital lacked the drugs to treat her. The Saudi Hospital offered to help and later admitted her itself, but the staff were unable to find a technician for an urgent blood transfusion. She died on May 31.

Sooraya's parents believed that she would not have died if Gedaref hospital had not discharged her, and later filed a case against it. I do not know the outcome. Meanwhile the *Sudan Times* article - which we reprinted in the first issue of our own magazine, later that summer - caused a bit of a rumpus, not unusual when Berhane put his pen to paper.

What Berhane had the good grace not to say or write was what must have been in his mind: that while the murder of the Rolfes and Sally Rockett made the front pages in much of the West, Sooraya Hussein Hadgai died quietly in a poor part of Africa, leaving the outside world largely untroubled by the issues that her death had raised.

Chapter Eight

Summer 1988: *Rain and sickness*

In June, during my second stint in Khartoum, it started to rain in Showak. The following year, I would be there when it happened. Throughout late May, after a few tantalising showers, it became hotter and hotter until you could scarcely breathe. The lack of humidity was usually a saving grace in Sudan, but as the rains approach, it did become humid; worse still, there were the *haboobs*. These are harbingers of a storm. As the season wears on they are sometimes accompanied by a clap of thunder, and finally a few drops of water. Then, in early June, it starts raining in earnest.

I remember one such storm, the first proper one of the following year, a few months before I finally left the country. The sky was overcast from lunchtime onwards; at half-past three the dust-storm started, and was so fierce that normally one would have taken shelter in the house. But I sensed that this one would be different, and stayed outside to watch. After 20 minutes the dust died down suddenly, and almost immediately I heard a strange, rustling sound like a curtain being dragged along the ground towards us. It was the rain, and it dragged across the compound, sweeping the last dust from the air.

It is a cliché but a true one that tropical rain comes in jets, not the dribs, drabs and drizzle of the English variety. In half a minute, the compound was awash. First I saw dark dots appear on the dusty ground, then they joined up, and finally the earth disappeared altogether beneath the weight of water, as yet more came in perfect rods that appeared to be boring holes in the ground. Then it was finished; the dust was damped down and cleansed from the air, and black clouds split to reveal, first perfect white ones, then a perfect blue such as I had not seen for days. The water made the straw rooves of the tukls glitter in the new sunlight against a skyscape of black and iron-grey, alternating with patches of blue and white. And that day, as sometimes happened, there was a fine rainbow.

Four in the afternoon was the time to expect such storms. Sometimes there was another deluge at eight, and there might be one or two more in the night. The evening storms would lower the temperature quickly, and I once watched in disbelief as the thermometer in my room dipped from about 105°F to under 70°F in just 15 minutes. The impact of this, after a day of extreme heat and dust-storms, may be imagined.

The thunder and lightning that accompanied these storms was equally spectacular. One night, I opened my door at about 8.30 to watch; at that moment there was a thunderbolt that made my ears pop and, simultaneously, I saw three great forks travel from heaven to earth. In that instant, the town power supply failed, plunging us into darkness until the morning.

Sometimes rapid action was needed when the rain began. The cushions, the tape-recorder, anything, had to be moved inside, sometimes with little warning. The lights might also need to be cut quickly. Like all houses and compounds in Sudan, ours had indoor wiring outdoors; the water would accumulate inside the light fixtures, causing shorts if nothing had been done, and a rubber-handled pair of pliers stood ready for the master-switch to be thrown if need be.

Any inconvenience cause by the rains was, for me at least, compensated for by the change in the landscape. It hardly ever rained in Khartoum, but on my way back to Showak in July 1988 I realised that something fantastic had happened as soon as we passed Medani. Out of the deep brown earth, itself a change from the baked dry dust, rose blades of green which seemed to have been sown in drills like a farmer's at home; there was always space between them through which the ground could be seen. Yet those blades were a luminous green, for when there is sun as there is in Sudan, a little rain will make everything grow with a vengeance. In the wood between Gedaref and Showak, the leaves were reappearing on the trees; I felt it was spring although the word *khareej*, for the season that begins on June 15, is more usually translated as autumn. Nothing is quite what it appears in Sudan.

The sky was better still. Where there had been glaring pale blue, almost white at midday, there was now a variegated patchwork of black, grey, white and strong, bright blue; a journey from Showak to Shagarab in late July felt more to me like a trip across Norfolk, the light bouncing this way and that on patches of water and wet earth and cloud, the great plains alive with green crops and grass, and the patterns in the sky constantly changing as the wind freshened. And it was cool; sometimes you could walk about in the open quite normally. Indeed, in the night, I found myself using a blanket, something which in winter was only needed for four or five weeks around

Christmas.

But the rains had their drawbacks. The most immediately obvious was a plague of insects; in the dry season, the great camel-spiders were a hazard and so, now and then, were the scorpions, but one watched where one put one's feet at night, kept the mosquito-net down during the day and need otherwise not worry. In the rains, it was different.

Amongst the seasonal hazards, there were the blister-beetles. These little bastards were round, jet-black and perhaps half the size of a man's fingernail. They crept up your trouser-leg. When one felt something moving and automatically brushed it away, it in its fright discharged urine that stung the skin, and would continue to do so for some days if you were unlucky. In extreme cases, quite unpleasant scarring and painful injury could be caused; a friend of Ian's had several blister-beetles crawl up his *djellabiya* one afternoon as he slept, and when he awoke they peed on him. The scars covered much of his chest.

But I think they were better than the stink-beetles, which were about the same size but narrower. Instead of discharging poisonous urine, the stink-beetle released a marker-scent so pungent that it smelled like gases of the gut, prompting one to look round the dinner-table for the culprit. And the mosquitoes, ever-present even in the dry season, multiplied horribly - but more of that in a moment.

Transport, too, became awkward. There was no problem on the main tarmac road, once you had got to it; but that could be difficult, although it was barely a kilometre away. The dirt roads, over which one could travel at 60-70kph during the dry season, became quagmires. This was worsened by the churning wheels of the Bedford trucks, and the large articulated lorries that occasionally dropped down into Showak. Even if your car kept going, as one drove into these ruts the centre line would rise up to meet the sump. This caused many more holdups than simple loss of traction, so even four-wheel drive was only of so much use in getting you out. Nowhere in Africa is travel as easy as it is in Europe, but Sudan is a special nightmare; even main roads may not be gravelled, and only the Khartoum-Port Sudan, Khartoum-Rabak and one or two shorter roads were actually sealed.

Motorcycles became a liability. But because, even at the height of the wet season, it only poured once every two or three days, there were times when the ground seemed firm enough to ride on.

Tempted, one would sling one's leg across the tank, only to come rapidly to grief. Usually this happened when you had got just far enough to make pushing the damn thing home impossible. After a heavy afternoon rainstorm, one could wade down to the souk in the evening and see all the Hondas used by the COR staff standing abandoned on little patches of damp but solid gravel, surrounded by water, like obelisks on islands in an inland sea.

I learned my lesson. One morning I left the compound at a quarter past seven and, instead of going straight to work, made for the UNHCR compound; I needed to see Robert Ashe, their head of office, who I knew would be leaving for Khartoum that day and would not be back for several weeks. Otherwise I should have left it, for the road to UNHCR was bad. Still, it was only a kilometre; I thought I should make it easily enough.

I steered onto the track that led there, riding gently, hand on clutch, humming along below a thick, grey sky. It felt like England on a dirty summer's day. Here and there a car splashed through the puddles. The track was badly rutted, and although it was possible to keep going at first by riding in the bottom of the ruts, they soon became so deep that the footrests and gearchange started catching on the walls of the depression. I noticed that, to the left of the road, there was a patch of unbroken, unmarked black cottonsoil between the ruts and the new grass. It looked perfect; the next time the rut shallowed, I left it and swung onto the cottonsoil, skimming over the surface at 20-25kph. I think I got two yards before the wheels started to sink, the back one first, sending up jets of black mud as my arse settled into Africa; the rev-counter showed a healthy 2,000 revs or so but I was going nowhere, the bike digging itself into the ground like a demented mole. When my knuckles were an inch or so from the ground, I admitted defeat. Too late. Two Hadendowa herdsmen walked by smiling slightly, their arms wrapped around their sticks, which were laid across the backs of their shoulders. I appealed for help, but they refused to become involved and sauntered off towards Showak, still smiling a little at the mad *khawaja*. I walked to UNHCR and persuaded two of their staff to help dig the bike out.

Later I returned to town the long way round, on a gravelled track that I hadn't known about; but, as I neared my compound, the road petered out into cottonsoil again and this time, before my bike could bury me again, I came flying off instead. Unhurt but so covered in mud that I looked like the creature from the swamp, I raised myself to the handlebars and cut the motor. Four young boys stood nearby; they laughed like drains but were friendly, and helped me wheel the machine the last few yards to the gate. I gave them a couple of Sudanese pounds and told them to go and buy themselves a Pepsi, then cleaned myself up and walked to my own office, seething. What really annoyed me was that the journey had been wasted. Robert had left for Khartoum the previous afternoon.

I had another problem besides transport: my roof. The others in the compound had been overhauled while I was in Khartoum, but mine had not been touched. With Ian's help I engaged three local thatchers to sort it out, knowing that a few more heavy rainstorms might finish it for good; I did not fancy several hundredweight of sodden straw crashing through its wooden frame onto me while I was asleep.

There were two problems, however. One was dura, or straw. Later, Ian Lunt, a former volunteer who had been responsible for the construction of some of the tukls four years earlier, told me that the straw for the original rooves had come from Hawata, some tens of kilometres south of Gedaref; a desperate distance to go for something so basic. Now even this was not possible. However, some was found; not enough, but mixed in with material from the old roof, it would just about stretch.

The next problem was to get the roof up between rainstorms. The men waited till it had rained heavily, then started work early the next morning, reasoning that it would be two or three days before the next deluge. The trouble was that the work would certainly take three days. They worked hard, starting at 6.30 in the morning and continuing until after 2.30; they were working in the open, and, as it was not overcast during those three days, the shade temperature would have been over 100°F. They just made it, stretching the limited supplies of new dura by twining it with the old. The results were excellent; there were one or two small holes near the apex, but they let in only thin streams of water. In any case, after two or three days' rain, the straw swelled to the point where the whole thing was impressively waterproof. They charged me S.360; about £36 at the official exchange rate, or £20 in practice. I wonder how much it would cost to rethatch a cottage in a Cotswold village today.

In the meantime, I had been sleeping in John's room in the new compound; John himself had returned to England a few weeks previously. I shared the room with Jeremy Hartley, a visiting British pho-

Thatching my tukl, *July 1988*

tographer who was later to take impressive black-and-white pictures of the Khartoum floods. Neither of us would have slept so well had we known that, three weeks later, the roof would cave in after a heavy rainfall; concrete and iron crashed into the room below. Happily it was unoccupied at the time.

*** *** ***

DURING JULY, it was Beiram Eid. This was the four-day holiday that marked the passing of 40 days since the end of Ramadan, and was really the main holiday of the year. Despite the chaos engendered by the rains, many of my colleagues left a day or so early to try and get back to their home towns, meaning to spend the holiday with their families. Frequently, they went for many months or even years without seeing them, as travel was difficult and expensive; and for several years now, Beiram Eid either had fallen or would fall at the time of the year when the roads were hopeless. Because of this, some people saved up their leave for several years and then took some months off, this being the only practical way to get to their homes.

We stayed put. Ian Lunt, the former Showak volunteer, came to us. He was still working in Sudan and was now in the north, some miles from Merowe; he was restoring ancient wells so that they could be productive again, and using local labour. It must have been a satisfying project. He once showed me some pictures of the wells (he was a good photographer); they were beautifully made, the lining being constructed of brickwork that would have done credit to a cathedral. They were hundreds of years old. Ian was sufficiently committed to the project to eschew the house provided for him in Merowe; instead, he lived on-site about 75 kilometres to the north-west, in a shack made of *biriish*-woven rush. He had also built himself an oven which was the size of the shack itself and in which he and his driver roasted a sheep every Friday, entertaining the sheikhs of the area.

That Beiram Eid they drove south-east across the desert from Atbara to New Halfa, and thence to Showak via the all-weather road from Girba. It was a hard journey, for the mud was deep, but they were lucky. They arrived with a sheep, purchased in the north; it had travelled in the back of the pick-up, and now grazed happily in the compound, unaware that its last hour approached. On the appointed day, the driver, a nice man whose name I sadly don't remember, slit its throat and bled it in the approved manner, and the two of them butchered it while our own Ian went off to round up all the mechanics from the workshop and invite them to the feast. Much *aragi* was drunk, and an excellent time had by all.

Ian brought something else besides the sheep. An inveterate reader, he ran through four or five books in four days without being in the least unsociable. He left them in Showak; the best by William Golding, J.G. Ballard and others.

Beiram Eid was marked by a stupid incident which, like most things in Showak, turned eventually into farce. There was a party given by someone at UNHCR; Ian Lunt and I did not go as we were tired, but two of the others did. They returned through a cloudburst at one in the morning, groping their way round via the souk on roads that had softened into nothing in a matter of minutes. Swinging round into the driveway of the compound, they clobbered a power-line pole and brought it down. Feeling that there was not much they could do about it at that time of the morning, they drove on into the compound and went to sleep off the excesses of the evening.

The next morning, I got up to find the pole collapsed, and a live electric cable carrying 400 volts lying across the ground. Ian Lunt's driver crouched anxiously beside it, warning away the local children. It was obvious who the offender had been; the pick-up's tracks swerved drunkenly towards the pole and then away up the drive to the rear wheels of the Toyota, which sat innocently by the shed at the top of the drive. Worse, the power-supply to the nearby COR chicken-farm had been cut, wreaking havoc with incubators that contained 400 eggs.

I had barely had time to take in all this when two policemen came into the compound and asked, politely, for the driver - by name; they knew perfectly well who it was likely to have been. I offered them tea and asked them to sit down while I tried to wake him up. Lazarus would have been easier, but eventually I elicited a series of grunts. I told the policemen that I didn't think he was there; could he come and see them later? They agreed and, still polite, returned to the police-station near the souk.

"I think you may as well get down there, mate," I suggested through the door. "You'll most probably be able to talk yourself out of it then. Otherwise they might come back and get stroppy."

"Ahhh, sod it."

Ian Lunt, sensing trouble, went off to see El Hadi, the head of construction with whom he had worked five years earlier. El Hadi, a kind man who had long had volunteers working for him, came down to the police-station with them and acted as an intermediary. In the end the offender was told that no further action would be taken provided he forked out for the re-erection of the pole. In the event, he did not even have to do that; the mechanics in the workshop held a whip-round for him.

People were not always so lucky. The same volunteer had been imprisoned briefly in the far west of Sudan after a man fell off the back of a pick-up he was driving, sustaining a brain injury that left him crippled. It really had not been the driver's fault. The man had been sitting on the edge of the pick-up, never a good idea; and another car had cut in front of them, causing an emergency stop.

There had been a similar incident involving another volunteer in Showak itself about 18 months earlier; in that case the man had died, and the volunteer was again held in custody, this time for three weeks. The conditions had not been bad; the Gedaref police had been friendly and had allowed him to sleep in the courtyard instead of a cell, allowing friends to bring him food, cigarettes, books and anything else he needed. But to actually get him released, VSO had to pay substantial blood-money, and the volunteer had then had to leave the country.

*** *** ***

BEIRAM EID ended, and the rain got heavier. There were now a number of practical drawbacks. One was food; as the roads got worse and worse, less and less produce could reach the markets from the gardens along the Atbara River. There were now no tomatoes, virtually no potatos, and less and less meat; just a few soft vegetables. Jew's marrow and aubergines were available, and onions. From these we made watery stews which hardly satisfied. Neither could we fill up the holes with bread, for the shortage was now biting badly. There was little domestic wheat to be had, as apart from the transport difficulties we were in the lean period of the year; the harvest would not begin in earnest until October. Pasta was available, but expensive; a packet of Greek spaghetti, just enough to feed four, was S.20 and that was what each of us earned in a day. It sometimes ran short as well, anyway. In the souk, there wasn't much for breakfast apart from plain *ful* with nothing to put on it. Knowing that work would take me back to Khartoum in a month or so, I dreamed fondly of a blow-out at the Hilton or Meridien.

There was another problem. The road to Abuda had been cut for some time; the ford became unusable in March, for the rains in Eritrea came ahead of our own and swelled the river. It was then still possible to cross by boat, but after June that year, this also was impossible; unusually, the river was so full that Hassen's deputy, Mohamed Tom, forbad anyone to attempt the crossing.

Hearing that the river had burst its banks completely, I went down to it one morning with Simon and one of the drivers from the Abuda school. The river was literally a mile wide, and fast-flowing. It was at this time that the pumping-station was swallowed up, despite attempts to protect it with *ad hoc* earthworks. However, in one places dunes stood proud of the water, and Simon and I climbed to the top of one and looked across to the eastern bank. The huge expanse of river took the light, which had been filtered through a carpet of dirty grey-white cloud, and flung it back and forth so that it felt as if one were standing between two giant mirrors.

Over the next few days, reports came into the office of bodies seen floating down the river. This was not so unusual. Flash-floods often catch people in Africa, and in the west of Sudan, it is common for people to be sudenly swept away while crossing an apparently innocuous river by lorry. This year, however, there were more than ever. After a few days the body-count had reached 30. Hughie, the Ulsterman who lived in the new compound, told me that he had seen a woman in a *toab* floating face-down in mid-stream. "Her *toab*, Jesus, it was flowing out behind her like it were a shroud," he said. "And her arms were stretched forward and her hands like this - you know? like she were prayin'."

One day Osman, a young journalist who was working for a while with myself and Berhane in Showak, came into the office after a trip to the police-station. "They have found a soldier floating in the river," he announced. "He is wearing an Ethiopian uniform."

Berhane looked up from the piece he was writing about the drowning water-pumping station. It was not so remarkable, he reasoned; the river flowed out from under Gonder.

"But I have thought of a headline," he said gleefully, sifting through his papers until he found a piece on recent refugee arrivals. He grinned. "*Even the Dead are Coming!*"

*** *** ***

"IF IT GOES on like this," said Gasim Awad el-Ray, "then the future looks green and bright."

Gasim was an agricultural specialist with COR. He was driving me over a stretch of land so waterlogged that it was a miracle the Twin-Cab kept moving; they were amazing, these machines, with permanent four-wheel drive through huge differentials mounted so high off the ground that they looked like mechanical storks. I never saw one stuck.

Gasim and his boss had responsibility for agriculture in the refugee settlements. Of the 234,000 refugees living in these and the reception centres, about 100,000 were in agricultural settlements. The idea was that they would become self-sufficient, but in 1988 they were still receiving World Food Programme (WFP) rations for about 30% of their number. (That was COR's figure; the number of refugees in the land settlements who actually grew enough to make a living may have been smaller than it implied.) The recommended ration was 1,900 k/cal a day, made up of 400gm of dura, 60gm of beans, 30gm of sugar and 10gm of salt. This ration was theoretical; the reality could be different, depending on WFP supplies, transport, administration and whether the moon was in Virgo.

The administration had, where possible, allocated 5-10 feddans (a

Sudanese children above the flooded Atbara river,
July 1988

feddan is about an acre) per family; it was this that my Californian friend had argued was inadequate, giving me a figure seven times the maximum as the minimum requirement. He was being unrealistic; there just wasn't the land available. It was strange, looking out across the wide expanse of the eastern Sudanese plan, to reflect that some-one had rights over all of it.

However, as the Twin-Cab slewed through the mud under a varie-gated midday sky, Gasim was a happy man. "To raise dura requires a minimum of 250mm rainfall," he explained. "We can expect 350-400mm annually in Showak. But at this rate, it'll be 500mm." In fact, 250mm had already fallen by July 17.

Gasim knew this because he had double-checked the rain-gauges at COR and Valmet every day. The farmers, refugees and nationals alike, preferred a more traditional method. They used the *dura'a* method. A *dura'a* was a man's arm; a stick was stuck in the ground, and when it was withdrawn with moisture to the depth of a man's arm, it was time to sow.

"We've got an arm and a half," said Gasim cheerfully, and talked of two and maybe even three harvests that season; in fact harvesting, he said, would not finish until well into the following year. Gasim could not know that the country was about to get more rain than it could possibly want.

But, rain or no rain, he had other crosses to bear. The previous year, much of the crop had been destroyed by rats. This time they were no worse than normal, but he was worried about *buda*, a pest that attacks the roots of the dura. Herbicides were useless for controlling it, and the dura had a substance in its root that caused *buda* to germinate.

And there was the *quila-quila*, the Sudan sparrow, which attacked the heads of mature plants. The Plant Protection Department in the region had dealt with this one by cutting off the tops of trees, or using chemicals, to destroy the birds' habitat. But now the PPD was worrying about locusts. Swarms were rising over much of the Horn of Africa, and on July 30 the Ministry of Agriculture declared Sudan a locust disaster area. Gasim said he hoped that the swarms would give the region a wide berth and go off causing trouble somewhere else. In fact, they largely did.

But, I had heard earlier, the previous year had also seen the refugees held back by a man-made problem.

Ploughing was done with tractors in the refugee settlement area. According to the agriculturalists (including Gasim), the ground was too hard for oxen, and a tractor-hire company to serve the refugees had been set up by Valmet, the Finnish firm, using tractors that they themselves made. Although set up in concert with COR, it was a commercial undertaking. I often wondered how much money it really made. Even if it did well, I couldn't see how it was repatriating its profits. Yet there must have been some motive for setting up the massive workshop that Valmet ran in Showak; perhaps the spreading of their tractors throughout Africa, replacing the Massey-Fergusons that once dominated, was the reason. Substance is lent to this idea by the fact that, in 1989, Valmet and the Finnish development agency, Finnida, embarked on a major aid project throughout the area that involved the extension of mechanised farming. This won't have made money as such, so it can't have been meant to.

The problem for refugees in 1987 had been that they couldn't get their hands on the Valmet tractors until the prime time for sowing was gone. Yet rich farmers, nationals with whom Valmet (quite legitimately) also did business, appeared to have had no problem. The following year COR, in the person of Hassen, cracked down heavily on this, suspecting that the richer farmers had paid kickbacks in addition to the officially agreed fee. Hassen was particularly keen to stop it after word leaked to the outside world; an article in a journal published by the Refugee Studies Programme in Oxford highlighted the incident, making me wonder if academics were as useless as they appeared. But in fact, action had already been taken.

I always had doubts about mechanised farming as a suitable method in the region. Our own *Showak Handbook* commented that the land was not rich in nitrates, and needed resting every four years or so. That wasn't happening, and the land was deteriorating. Mechanisation did nothing to improve the situation. It was not new; the British had started it in the 1920s, and many fortunes in Gedaref had been built through it. Yet the topsoil was disappearing very quickly. Every time there was a *haboob*, that was Sudan in the sky.

Environmental degradation had been recent and rapid. The wood on the way to Gedaref was called Elephant Wood, for it seemed that elephants had once been numerous there; I was amazed to hear that they had been seen in the area as recently as 1964. They would certainly be wasting their time now, for the countryside around Showak was totally desolate in the dry season, apart from the wood itself - which only went back half a kilometre on either side of the road.

The climate was changing, too. In Showak I heard that there had once been 'small rains', as there were in Kenya; this had been in March. Now, no real rain fell until the end of May. And in Khartoum, someone told me, the winter had been longer and colder 10 years earlier. Was something sinister happening?

There was another, more immediate consequence of mechanised farming, and the cash-cropping system that went with it. This was that the old system of peasant husbandry had broken down.

A rare sight along the road to Gedaref, but once I guess more common, were the small mounds in the ground beneath which the farmers had buried their crop surplus. There it would remain for up to eight or nine years to help them through bad harvests if necessary. But when the famine struck the Horn of Africa in 1984/85, many people in the area had been reduced to day-labourer status on the mechanised farms; these sent their surplus for export abroad, or to the cities. There was thus no personal surplus for the peasant labourer to bury, then recover if things went wrong several years hence.

Moreover, their conditions of work were harsh. Obviously they would never have been very easy, but now they would go eight or nine miles on foot to a rich farmer's land at five in the morning, hoping to be employed for the day. If they did a day's work, they would be driven back to their village or town at two. If they did not, they would walk back through the blazing sunshine at mid-morning, having earned nothing. It was a powerful incentive to accept whatever poor wages were on offer.

Why was COR so heavily involved in mechanised farming-making the refugees dependent on Valmet tractors, rather than encouraging them to plough with beasts? Perhaps the ground really was impracticable for animal traction, but this wasn't universally accepted. There may also have been a genuine need to save labour; it seems unlikely, but this is actually a problem in many parts of Africa. However, it may be that, when a benefactor like Valmet or Finnida steps in with an offer of hundreds of thousands of dollars' worth of machinery, it is hard for a responsible official to turn it down. So COR took it, and that equipment supplier supplanted his rivals in that part of the continent. Meanwhile, the venture would be subsidised by the donor development agency, which would thus kill two birds with one stone: fulfilling the aid quota expected of a European state, and subsidising a domestic industry at the same time. The Finnish representative of Valmet, Hekki, once told me proudly that Finland donated twice the percentage of GNP in aid that Britain did. No doubt this was true as far as it went.

*** *** ***

RAIN WAS rotten new for some people. Between July and December 1988, a malaria epidemic killed 10,000 people in the Eastern Region of Sudan, including about 800 of the 234,000 refugees in the settlements. There were 174,000 cases in the settlements and reception centres alone; how many there were in the region as a whole I did not know, but by November the victims were three to a bed in Kassala hospital.

One day Omar, a driver who had once been seconded to me in Khartoum, joined me for breakfast in the souk. He was so weak that I urged him to go home and make arrangements to see a doctor; a car was found to take him to his village, about five miles away. There he saw a traditional healer, who bled him. The following week he had massive crossed-swords scars on both wrists, but a big smile on his face. "Thanks be to God I am well again," he told me over the morning *ful*, showing me his wrists. He was.

Little Ahmed, son of Miriam the cleaning lady, was one of the victims. For a long time, I was one too. Buoyed up by a lifetime of good food and having ample supplies of chloroquine, I was never in serious danger of losing my life, apart from that one early incident. But for others it was different.

The epidemic caused problems for Jose, the Californian. SCF ran a clinic in the agricultural and predominantly Moslem settlement of Karkora, about 30km north of the tarmac road between Showak and Girba. In August Jose found himself under pressure from UNHCR, which claimed that he was bringing insufficient drugs into the settlement. In that month, 13 people died there; in September it was 40, and the following month it climbed to 64. The population was 11,000.

Jose argued that SCF had done everything it could, borrowing a doctor from another agency and running the clinic for 24 hours a day. He questioned whether it was solely or even mainly malaria, anyway. "We had plenty of quinine, chloroquine and blood transfusion kits... I started to ask a lot of other questions," he told me later. First of all he suggested a virus. But the origin of the illness was malaria. COR's head of medical services in Showak, Dr Omer Mekki, arranged for laboratory tests which showed that although there may have been some other contributory cause, the nature of the disease was clear enough.

However, Jose also pointed to the fact that no food rations had been delivered to Karkora in July or August. UNHCR replied that this was due to problems with a bank transfer between the World Food Programme and the Agricultural Bank of Sudan. This was true, but UNHCR also told Jose that they didn't think there was a correlation between malaria and malnutrition, and that studies in Somalia and Thailand bore this out. But how can it be argued that someone who is well-fed is no more or less likely to be unwell than someone who isn't? I wondered if the research to which UNHCR referred had looked at the incidence or prevalence of malaria, rather than mortality; it was the latter that was at issue here.

Jose was not the only foreign aid worker put under pressure because of the epidemic. In the large reception centre at Safawa, near the border, the American Refugee Committee (ARC) ran a clinic. During September 1988, ARC's doctor, a heavily-built, bearded Latin

American who I often saw at the monthly coordination meetings in Showak, found out indirectly that the Relief Society for Tigray (REST) had complained to COR about the way medical services in the camp were being run. REST is the humanitarian wing of the Tigrayan People's Liberation Front (TPLF), which was fighting the war in Tigray. As Safawa was a reception centre for Tigrayan refugees, it was powerful in the camp.

REST had apparently told COR that there were no medicines, mortality was abominable and insects multiplying, and that sanitation and hygiene were poor. The doctor was horrified to find himself being hauled over the coals for things that he felt were not his fault. He was reluctant to talk about it when I first asked him. But later, when it had all been sorted out, he told me what it had really been all about. It is worth repeating because it exemplifies the problems and misunderstandings encountered by foreign medical staff in such an environment.

ARC had not, he told me, been niggardly with drugs. It was simply trying to control their flow.

"We wanted to stop people wandering out with armfuls of drugs," he said, suggesting that previous agencies working in Safawa had been a bit liberal. (I understood it had also been alleged that REST or some other body had been smuggling surplus drugs over the border into Tigray, but when I asked the doctor about it he said he had no such evidence.)

What had sparked off the arguments, according to the doctor, was that the family of a Tigrayan refugee who was ill in the clinic had visited him one night and found that the intravenous drip had been removed. They then complained to REST that ARC wasn't giving their relative proper medical care. In fact, the staff had removed the drip for clinical reasons.

It brought to a head a series of misunderstandings arising from the way refugees (and some Sudanese) regarded medicine. They wanted chloroquine injections, not pills, for malaria, as the jabs were seen as doing more good; whereas Western doctors, fully supported by Dr Mekki, regarded the injections as unnecessary and even dangerous.

"If you treat a malaria patient with injections, you are giving him perhaps 150/200mg over five days," Dr Mekki told me. "With tablets, you are actually giving a much bigger initial dose of 600mg." Despite this, he explained, tablets were safer because the body rejected, through the stomach, what it could not deal with. If chloroquine was injected straight into the bloodstream, it could become toxic. That was partly why ARC's doctor had tried to crack down on the movement of drugs.

What had angered him was that private practitioners were giving patients massive doses of chloroquine by injection. This had two consequences. First of all, no doctor approved of abuse of chloroquine, because of the rise in multiple drug resistance in malaria was worrying throughout the region; and second, the doses being given were sometimes so big that by the time the patient reached the ARC clinic, it was too late.

ARC's doctor solved his problem through diplomacy, and by the time he spoke to me, he was holding regular meetings with REST, COR and the camp elders to discuss any problems that arose. But it was not an isolated incident.

*** *** ***

WHAT was more worrying in retrospect, however, was that so little was being done to prevent another epidemic in the next *khareej* too. Certainly Dr Mekki thought so. In June of the following year, I sat down with him to ask about the overall health picture for refugees in the settlements. The result was an article which was never published, as the third issue of *Showak Magazine* was lost to the military coup at the end of the month. The following extract comes from that interview, which would have been headlined *Waging War on the Silent Killers*.

Dr Omer Mekki holds a test-tube full of water to the light. On the surface can be seen mosquito larvae: "Anopheles," he says. It's the larvae that hatches the mosquito that bites the human who receives the parasite that killed nearly 1,000 victims in the refugee settlements of the East in 1988. And in the region as a whole it will have killed many, many more than that [actually 10,000].

COR is doing its best to find potential breeding sites and clear them. Dr Mekki is asked where this larvae came from. Safawa? Wad Sherife? Abuda? "Well, actually it came from the General Project Manager's [Hassen's] *house," he says, roaring with laughter.*

He becomes a lot more serious when he explains just how large the malaria threat could be this year. In 1988's wet season, the region suffered a catastrophic outbreak... but 1989 will be worse.

"Last year, we started with a mosquito density that was very low. In a settlement of 10,000, you might have had five or six people with the parasite in their

blood. Now it is three times that." The parasite is transferred from one person's blood to another when they are both bitten by the same mosquito.

Dr Mekki's supposition is borne out by the number of cases COR has seen so far this year. In the first three months of 1988, there were 10,998 malaria victims; this year's first-quarter figures were 36,336 -a more than threefold increase.

There is another threat. In 1988 just 4% of cases treated at Gedaref Hospital were chloroquine-resistant. In 1989 it has been 16% and Dr Mekki thinks there is now about 40% resistance.

"If we do not do our malaria control work now, it will be too late," he says flatly. It is June, and the rains have started.

But it seems that when it comes to malaria, COR is expected to wage war without weapons. COR has been looking for and destroying potential breeding-grounds in the settlements. But: "The major effort should be spraying," says Dr Mekki. "But that wasn't done in 1988 and may not be done this year.

"Residual spraying should be done in June. If it's not, it's useless."

This is the process by which the inside of living quarters will be sprayed before the rains begin so that the mosquitoes cannot gather there. COR had intended to follow this up with space-spraying; in July, when the mosquito density is high, the air is filled with insecticide at peak times of day to kill as many as possible.

But COR hasn't got the spray for residual spraying. And for space-spraying, it needs Aqua-Presatin equipment. This is ULV (ultra-low-volume), delivering a very fine spray. It hasn't got it.

According to Dr Mekki, an entomologist with UNHCR agreed to most of these plans after spending a month here last November. But the insecticides and machines still have not arrived. [UNHCR was supposed to supply all of this.]

There is another problem. "We don't have a single tab of chloroquine as a buffer stock," says Dr Mekki. "The spraying is supposed to be carried out in June but we still don't have the sprayers, although we ordered them early in 1988. We are supposed to be using insecticides for the 1988 season, but we haven't got them yet."

So it looks like being a repeat of last year, but worse. "We were not prepared last year when the rainy season started. There was no preventive work. Most of the NGOs were short of drugs. UNHCR emergency advisor Dr Bernard was here, fortunately, and he did his best to get the drugs airlifted. We used to go to clinics together and find that half the staff were sick." The blame for the drugs famine belongs, he feels, to UNHCR, and it is not just malaria that is involved. "There is cholera in Angola. It will travel. We are supposed to have buffer stocks for that, for meningitis and malaria."

All Dr Mekki's meningitis vaccines at present have come on loan from the Ministry of Health, which needs them - so he has to give them back. The same

applies to supplies of oral rehydration solution. As if to prove his point, a col-
league from an NGO comes in to borrow 12 drugs. He can give her just two;
they're for cholera, and they're 1988 supplies.

There is a further problem with malaria drugs. As he has said, chloroquine
resistance is high, the massive effort of last year having wiped out much of the
non-resistant strain. "My impression is that Fansidar must now be used," com-
ments Dr Mekki. This is the answer if the patient does not respond to chloro-
quine; and if the patient is a child, or in obvious danger, he thinks it is sometimes
better to use it immediately.

Questions have been raised about Fansidar, as some patients may suffer an
allergic reaction. Dr Mekki explains that it is composed of sulfa and poriv-
inethamine, and that some people are sensitive to sulfa drugs. But COR has been
using it since last year, and the NGOs have not reported any problems. He does
not however recommend its use as a prophylactic.

But again, COR has no stocks of Fansidar. NGO stocks are being checked,
and they are being advised to carry buffer stocks.

The whole question of drugs is obviously a bitter one. Asked why Showak
UNHCR is not bringing the drugs in, Dr Mekki answers: "I don't know -
nobody's telling me. Whatever they get from Geneva, they pass it on but they are
not decision-makers...

"It's a matter of life and death-you need a high-ranking person with influence
who can get the drugs."

It was indeed a bitter question. UNHCR came in for some criticism over mismanagement elsewhere in the Horn of Africa a year
later. They do not have an easy job, but they did seem bureaucratic at
times. A small example of this - and only a small one - was the
UNHCR international staff member who wanted to swap the radio in
a crashed car with the one in his own, which did not work. The then
head of UNHCR Showak (not Robert Ashe) wanted to refer this to
Geneva. For professionals like Dr Mekki and, one suspects,
UNHCR's own staff, this insistence on procedure could provoke
screaming frustration. But the international staff at UNHCR had little incentive to rock the boat.

But Dr Mekki's real problem was of course not UNHCR, which,
whatever its faults, was trying to help (and had huge commitments not
just in Sudan or even in Africa, but all over the world). Dr Mekki's real
problem was the presence of hundreds of thousands of refugees in
what was already one of the world's poorest countries. That this was
the case was emphasized by the fact that tuberculosis was still a seri-

ous factor. New cases were then running at six per 10,000 a month; reported cases had been 505 among the refugee population in the first quarter of 1989, as against 347 in the corresponding quarter of 1988. It was, said Dr Mekki, an important indicator of poverty, malnutrition and overcrowding. Prevalence, at 5.5 per thousand, had not gone up; but it was high in relation to incidence, he said, because the treatment could take 10-18 months.

Although the drugs for tuberculosis were expensive, Dr Mekki felt that in this case it was diagnosis, not treatment, that was his main problem. TB, he explained, was an emotive disease and a refugee working with food, or in a house, could lose his or her job if known to be a sufferer. So he was pleased at the low default rate - 155 - among those undergoing treatment (although it seemed quite high to me). I reflected that it was lucky that the sufferers no longer had to be packed off to a sanatorium in Switzerland. At least that would have solved the diagnosis problem, though; Dr Mekki would have been trampled to death in the rush.

Poverty and overcrowding are also responsible for diarrhoea. Adults of course are not immune, but wherever people live too close together and have inadequate sanitation, children are very vulnerable. Those in the refugee settlements and reception centres of Sudan were no exception. Dr Mekki told me that there had been 20,475 reported cases in the first quarter of 1989; again, that was up on the previous year's first-quarter figure of 12,792, but this could have been ascribed to better reporting. To put these figures into perspective, imagine that you are a British GP with a patient list of 3,000; in a given three-month period, nearly one in 10, or nearly 300, presents with diarrhoea. In practice the figure will have been higher, as medical services were overstretched, and there was no way of knowing what percentage of victims actually reported to a clinic.

If sanitation had been reasonable, Dr Mekki told me, about a tenth as many cases might have been expected. Out of perhaps 300,000 people (no-one really knew if the refugee-settlement count of 234,000 was really accurate), 150,000 were defecating in the streets of the settlements. He thought that perhaps 12% had access to pit latrines. To make matters worse, UNHCR had just announced massive spending cuts, and were axing many of COR's staff positions. In the huge reception centre at Wad Sherife near Kassala, it was proposing to reduce the number of sanitation workers from 141 to 38.

Rather than complain about this, however, Dr Mekki linked the diarrhoea rate to the problems of the developing world in general. As he had made clear, prevention rather than cure was the real goal. A year or two later Hannah, who took up medicine on her return to Britain, was irritated to hear one of her lecturers crow about the use of oral rehydration solution and the way in which it had reduced child mortality in the Third World by preventing diarrhoea from being a fatal disease. What, she asked him, would prevent those children from simply getting diarrhoea a second and a third time? The disease arose from living conditions, and it was those that needed to be improved.

Dr Mekki and I talked about a lot of diseases that day. Meningitis, too, was a serious menace, and we barely touched on typhoid, cholera and hepatitis (the first and last of these were an ever-present problem, the second an ever-present threat).

Shortly before I had left Britain in 1987, the government had thrown itself into an orgy of publicity to prevent the spread of AIDS, a subject which seemed to touch some morbid nerve in the collective unconscious. Many people were convinced that the disease was spreading, unchecked, in Africa, thus presenting more of a threat elsewhere. What, I demanded, was Dr Mekki doing about AIDS? Was he concerned about it?

"I'm supposed to be concerned about it, yes!" he said, and threw himself back into his chair with a weary grin. In fact, he went on, no evidence of seropositivity had been found in 1987 when a survey had been carried out in Tawawa, the semi-urban settlement notorious for its prostitution.

Dr Mekki did not think that that would be the end of the story; neither did he imply that it should be, and said that he would co-operate as fully as possible with any agency that wanted to carry out more extensive tests. He also said that he'd like to screen new arrivals, simply because the local population tended to blame refugees for everything.

But look, he told me, he was dealing with mass-diseases like meningitis that could "kill the patient on the way to the dispensary". He had limited resources available for fighting a disease that had so far not even appeared in the refugee population. In this context, it is useful to compare figures; in Britain, at the end of 1990, out of a population of around 60 million, about 3,000 people had so far died of AIDS. In the Eastern Sudanese refugee settlements, out of (officially) 234,000, 505 had presented with tuberculosis in the first three months of 1989. It was a potent illustration of the gap between the agendas of rich and poor countries. To be sure, the AIDS epidemic eventually became more serious in Africa than even skilled observers like Dr Mekki could have envisaged. But there was probably not much they could have done about it at that time.

The rains stirred some appreciation of fundamental truths for me: bringing life and death, good news for some, rotten news for others. I suppose I must have been thinking along those lines when I wrote about the rains in a novel I produced when I returned to Britain:

...Trees strengthened and gave shade to herds of camels whose flanks were now stained grey-brown with mud. And hundreds of thousands of farmers, poor men in goateas of straw and rich men with Massey-Fergusons, got ready to sow, and prayed that it would rain like this for two months so that they might have the best wet season for a decade, and maybe bring in a second or a third harvest.

The rain made other things grow, too. Beneath the hedges where the children played, waste matter no longer shrivelled and died harmlessly on a sterile earth. In the cities, the drainage ditches that ran beside the streets, green and opaque, filled and sometimes overflowed. Mosquitoes prospered. Multiple drug resistance spread. And right across the region, hospitals were packed with men and women who slept in corridors or three to a bed, touched by fever with its cold, bloodless hand.

Chapter Nine

August-November 1988: *A flood; echoes of war*

Neither VSO nor COR ever seemed to know what I was supposed to be doing in Sudan. By the time the rains set in, I had decided that the post had been invented for the volunteer that VSO had not accepted, and when VSO decided to fill the post anyway and I turned up instead, people were nonplussed and a little irritated. But I was there, and had either to do something useful, or decide that I couldn't, and go home. After giving up my job, travelling 3,000 miles and suffering repeated bouts of malaria, I was grimly determined it should not be for nothing. I decided I was going to justify my existence. I am not sure I would make the same decision today.

We did know that I was supposed to be producing some sort of newsletter. Nominally, the proposed nwsletter was to be one for COR staff and the refugees. But it evolved into also being a PR job representing COR's, and the refugees', situation to the outside world. I drove that change. Berhane seemed comfortable, or at least, not uncomfortable, with it; but he left in the autumn of 1988 to take up a full-time place as a postgraduate student at the University of Khartoum. His thoughts had been elsewhere for some time anyway. I found myself effectively in charge of the department - which was me and the tea-boy, for now - and of the newsletter. But others helped; Yassin in particular took a lively interest.

I realized that, since the 1985 famine and BandAid, the western world had largely forgotten what had happened. But throughout 1988, more refugees were crossing the border into Sudan. Their numbers were small compared with those of 1985, when Hassen and his staff had found themselves coping with as many as 25,000 new arrivals a month. Nevertheless, in the nine months to March 1989 about 45,000 people, mainly Eritreans, sought safety in Sudan. Moreover it was a constant struggle to find food and jobs for those already there - of which more later. There was still a crisis. My idea was to get this across by producing, not a simple newsletter, but a lively and well-produced magazine about refugees and development, and get it to as many people in the aid business and the overseas media as possible. I even envisaged selling advertising space to support it, and for the second issue, with Ibrahim El-Bagir's help, I did sell a half-page, to one of Khartoum's many travel agents. I think that had we continued, we might have had an effect. Volunteers are warned that they are not going to change the world. I think I probably made a contribution, and have learned in the years since that few people in development can hope to say much more.

*** *** ***

IN ANY case, by the end of July 1988 Berhane and I had assembled just enough material for a magazine. One day I did a word-count, then cast off a 32-page magazine and pronounced myself satisfied. Berhane went to see Hassen, who sanctioned the spending of about £1,000-worth of local currency and told us to go to Khartoum and print it. Adem Schitta was assigned as driver.

We left on August 4. As usual, it was nearly lunchtime before we left Showak. It was a full car; besides myself, there was Mohammed Khair, the head of veterinary services, and Ibrahim, the radio operator, who was going to Khartoum to get spares. We arrived in Gedaref about three, had a late lunch, and then didn't leave for Khartoum until about four. We knew that, since the murder of Chris and Clare and the others, there had been a guard on the main roads into Khartoum that prevented traffic from entering the capital after 10.30. But we thought we could make it by then.

Some miles short of Fau, as the first of the weirdly-shaped jebels rose out of the plain, the road had been partially swept away by flooding over a 200-yard stretch. A number of lorries had tipped over at that point; it must have happened in the dark. In fact, I had heard of it two weeks previously. The trucks were still lying on their sides by the side of the road, like decomposing dinosaurs, the ribs showing on the undersides; at least one man had apparently died. A crane was in attendance, but work seemed slow. It was impossible for a large vehicle to get through, and there were long queues on either side. We were able to pass, but stopped for nearly an hour while Berhane took photographs and chatted to the crane-crew. I wished he had not; I had another attack of malaria, and sat and fretted in the afternoon sun, looking at my watch.

It was nearly sunset when we passed Fau. We stopped again for a pee-break and I went on to a nearby jebel, green in the wet-season growth, the blades of new grass lit from the side by the descending sun. It was a beautiful scene; so peaceful. We cruised on as darkness fell, reaching Hasaheisa at about eight.

Here, we stopped again. Adem thought the headlamp alignment was bad, and he and Ibrahim wanted to adjust it. We had a quick meal: *chaya, kibda* (liver), *ful* and *jebenah*. Afterwards, Berhane and I crossed to the beach beside the Blue Nile and looked across towards Rufa'a, invisible in the darkness. The river was utterly still, but there was a closeness in the air. To the north there were periodic lightning-flashes, but what thunder there was sounded quite far away.

"Are we going to make Khartoum in time?" I asked Berhane.

"Oh, I think so. I am not worried." He looked at the water. "You know, before *Shari'a* you could sit and enjoy a drink here, beside the water, with the cooling breeze." He stretched. "We will go back. I think they will have finished the lights now."

Adem and Ibrahim had balanced a two-gallon tin of diesel on the wing and were feeding it into the tank through a flexible pipe. All around us the Austin buses were pulling in and out, depositing and collecting passengers. There were lights all around us, and the stands were doing brisk business selling food and cola. Boys sat or squatted on the ground before pale-blue hardboard stands with grilles across the front, displaying the goods; mostly cigarettes, matches and the chewing-gum known as bazooka. It was a cheerful place, Hasaheisa.

It was in the town on the opposite bank, Rufa'a, that Nicholas Gordon had worked as a volunteer nearly 20 years earlier. I later heard him describe how one day he crossed to Hasaheisa on the ferry in search of something for a bad stomach; he decided that he'd damn well have a brandy to settle it. (Shari'a was many years ahead.) He went into a bar run by a Greek and was staggered to see on the shelf bottles of Courvoisier, Grand Armagnac and Hine. "Which would you like?" the Greek asked him. Feeling flush, he chose the Courvoisier. It was poured, and he drank. "This," he said, "is Ethiopian cognac." The Greek nodded. "They all are," he replied.

We left Hasaheisa. About two miles to its north-west, the wind strengthened and swirls of dust started to collect in the columns of light from the headlamps. The swirls became thicker. Ibrahim, who was driving to give Adem a break, slowed down. We all remarked on the strength and suddenness of the dust. Then it ended and was replaced for a few minutes by calm; and then by rain.

I had never seen rain like this, even in Sudan; I never have since. Soon Ibrahim could not see much. He slowed down to about 30kph;

the windscreen misted up and he fiddled with the demister switch, uncertain of how to use it, for he had never had to before. We settled down to a slow cruise about 30 metres behind the car ahead; behind us, another car followed, equally blind.

The lightning was bright and frequent now. Every 20 seconds or so it lit the empty landscape to either side, and the picture it showed us was changing. The water had now formed an unbroken sheet across the dust, and the jets of rain were making densely-packed circles on it. Before long the water had reached the level of the road, and risen over it. We went through a village, and I saw that it was halfway up the doors of the parked cars; then I remembered that the road was only a foot or two above ground level, and realized that we could be in trouble. Soon the water was swishing against the underbody of the Land-Cruiser. We passed a yellow Khartoum taxi that had gone off the road; its rear was pointing in the air, and it reminded me of the passengers I had seen flying through the back windows of the Khartoum buses, their legs flapping in the ether. A mausoleum, some yards away from a small village, passed by on our right; I could see it clearly in the lightning-flashes, shining a sort of luminous green in the electric-blue light. I turned and watched its flickering image disappear through the steamy rear window.

After half an hour or so we were all worried. I think we must have been heading in towards the city in the vanguard of the storm, and that was why the water reached our sills and then never got much higher. We were lucky, because a stretch of road about 40km outside Khartoum was washed away at about 11, and we cannot have passed it much before 10.30.

It was shortly after that point that we reached the Khartoum checkpoint. A soldier came out of his hut dressed, surprisingly, in a plastic cape. Perfunctorily he checked our passes. He waved us through, although we were not all Sudanese; but we were irritated that, in such weather, he should have bothered to check us at all. "They never give up," grunted someone in English as we pulled away. We settled back into silence.

The number of cars and lorries abandoned by the road was growing. We were increasingly alone. I doubted whether we would make it to the city, as we had no overhead exhaust. But we did, at about 11, to find it awash.

We came in by way of Africa Road. Parallel to it, a kilometre to the left, was Cemetery Road. At about nine or ten, Ian Lunt, who was in

Khartoum for some reason, had driven down it and was alarmed to see a taxi coming towards him on the wrong side of the road, lights blazing. He sounded his horn; but the taxi continued towards him, inexorable. He swerved and realized that the taxi had no driver. Abdandoned and floating, it had simply drifted across the carriage-way.

Our own route into the city was choked with abandoned cars. The water had sloshed through their grilles, soaking the ignition. But diesels kept going as long as their exhausts could cope. So we weaved our way in and out of the abandoned hulks; everywhere, masses of stranded pedestrians waded through water that was now up to their hips in places. Women with *toabs* lifted them up and stepped delicately through the flood like cats. The electricity was still on, and I heard later that of the 60 or 70 people who were killed that night, about half were the victims of falling power-lines that electrocuted them through the water. However, no-one yet knew anything of this. It rarely rained in Khartoum, and there had not been a flood as such since 1947; I think they were enjoying the novelty, and almost every-one I saw was smiling and laughing, despite the chaos. They did not know how much damage would be done by dawn.

We made our way up past the Meridien Hotel, having bumped across the level crossing east of the marshalling yards. North of the Meridien we crossed Gamurihiya and swung left off Mek Nimir into Jama'a, making for the VSO rest-house in Mogren. Most of the Ministries that lie between Jama'a and Nile Avenue were under a foot or two of water, and I wondered if the Nile had burst its banks. (It hadn't; what we were seeing was the result of rain alone.) Berhane was busy taking photographs, a profitless exercise in virtual darkness; but he would not be convinced, so I left him to it. But we quarrelled when he insisted on stopping for a long time near the Foreign Office. I pointed out that the rain was still falling, and the water had reached our headlights; if the engine stopped we would never re-start it, and soon we would be going nowhere. Eventually he gave in, and Ibrahim eased the car forward through the waters towards the Zoo.

We reached Mogren. I wanted Ibrahim to drop me some yards from the rest-house and let me wade my way towards the *hosh*, but somehow he found his way aross the rail-less bridge that took the road over a drainage ditch a hundred yards away, and set me down outside the gate. The car pulled away; they meant to reach the COR house in Omdurman. I thought they should have stayed with me in

179

Mogren. But I heard the following morning that they had made it in safety.

I sloshed through the two or three feet of water that had accumulated in the hosh. Incredibly, the electricity was still on. Moreover, Ngusi was in the rest-house; no water had entered it, but he told me, after greeting me warmly, that his own room was completely flooded. Kindly he made me some hot food; we ate, and then set up our beds. It was a tatty hole, that rest-house, but I was never so pleased to see anywhere as I was to see it that night. I had some affection for it thereafter.

In fact, the flood marked a turning-point for me personally. Prior to August 4, 1988, nothing ever went right for me in Sudan; after that day, nothing much seemed to go wrong. It was a miserable day for the country but an oddly good one for me.

Right now, though, I was incredibly tired; my stomach had gone, and my legs were almost immobile with weariness and malaria. I settled under my net, turned off the light (and the fan; it was amazingly cool), and went to sleep, oblivious to the bits of plaster that detached themselves from the rain-damaged ceiling and floated and twisted, like autumn leaves, onto the mosquito-net over my head.

*** *** ***

I AWOKE at about nine on August 5, and looked around me, puzzled as to why there should be great dark patches in my field of vision. After a while I realized that they were the flakes of plaster that had fallen during the night and caught on my mosquito-net. I felt a bit better: I stretched; then I heard a sound in the living-room outside, beyond the partition, and realized that someone was there. Whoever it was, they must have woken me up.

"Hallo?" I called.

"Hi, who's that?" An English voice called back.

"Mike. Who's that?"

"Mike."

"Yep," I affirmed. "Who're you?"

"Mike."

"Oh." I thought for a moment. "Oh, yes. Mike."

It was Mike Morris, VSO's field officer for the West of Sudan. "What are you doing in the office?" I called. "It's Friday."

"Oh, my house has fallen down," he replied through the partition.

"Oh," I said. Then:

"Isn't that a bit inconvenient?"

"Yes, it is, rather," he replied. "Would you like some tea?"

I got up. Mike fiddled with the kettle, but discovered that the electricity had finally gone off during the night. Ngusi appeared and announced that he would light the *kanoon*, if he could find some dry charcoal. He wanted to remove his books from his room next door and dry them in the sun. But there wasn't any sun. I dressed, and went out; there was indeed no sun, for it had been raining heavily until only half an hour earlier, and was still drizzling. It had rained on the capital for 13 hours without a break. The floor of the rest-house was a mess; the water had mostly been stopped by a raised lip at the door, but the amount of plaster that had fallen during the night was horrendous. It occurred to me that the roof could have come crashing down on top of me as I slept.

The *hosh* was awash; so completely was it flooded that there was no way of getting out to the street without getting wet up to the knee. I waded out the way I had come the night before, thinking that I might be able to find us all some breakfast.

But there were no shops open that morning. In all the nearby streets, the outside walls of half the houses had crumbled down into the water, leaving piles of rough-hewn bricks that in some cases would remain for months afterwards. Quite a few houses had sustained serious damage and a few had collapsed altogether. Families picked around on heaps of rubble that had been their homes the night before and tried to salvage what they could; they looked broken and listless. The street where the *ful*-shops were was doubly flooded, for the drainage-ditches down both sides had burst their banks, the foul contents mingling with the flood-water. There was hardly a patch of completely dry land.

I retreated to the *hosh*, where we tuned my portable radio to the BBC. The disembodied voice crackling at us via the Indian Ocean relay-station sounded weirdly homely but remote. At mid-morning, it told us that Khartoum had suffered its worst-ever flood, and that a million people were homeless.

Mike was one of those, having returned home with his girlfriend, Amanda, to find that three of the four walls had fallen down and that the roof was hanging by a thread, making it unwise to seek shelter in what was left. His neighbour, and landlord, was even worse off; his house had been completely destroyed.

They were not typical. Most brick-built houses were still standing on the morning of the fifth, although most had suffered some damage and had often lost their hosh walls. The people who had actually been made homeless were the dispossessed from the south, and the poor. Khartoum's population in 1980 had been about a million; it was now reckoned to be three or four times that, swollen partly by southern and Ethiopian refugees and partly by the nomads and farmers who had fled the countryside in the great famine three or four years earlier. They lived in shacks and lean-tos constructed of cardboard boxes or, if they were relatively wealthy, corrugated iron. Their possessions would be confined to a few pots and pans, a *kanoon*, a rush mat on which to say their prayers, and an *abrique*. Most people associated this underclass with the great stretches of wasteland such as Hag Josef, or the far north of Omdurman, where the railway-line embankment had provided a refuge for thousands of people that night; or the open area between Riyadh, the airport and Souk Two, where the number of shanties had increased enormously over the last six months. But people also just bedded down where they could. I had seen shacks built against the outer walls of mosques. One day a few months earlier I had walked out into the early-morning light after a night spent in Mike's then-standing house and passed a huge building site on the corner of Souk Two. Probably they were building a new office-block for the use of an aid-agency. The site was surrounded by sheets of corrugated iron and, curious, I decided to look through the cracks between them.

The foundations had been dug, but the building not begun yet; perhaps the contractor had gone bust and left a huge hole in the ground, as had happened elsewhere in Khartoum. In the centre of the hole, some 30 yards away and 10 below me, a family had built a shack and were living in it, a green plastic bowl and yellow plastic *abrique* standing beside a kanoon that smoked slightly in the thin peach-coloured light of the morning.

The whole area was now flooded badly, and water must have poured over the edge of the foundations and into the depression below. I hope it spared them.

*** *** ***

WESTERNERS who were in Khartoum in the days that followed the flood often commented on the fatalism with which the people seemed to accept the catastrophe. I only once saw real fear in people's eyes. That was later, on August 14. Storm clouds gathered just to the east of the city in, unusually, mid-morning. I was on the back of a pick-up on which I had hitched a lift, driving down Gamurihiya past the Cairo University building, when I saw the clouds hovering blackly at the end of the road. That morning, I remember, people did lift their eyes to the sky and seemed to ask: surely it has finished with us?

But by and large they went about their business as best they could. Rumours flew around the city, of course. There had been cholera reported in such-and-such a suburb (there had); the World Health Organization had instigated a programme of spraying from the air (it had. Helicopters passed overhead and the next day there were fewer mosquitoes than usual); the Government had forbidden uncensored reports by journalists from Khartoum to the outside world (it did). But the real fear was the Nile. It had not burst its banks on the night of the fourth, but now there was a possibility that it might, setting off a round of flooding that would be much worse than the first.

This was not empty supposition. It had risen; passing the May Gardens one afternoon, I noticed that a pleasure-cruiser parked there had its freeboard level with the lawns. In the meantime, staff at the lock-gates at Roseires, on the Ethiopian frontier where the Blue Nile entered Sudan, metered the flow as best they could but warned that the river would overflow in Khartoum on August 16.

The British Embassy had already pulled all the staff of the Overseas Development Administration (ODA, later renamed DfID) out of Atbara, some hundreds of kilometres to the north. This was because the whole country was affected, and Atbara was isolated and running short of food. There was nothing left to eat but the local diet. This caused some embarrassment to the VSO volunteers in the city, who ate it anyway. However, as the ODA was to a large extent VSO's paymaster, they obediently trooped onto the plane to Khartoum and spent the next few days trying to get back. The embassy was now laying plans to get the entire British contingent out of the capital. Someone decided that they would have to be ready to evacuate everybody by helicopter. Where the helicopters would come from was not specified, but someone was sent to pick up some maps from the Government's Survey Department, so that the British staff could mark all the high points suitable for a landing. He returned empty-handed, having found the Survey Department under water.

For the Sudanese, however, the Nile breaking its banks was a real threat. It had already done so at Merowe, a few hundred kilometres downstream, wrecking the market gardens there and causing a shortage of fresh vegetables in the capital that would persist into the autumn. And the steady rise of the water beside Nile Avenue suggested that the people at Roseires were right; August 15/16 would be the day of the second, greater, flood.

Mike took it seriously. A day or so before that date, we took an evening ride in his Land-Rover to the conjunction of the Blue and White Niles at Mogren. The fields between the ring-road and the rivers had flooded already. Where once there had been oxen in the centre of the city, now there was a sheet of water, burning orange in the sinking sun; and the row of date-palms that led down, usually, to the riverbank now stood out of the water like obelisks.

He was hungry, he told me; hungry and fed up. "Let's go to the Hilton for dinner," he said.

The Hilton Hotel was several tens of storeys high, dwarfing the tatty city. It was a square modern building with little architectural merit from the outside. Its site was on the Mogren spit, and both the Blue and White Niles were within a kilometre on either side. There were few other buildings near it, and the road linking the hotel to the rest of the city formed a causeway; the ground on which the hotel stood was dry for about 50 yards around it. Beyond that, there was now only water. On the roof was an ITN camera crew, busy transmitting via satellite to London. They must have had a tremendous view from the top of the hotel, for the water was still ablaze in the sunset.

We pulled up outside the doors. Someone had erected a shack a few feet from the walls, and was living there. One or two goats picked about on the damp patch that was not actually flooded. I noticed this as we went through the doors, and then we were in the lobby area; it was vast, with a high vaulted ceiling that went up several storeys; it was completely air-conditioned, to the extent that I started to shiver. It cannot have been more than 65°F; outside it was still over 100°F, despite the evaporation of the water that still, after 10 days, lay across the capital like an inland sea. Here and there, smartly-dressed businessmen in slacks and immaculate shirts drifted in ones and twos, talking contracts; Middle Eastern figures in robes and headbands, distinct from the Sudanese with the latter's simple way of dressing, swished in and out to sumptuous cars that drew up before the automatic doors. An American car of indeterminate make; a Mercedes S-

Class; all with the lights glimmering off their deep paintwork, as if they were dropping stars at a theatre for a Broadway premiere. Behind the reception desk was a neat African who spoke to everyone in perfect, unaccented English; he could have been Sudanese, but I suspected he was Kenyan. He was wearing a light-coloured European business suit with a red tie; the suit would have stewed him if he had stepped outside.

We went down the hallway to the second of the two restaurants, where a buffet could be had. A poster outside advertised the menu for this; "Seven Days: Seven Ways", it proclaimed, for the buffet changed every night and rotated between Italian, English, Korean, Chinese, seafood (which Moslems do not eat), and a couple of others I do not remember (not Sudanese). Somehow it always tasted the same apart from the English food, which had a certain individuality. I ate several times there while I was in Sudan. It was a special dream you had while at your post, food; and there was something of a ritual. When someone was leaving the country, they were only allowed to change up to £200-worth of local currency, and few volunteers had that much anyway. As changing what you did have was a paper-chase, most people took their friends to the Hilton for a blow-out instead.

Although he lived in Khartoum and was paid in sterling, Mike was not super-wealthy, and he was himself quite hungry. I was ravenous. He, Amanda and I dove in and piled our plates high with fish and chips, Lancashire hotpot, steak and kidney pie, roast beef and a multitude of vegetables. As we sat down I glanced across to the next table, which had been abandoned; there was a plate of chips and a half-eaten steak, enormous, lightly charred on the outside and just a little bloody within. I could scarcely believe my eyes. The steak had probably been flown in from Europe; it would have cost about £15 sterling, or about eight days' wages for me (and I was quite well paid by local standards). To put that steak into perspective, one must imagine that a rich foreigner has gone into the Hilton in Park Lane and paid £200 for a meal which he has not then bothered to eat - and has done so in the wake of a major civil disaster that has left Smithfield empty and cleared the shelves at Tesco.

This is not an exaggeration. A few days later I went with Adem and Yassin to a restaurant in the souk where one could normally get a bowl of *ful* with with trimmings, or a plate of *kibda* and *addis* (liver and lentils). For some reason it did still have some food, the only restaurant in the area that did. It was surrounded by crowds who were pushing and shoving to get in; every now and then, they would be barked back into line by the two armed policemen who were guarding the door. When we did get in, there was nothing but *kisera*, a bitter vegetable dish which resembled spinach but was make from okra, and *waka*, tissue-thin folds of bitter unleavened bread that I heartily loathed. We ate it happily enough; there was nothing else.

I enjoyed my blow-out at the Hilton, but it was an uncomfortable reminder that I was never going to starve. If I had to, I could go to the Bank of Khartoum in Gamurihiya and cash a cheque, change it, and then go to the Hilton. I had enough in my account in England to keep me going like this for several weeks, provided I did not have to stay in the hotel. If after that the situation was still desperate, we would probably all be flown to Cairo or Nairobi anyway. I was often hungry in Sudan, and have never forgotten it. But there was little to be afraid of in the end, for me.

*** *** ***

BUT THE Nile didn't burst its banks at Khartoum.

Anyway, life had to go on. I asked Ibrahim El-Bagir if I could do anything useful in flood relief, but he said no. Looking back, I realise that there were already quite enough Europeans hanging around the airport trying to bully plastic sheeting through customs; I am not really sure what I could have done. I decided to get on with what I was supposed to be doing, which was preparing a magazine.

For the next two weeks, Yassin and I toured the city with Adem at the helm. We were looking for a printer. Berhane left us to get on with it; he was searching for other ways to use his talents. On the whole, I was happy about this. Berhane could be inspired, but also erratic and impatient. His touch brought some of the magazine's contents to life, but the meticulous mechanics of production were not for him.

The city was still largely flooded. Every now and then, we would cut through some quiet street somewhere to find that the only dry land was at its edges. One day, at mid-morning, under an overcast sky, we cruised onto a patch of land about 400 yards square. It was surrounded by houses with low walls, many of which had toppled into the mud. The entire square, bar a yard or two around the perimeter, was still awash with muddy water a fortnight after the downpour. I remember that there was a mosque on one side, and the multicoloured minaret was perfectly reproduced in the stagnant water; I saw the reflection first and thought that the world had been turned upside down.

At times, we would creep slowly up Huriya towards the marshalling yards, only one lane open to the chaotic Khartoum traffic because the road-surface had been largely torn apart by the weight of water that had settled on it. When the water drained away at last, they filled in the holes; but that was later.

Communications and power were a shambles. I have said that the flood did for much of what was left of the telephone system. Often one would pass an engineer on a corner, struggling with a mighty mass of twisted wire beneath a baking sun; yet many lines were simply never reconnected. And the power remained off for days. The one area where it was quickly restored was Mogren, as the main pumping-station for the city's water supply was there, and it was back in action in two days. The water that came out of the taps was filthy, but it was water. For the first two days, Ian - who had business in Khartoum and had made it there with difficulty the day after the flood - and I managed quite happily with candles, using what was left of the water in the overhead tank.

In industry, the loss of power was a serious blow. One printer expressed despair at being unable to run his presses. He did have a diesel generator, which he used in normal times to fill in the gaps in regular power supplies, so that he could keep delivery-dates. But he couldn't run it all the time, and had been forced to stop work.

The next time I saw him, however, the machinery in the shop was whirring merrily. He had come together in a consortium with several other local businesses, he explained, and between them they had raised enough in bribes to get the service restored. There were the usual manic voltage fluctuations, but he was back in business.

Here, private enterprise had the march on everyone else. The Ministry of Culture and Information told me that they did not expect to have power for their presses for three weeks. I expressed sympathy, but the place was a shambles anyway. Much of their machinery was old-fashioned hot metal; it was barely operational before the flood, and they were making a patchy job of the Government English-language information magazine, *Sudanow*. Their print-shop would not even quote for us unless we supplied the paper. As we left the building the manager asked me if I knew where he could get international aid to install modern Linotron equipment, but I didn't, and felt that such hardware could be better used elsewhere. I did not say this;

Government salaries were miserable, and it must have been very hard for him to motivate his staff.

I had better luck with the smaller, private-sector printers. Several were enthusiastic, and anxious to supply a quote. Some I rejected because they wanted (for instance) to set the text on an electric typewriter; they swore it would look fine. No, I said firmly, and went off knowing that I would probably have to place the typesetting and printing contracts separately; and that in the end was what I did.

One public-sector print-shop did impress me. This was the Army's, in the far north of Omdurman. After a courteous reception, we were shown into the comfortable air-conditioned office of the manager. Instead of a sharp, fast-talking businessman in razor-crease slacks, I found myself talking to a beautifully-turned-out major in full uniform. My quote arrived in five minutes, and was delivered by an equally well-groomed corporal who saluted and came to attention as he delivered it, stamping his boots smartly on the hard floor. The quote was competitive, and the quality of the samples they showed me was very high by local standards. Much of the machinery in Sudan was knackered, and the staff are often poorly-trained. But the Army was by no means bad even by European standards. The major wanted to print my magazine by letterpress, to my amazement, although he knew exactly what would be involved. But he was itching to do it, and could clearly have done so. I rejected the quote in the end because I was unhappy with his half-tones, and because the plant was so far out of Khartoum that supervising the work would have been difficult and expensive. But I was impressed, and wished them luck.

Over the next few days, we drove for miles through the flooded, congested city. I settled eventually for a more modern lithographic printer in Khartoum Three. The typesetting would be done on AppleMac by a company based in the air-conditioned splendour of the Faisal Islamic Bank building. It proved to be a good choice in several respects. As for the print-works, its owner was completely bilingual in English and Arabic and had diplomas from a business college in Pennsylvania, in calligraphy from Cairo, and a general one from the London College of Printing. He was a competitive businessman, but a charming one, and no battle of wits has ever been so much fun. Better still, there was an Eritrean restaurant between his works and the Faisal Islamic Bank building; and, as I was to find out the following year, it was open throughout Ramadan. Intriguingly, the typesetting company had some connection with the National Islamic Front.

(The NIF was, in fact, largely business-based.) It never bothered us. But laser-printers were then in their infancy, and could not reproduce text satisfactorily above about 12pt. So Yassin and I got the *Sudan Times* to set the larger headlines on IBM-Linotronic equipment and output as photoset artwork. The whole lot was then pasted together by the head of the printshop himself, using scalpel and Cow Gum; he rather liked being "back on the tools" and did an excellent job.

My next hurdle was to get the money cleared by the Commissioner for Refugees office in Khartoum. The cash was actually ours, but had been transferred to the Sharia Jama'a office on Hassen's orders so that we would have access to it. That was exactly what we did not have. In order to get at our cash, I had to go through a bureaucratic quadrille that lasted a month and involved writing endless position-papers on the various printers we had seen. In the end I wore them out and they let me have my way, but I was nearly worn out myself by then. The irony of this dance was twofold. First of all, the procedure was intended to stop corruption. It didn't; it just stopped the work. Sudanese bureaucracy was not nearly so corrupt as Westerners liked to suppose, but it was not clean, particularly at the highest levels; this was to be a factor behind the June 1989 coup. Second, the procedure was used to drag me into a power-struggle between two offices of the Commissioner for Refugees, which I resented. When I printed again in the spring of 1989, I proposed a deal with Hassen's head of budget; I would bring back comprehensive documentation from Khartoum, and he in return would simply let me travel to the capital with all the cash I needed stuffed into a holdall. He agreed, and it was a lot more satisfactory.

I kept my part of the bargain, and there is a piece of paper before me which is worth reproducing. It is the account for the trip I made to print the second magazine, in March/April 1989; in it I showed Hassen exactly what I had done with his money. It is for the typesetting of the magazine, which was 32 pages, in separate English and Arabic editions; the printing of 1,000 copies of each; binding; and artwork assembly, this time done by a freelance we had tempted away from one of the nationals to make up the pages to my design. It runs:

Typesetting, English:	*S.2,100*
Typesetting, Arabic:	*S.1,272*
Late setting and headlines:	*S. 390*
White paper, 65 grammes per square metre:	*S.24,000*
Total:	*S.27,762*

This was about £2,000 sterling, and it can be seen that the Third World economy runs to a different scale. If we had done the job in Britain, it would have cost three times as much. Moreover, I enjoyed the work. We hit many problems, especially with the second magazine, which was produced during Ramadan; the film for the litho plates was badly assembled, and the pictures badly cropped. We had to throw a lot of it back. But in the end it came right, and we were getting better at it. Not only that, but we were getting ready to beat Western journalists at their own game. This, for me, was the underlying idea. Transferring media technology and writing techniques to colleagues in developing countries is a form of empowerment, to use a piece of development jargon. It can make a real difference in the business of sustainable development. Indeed, writing this has reminded me how very sorry I was when the coup brought it all to an end.

But it was always going to. Perhaps I got so involved with the work that I rather forgot the tensions that were driving the country apart.

*** *** ***

IT WAS, of course, impossible to forget the floods themselves.

Normality had returned to some extent by the end of September 1988, but the city was never quite the same again. The great holes in the road, water sloshing round your feet or the sills of the car, were reminders, as were the shortages of commodities and vegetables in the souk. And then there were the people picking over the skips in which the wealthier households in Khartoum Three dumped their rubbish. And if all that were not enough, on an overcast day the sun that shone dully through the clouds picked up reflections from the sheets of water and bounced them back and forth, so that the city was a prism.

In early September, a series of radio messages summoned me back to Showak. Hassen had a job for me to do, and said it would not wait. I stalled for a few days to get a few urgent bits and pieces done and then told Adem to get as much diesel as he could; then I went off to get a travel permit from the alien's office near the Meridien.

"Showak tomorrow," I told him one morning as we ate breakfast together in the little canteen behind the COR office.

"Thanks be to God!" he almost wailed. He had had problems living in Khartoum in the first days after the flood, as we all had; but was now settled comfortably with a family in the Islamic housing development south of Amharatt. It was a beautiful flat, and I think they were very kind to him, but he missed his wife, and his daughters)he had three). Later, before I returned to Khartoum, I told the head of the workshop that I would have liked Adem with me again (this was true), but thought he would probably prefer to stay with his wife and family; this was arranged.

I had business to do in Khartoum the day we left, and we did not leave the capital until after one. Yet again, we were a full car. A member of the family that had been looking after Adem came with us, a pleasant man who wanted to find work in Showak (he did; he became a radio operator, and later went to work for the EEC). There was also a woman who wanted to join her father in the huge reception centre of Fau V, about 80 miles short of Gedaref.

The girl's father had intended to meet her at the junction with the Medani road; he didn't, and Adem attempted to reach Fau V over the dirt tracks. It had been raining heavily all over the region, and although it was a fine evening, the ground was slippy. After the sump had stuck on a rut just before sunset, I insisted that we turn back. There was some argument, but I refused to let us go on, although Adem insisted that it was only another four or five kilometres to the camp. However, he had said that four or five kilometres earlier. "We've got no food on board," I told him, "and no water. If you want to be stuck out here all night and maybe much of tomorrow that's your problem, but I don't." With sudden good grace he gave way, and we took the woman on to Showak, where we knew that she would be able to arrange a lift back to Fau with the next maintenance truck.

It was odd, bumping over the mud and looking to the horizon, knowing that a camp of 4,500 people lay just out of sight in the middle of nowhere. It was odder still going back towards the main road past a series of hummocks that had once formed the outer boundaries of Fau I and Fau II. These were the great reception centres to which the Tigrayan refugees had been trucked from the border in 1985. Many had died in Fau before the Tigrayans had marched them all back into Tigray in May 1986. Now, there was nothing but a flat field surrounded by raised-earth windbreaks. If places could speak, this would have had a certain eloquence. That night, as the sun sank into the damp green landscape and the sky turned from blue to silver, I think it did.

The task that awaited me in Showak was a position paper on

Sudan's support to refugees. Yassin and I worked on it together. Hassen told me that it was intended for a seminar, which in a sense was true. I later learned that he had taken it to the Executive Committee meeting of UNHCR in Geneva, where it helped him wring a couple of million more dollars out of the international community. I found the work well worthwhile.

However, I was in a hurry to get back to Khartoum and finish the magazine. Abdel Jallil, who was going to Gedaref, kindly offered to take my passport with him and get clearance from the police for my return journey. He returned in mid-afternoon. "Sorry," he said gloomily, "I couldn't even get near the police station, even on foot. They've closed the entire city centre."

The following day I hitched a lift back to Khartoum with Suleiman, the head of water, hoping to get a permit in Gedaref on the way. Once again we found the city centre turned upside down; there had been riots, which had now stopped. It was not anti-refugee vioence this time, Suleiman told me; everyone was involved, against the police.

"Why are they rioting?" I asked him.

"The people have no bread," he said simply. It was nothing more or less than the truth.

With a colleague from the Gedaref office, I shuttled between the police station and the Army depot, trying to get my papers stamped for the journey. Eventually a policeman wrote out the permit by hand, apologised for its unprofessional appearance and refused to accept the usual administration fee. Somewhere in my papers I still have that tattered sheet of foolscap, covered in fluid, elegant Arabic script.

*** *** ***

IN KHARTOUM, a new group of volunteers arrived. One Friday in October, just before I returned to Showak, Ngusi and another member of VSO's staff, Hyatt - herself a South Sudanese - hired a minibus to take the new volunteers to Jebel Aulia, south of Khartoum. There was a river crossing and a hydro plant there, constructed by the British in the 1930s. It was a favourite spot for a day out beside the White Nile, and Ngusi and Hyatt invited me to join them. It was a pleasant day; we sat on a patch of shaded grass at the rear end of the river barrier and watched the murky waters of the White Nile break and cascade through the gates, while around us the Sudanese drank Pepsi,

VSO's volunteers and staff in Sudan pose for a group picture on the roof of the Yugoslav Hotel in Wad Medani, during a VSO conference in late December 1988. Ibrahim El-Bagir is on the extreme left, Mike Morris second from right at the back; Elaine is in front of him. Hannah is crouching second from right at the front. For some reason no-one from Showak is there, apart from me; I took the picture

played with their children and fished off the dam, much as an English crowd might do in a park on a summer's afternoon. I remember looking at the new volunteers with their expanses of white flesh, new cotton print dresses and wide-brimmed hats, and deciding that there was something very time-out-of-place about the gathering. "I thought," I wrote my parents a few days later, "that we rather resembled an outing of memsahibs from some second-class hill-station of the Raj. Ootacamund, perhaps; but not Simla, oh no."

But the day had begun badly. Hyatt and Ngusi must have forgotten that there was a police checkpoint on the Rabak road, which one followed to reach Jebel Aulia. Or perhaps they had assumed that travel passes were not needed for Jebel Aulia, but it seemed they were. Maddeningly, the checkpoint was right before the dam; presumably it had been placed there for that reason.

I found officialdom was frequently labyrinthine in Sudan, but not usually spiteful. At Jebel Aulia that day, we met an exception. The police officer, a small, thin, rat-like creature in his thirties, in slacks, shirt and dark glasses rather than uniform, prowled around the vehicle, barking at us to give him our passports.

Ngusi explained that most of us hadn't got them.

"You should have," said the rat. He glared at us. "Very well. You will write down all your passport numbers and give them to me. You will agree to take no photographs at the dam. If you do that I will let you through, this time."

The dam was only 300 yards to the south. However, we complied. I had not got my passport, and had no idea of the number, so I wrote down my parents' telephone number instead. Bizarrely, they turned out to be nearly identical.

While we did this, rat-face gave Ngusi and Hyatt a hard time.

"You!" he barked at Ngusi. "You are a refugee, aren't you?" For our benefit he did this in English, although Ngusi was word-perfect in Arabic.

"I am a refugee, yes," replied Ngusi in English, very quietly.

"Say it louder!"

"I am..."

"Properly! Repeat after me! I-am-Ethiopian-refugee!"

Ngusi did as he was told, not a muscle in his face betraying what he must have felt. The policeman turned to Hyatt, and now he spoke in Arabic.

"You are a refugee, you are Beni Amer," he said.

"No, I'm Sudanese," she said indignantly. It was the truth; her family were from Juba. I am not sure why rat-face thought her looks identified her with the Beni Amer; some Ethiopian tribes do have a more African appearance, but they are not one of them.

In any case, he gave up and lectured us about the need for passports "because of the security situation". Then he let us go. We went.

*** *** ***

THE SECURITY situation to which rat-face referred was the war in south Sudan, which was now five years old. It had entered a grim new phase during 1988, and no-one working in Sudan could have not known this.

What had been new during this year was the extent to which the civilian population in the south was being uprooted; they knew that, if they stayed in their villages, they could face harrassment from the Government-sponsored militias, but could hope for little protection from the SPLA, which was a threat in itself - especially to those who refused to part with their food and cattle. So they fled. They tramped north to the railhead at Babanusa; or, increasingly, abandoned Sudan altogether, walking many hundreds of miles across country to the reception centres at Gambella in Southern Ethiopia. Many died on

the journey. By the year's end, the death toll since January was estimated at about 200,000. Attempts by the World Food Programme to
force emergency supplies in by air from the north, or overland from
troubled Uganda, were only partly successful. The record harvest in
the north of Sudan was of little help.

The political balance was changing, making peace seem farther
away than ever. Late in the year the Democratic Unionist Party of
Othman Mirghani, unable to budge its Umma partners on the war
question, decided for the time being to leave the government. This
split had probably been inevitable, but the occasion for it was the
DUP's Peace Plan, thrashed out with SPLA representatives and then
rejected by Umma. It seems extraordinary that one half of a coalition
government should negotiate with an internal enemy without the participation of the other half; but then Sadiq himself, who besides heading the government was the Umma leader, had met with SPLA leader
John Garang at Koka Dam in Ethiopia some months earlier.
However, the two men had not liked each other, and the understand-
ings reached there had not been implemented.

To an extent, the impossibility of ending the war also reflected the
SPLA's ultimate aims; it wanted participation within Sudan's power-
structure, not a separate state. Like the Tigrayans in Ethiopia, they
knew that an independent nation might not be practicable, and aimed
for a federal state instead. Had independence as such been sought, it
is possible that Sudan's far-right Islamic fundamentalists might actually have pushed for such a split, which would have left them with a
unitary Moslem state in the north.

Whether federalism or separatism was the issue, Mirghani's DUP
must have felt that a turning-point had come. When Umma refused
to follow them down the peace road, they gave up their position in
government to the National Islamic Front, led by Sadiq's own broth-
er-in-law, the able and articulate lawyer Dr Hassen Turabi; he took the
justice portfolio in the new line-up, making entrenchment of Islamic
law inevitable. Never had a settlement looked so far away.

But the DUP held demonstrations for peace, and one of their
biggest public meetings took place in Kassala in the late autumn of
1988. Like Umma, the DUP had a leadership who were religious figures also, and Kassala was their power-base. I was there that day in
Kassala. In fact I was with Hassen, who had gone to see the provin-
cial governor in the company of the deputy commissioner for
refugees, Frank, Doug McClure of the EEC and others. The meeting

was a hurried one. All then adjourned to a stretch of open land below the Kassala jebels to see what was going on.

The demonstration wound its way into the park slowly and good-humouredly, led by men on massive bull camels. They held banners. Outriders rode small Japanese motorbikes. People laughed and ran beside them, children skipping about on the edge of the drainage ditch that lined the road. It was 11, and the sun was high, but no-one seemed concerned; I remember that it was a cool day by Sudanese standards. A series of speeches was made in the park. There was one heckler, an old man who appeared wheeling a bicycle and yelling that the demonstrators were traitors, and blasphemers against Islam. He was shouted down, but not unkindly, and left in a huff.

Frank and I went off afterwards for a splendid lunch. It was the last I remember in a Sudanese restaurant, for by now the economy had gone into severe decline. Then we travelled back to Showak in Frank's Land-Rover. The two-hour journey was a pleasant one. We were going at my favourite time of day, when the sun starts its down-ward curve in earnest. The day was still strong, but life had returned to the sky. The harvest had begun (it was November), and the land to either side of us was cloaked in thick, gold, high dura. People were speaking out against the war. It might end, and then the USA would resume grain shipments. With a good harvest in prospect too, we would have plenty of bread. Everybody would look less tired, no longer forced to queue at the bakery in the early hours, and the hel-ter-skelter collapse of the currency would cease.

I was wrong. In fact, the events of the last few weeks had settled the fate of Sudanese democracy. It would linger along for another seven or eight months, but the die was cast.

But it didn't look that way that afternoon. At Khashm el-Girba we stopped to buy cigarettes, and as we accelerated away again on the main road I saw a Bedford souk-truck parked some yards away in a patch cleared of dura. Three or four men in white *djellabiyas* hacked around the edge of the clearing with scythes, and the back of the Bedford was already piled high. The dura was gold, the ground where it had been was green; the sky was mid-blue, the cab of the truck a bright royal blue, all rich in the afternoon sun which lit the faces of the Kassala jebels that faded behind us, sheltering their rich oasis of dark-brown earth, date-palms and ploughs pulled by oxen.

"I hear it's a record harvest," said Frank. He was right; it was; but it would do precious good for some people.

Chapter Ten

November 1988-February 1989: *Hunger and plenty*

"We never expected a harvest like this," said Hassen. He was standing in the conference room behind the Showak office. It was imposing; high ceilings, cool, with ample fans and swamp-coolers. Here, the representatives of the 32 non-government organizations-NGOs, or Volags-gathered once a month to discuss matters of mutual interest. It was a mini-United Nations, attended by people from most parts of the world.

Today, however, Hassen was not addressing an ordinary NGO meeting. Today was the assembly of the Food Assessment Mission.

It was November 1988 and the 1989 FAM report was in preparation. Fifteen people each from COR and UNHCR, drawn in both cases from the Khartoum and Showak offices, would look at the nutritional status of the quarter-million refugees in the reception centres and settlements, working under the leadership of Hassen's deputy, Mohamed Tom.

Hassen warmed to his theme. There was not only an excellent harvest, he said; there was an excellent market for wage-labour as well. There was no mystery as to why; the rainfall in one settlement alone, Um Rakuba, had been 726 mm instead of the usual 400-odd.

The meeting started me thinking about nutrition.

*** *** ***

I HAD to start thinking about something. I had returned to Showak in early November; Berhane was gone for good now, and my first task in the office was to open the door. The key refused to turn in the lock and much brute force and ignorance on the part of myself and two of the office *gafirs* was needed to burst the door open. Inside, there was darkness. There was an unpleasant dampness. The wooden shutters that we used in place of glass windows had been closed for two months; moreover, there had been a plague of insects during the rains, and they had flooded in under the door and died. They were now lying all over the bare tile floor like a grisly, rotting carpet.

I decided to get it all cleared up, and managed to recruit a new office-boy from the Administration, the previous one having left. The new one was probably about 13, but looked about eight to me. He was also a halfwit. I begun to have a liking for the boy after a month or two; he was remorselessly dim but meant well, and I was not sure who else would have him.

I had trained him to fetch me a *jebenah* from the small shack outside the office gates, where a friendly man called Salman made tea and excellent coffee. When I returned from the FAM briefing I sent for one, and sat drinking it, drumming my fingers on the bare metal of my desk and staring out of the window towards the shop opposite. A number of customers gathered there to drink Pepsi between its bright purple zinc shutters; every now and then a camel lumbered past, surmounted by a Hadendowa or Rashaida tribesman on his way to the livestock market up the road.

I drank my coffee and thought for a while. Then, tired of the stink left from the rotting cockroaches, I stood, stretched and went to see Salah in the office upstairs. He worked for Zahra Mirghani, the head of nutrition at COR Showak. Salah was her nutrition surveyor. Between them they had a watching brief over the nutritional status of the refugees in the camps. It was a huge task for two people; they managed with the wholehearted cooperation of the NGOs, who helped Salah with his weighing and measuring.

About 30, slim, rather young-looking, Salah was sitting behind his desk perusing a vast pile of survey returns from one of the reception centres.

"Peace be upon you, oh Salah."

"And upon you be peace, Mike." He stood and extended his hand. "*'Itfadl -*" he indicated a seat - "how about some tea or coffee?"

"Thanks, Salah, I've just had some," I replied, putting my hand on my heart. "How are you? How's work?"

"I'm well, thankyou, and work is not bad." He switched into English, which he spoke perfectly. "I'm going off to Central Region next month, and I'll be away for about 17 day s. I'm doing Fau, Salmin and all round there... I'm afraid it'll be tiring."

"It sounds like it," I said, knowing that he would be sleeping where he could and eating what he could get and having little chance to rest. "Are you going anywhere closer at hand before that?"

"Oh yes. I'll go to Um Gulja, just for a couple of days," he said.

I thought quickly. Um Gulja was an interesting settlement, mixed agricultural and wage-earning, mid-sized, middle-aged and about four kilometres from the sin-bin of Tawawa, the vast sprawling semi-urban settlemrnt on the edge of Gedaref that had become a byword for prostitution and liquor.

"Do you mind if I join you?" I asked. "I'd like to see how this is done." I added that it might also make a good feature for the magazine. Salah agreed cheerfully, and a few days later we left for Um Gulja.

*** *** ***

A FEW hundred yards from the Um Gulja settlement office was a *tukl*, a little larger than the domestic type but still only 15 or 20 feet in diameter. There were two windows, and they let in squares of flaming sunlight that bounced off the mud-and-rush walls opposite. It was intensely hot; although it was late in the year, winter wouldn't really start until mid-December, three weeks hence. Even then, the midday shade temperature would rarely dip below 95°F. It was now mid-afternoon, and hotter than that. At this time of day, the heat stored in the baked-earth plain and in the fibres of the buildings started to radiate back towards its source; everything you touched was hot, a slow, lazy heat that ate into your soul.

Today it was hotter than usual inside the *tukl*, as there were 10 or 15 people crowded into it. All were paramedics or administrative staff detached for two days from the NGOs in Gedaref. One or two worked for European NGOs, but none of them were Europeans; most were from indigenous Sudanese bodies such as SudanAid or the Sudan Council of Churches, or from the Association of Eritrean Red Cross and Red Crescent Societies. One or two were Sudanese, but the majority were Eritrean, Amharic or Tigrayan. They were split roughly half and half between male and female. Most were young, and all were quite smartly dressed. They were listening hard to Salah, the more so because they didn't all speak the same language, forcing him to speak in either Arabic or English. He had chosen the latter, perhaps partly to help me but more probably because the technical content of his talk translated better that way.

He was explaining to them what they would have to do in the morning, when they would go out in teams to survey the nutritional status of the refugees. They would do this by looking at the children, and taking a figure from a combination of their age, weight and height which could then be used to extrapolate a picture of what the refugees' health in general was like.

"You have each been allocated a cluster," Salah told the surveyors. "When you start work on your cluster, you will take a pen. Stand in the middle of the cluster. Toss your pen up in the air." He waved his biro about. "When it lands, it will be pointing at the first house you should investigate. Start there. Don't worry if a health visitor or a neighbour says to you that there are no under-fives in the house. Enter anyway to satisfy yourself. If you find not enough children in the cluster, then that is too bad. By law you must not complete from another cluster." If the statistics were not compiled on a genuinely random basis, he explained, they were meaningless.

When they got inside the house, besides weighing and measuring, they were to check the vaccinations had been done, too. "Check the BCG scar. Check both arms." The Sudan Council of Churches, which ran the clinic in Um Gulja, always used the same arm, but if the child had been done in (say) Tawawa, its scar might be in the other arm. "So check," said Salah crisply. "Next, check the Road to Health card." This, he later told me, was a document for each child issued either by COR itself or sometimes by the Red Cross. It should list all inoculations and any periods of supplementary feeding. How many children would have such cards, I asked him? He replied that 85-92% of children had them, and if he found it to be below 80% he would refer the matter to COR, which would investigate. The card was invaluable, as it made it clear exactly what inoculations the child had had; these should include oral polio vaccine and diptheria inoculation.

Next, the team would go to the heart of the matter; they would check the height-to-weight ratio of each child. They would be measured by a sliding cursor on a board, and the weight would be a certain percentage of the average that it should be for that height; a median of 100 had been fixed for that purpose. All children of under 110cm would be measured, as it was impossible to know their exact birthdays. The height had to be measured with care, Salah told his audience, and he waved his hand vigorously at the blackboard on which he had been writing in English a few minutes earlier. "Bring the cursor right down to flatten the child's hair. If the child is wearing shoes, take them off." We would not run into that problem very often.

The teams noted all this down carefully. Later, Salah told me that they would check how the children's weights measured up against the medians to find out exactly how many were malnourished; they wouldn't be looking at every child - they couldn't, and that was why it was so important to get the random nature of the survey right. The maximum weights, he thought, would be 130%. Below 80%, the child would be malnourished, and below 70% s/he would be seriously ill. There was an absolute minimum of 50%, below which the child could not survive.

The briefing took time. I did my best to concentrate, taking notes as rapidly as possible in a ring-bound notebook. Now and then, water was brought up to us from the COR project office. After two hours or so, Salah wound up, explaining where the measuring and weighing equipment would be handed out, and when and where they should start.

The teams dispersed. It was after four when we started the half-hour run back across the plain into Gedaref. We would return at 6.30 the next morning.

I turned and looked at the landscape. Um Gulja had disappeared behind us, but now Tawawa was started to appear. We rattled through the souk and out again, towards the two or three kilometres of open land that separated Tawawa from the city. I remembered that the last time I had been along this dirt road, the driver had jerked his thumb towards the *tukls* on the right, grinned at me and said: "Prozzies!" It was here that the Eid riots had started in 1980, when five men - apparently soldiers or policemen - had come in for a day's drinking, and then refused to pay their bill. It was the rumour that the refugees had killed them, I remembered, that had started the riots; they had not been killed at all, but by the end of the day 35 other people had.

COR ran a rest-house in Gedaref and it was to this that Salah and I went to stay the night. We dumped our bags, and rested for a while after the heat of the day; then Salah said his prayers. I sat outside on the verandah, enjoying the relative cool, drinking water from the refrigerator and smoking Bringis, the best of the Sudanese cigarettes.

Salah re-emerged, dressed now in a *djellabiya* instead of shirt and slacks.

"Let's go to the cinema."

"Fine," I said. "What's on?"

"Let's see."

We drove to the cinema, a huge open-air stadium-like place with a tall screen not unlike those in American drive-ins. Row upon row of iron-framed, canvas-slung chairs ringed the upper balcony, where we perched on the uprights in order to be able to see across the people in front of us. There were several thousand people there; not a single

woman, just row upon row of men of all ages in simple white
djellabiyas and *sirwals*, chatting, calling to each other and laughing. It
was still very warm, but not oppressive; once again the velvet cloak
that drifts across your shoulders after sundown. A huge gold harvest
moon hovered above the screen. I lit yet another cigarette and waited
for the film to begin.

It was Indian; many of the films in Sudan are. Surprisingly, there
is quite a large community of Hindi-speaking people in Sudan, mostly in Port Sudan and Wad Medani. But it was with the Sudanese themselves that the films were so popular. They had been made for an audience that is largely poor, and likes to be taken out of itself; moreover
the audience doesn't wish to see the blatant representation of sex on
screen, so that whenever a couple seem about to kiss, they burst into
a big song-and-dance number instead. The film we saw that night was
a typical example. It was in Hindi, but there were Arabic and English
substitles. A product of the huge Bombay film studios, it concerned
a beautiful young woman of limited means who by happenstance
marries a millionaire, and is then split apart from him by the machi-
nations of his family and business cronies. White telephones and
Japanese cars were much in evidence, and the song-and-dance numbers were spectacular; there was a change of costume for every verse.
The audience loved the songs, and several got up on the stage before
the screen, stood in the path of the projector and did their thing; their
shadows fell ten feet high on the screen behind them, making crypto-
Indian dance movements and generally showing off. Far from mind-
ing, the rest of the audience cheered and jeered enthusiastically. When
the fight scenes came on there was massive applause whenever the
hero landed a punch. There were boos and catcalls whenever yet
another villain appeared in the background with a chair or knife,
poised ready to strike. The film was of epic length, I think of three
and a half hours, and all this time I was balanced on the edge of my
seat-back. But I enjoyed myself immensely. I had not seen a television
properly, and not seen a film, for over a year apart from part of *The
Bostonians*, seen on video on the ill-starred roof of the Acropole some
months previously. The colour and the cheerful atmosphere lifted my
spirits. We sauntered into the snack-bar over the road afterwards and
treated ourselves to a special luxury, small bowls of custard. We went
to bed late by Sudanese standards, about 11; I was tired, but happy,
and I slept well.

*** *** ***

JUST AFTER dawn the next morning, the Twin-Cab weaved its way through the narrow streets of Um Gulja settlement. We were late; it was after half-past six, and Salah knew that the nutrition teams would already be at work.

We swung off the main thoroughfare and down a narrow track between two straggly hedges of mesquite, thin, and no higher than a man's hip. They were festooned with bits of rubbish, old plastic bags and bits of paper. Behind them were compounds of three or four tukls, some in much better condition than others. Often they were joined together by *rakubas*, below which sat women with children; now and then there was the white-clad figure of a man, but they seemed rare.

"Stop here," said Salah to the driver, and climbed out, holding a clipboard under his arm. Just ahead of us he had seen two team members walking into a compound, carrying a measuring-board and what looked like a pair of blue plastic children's shorts with very long braces.

I left the car too, a camera hanging over my shoulder. I followed him into the compound. Below the rakuba that linked the two *tukls*, one of the surveyors was talking to the householder, possibly in Tigrinya but more likely in Amharic. The surveyor was petite, pretty, with hair braided in furrows along her scalp in the Ethiopian fashion. The refugee looked cheerful and open and greeted us warmly. His wife was marshalling the children, a girl of five and a little boy of about three.

The male surveyor strode up to the *rakuba* and took out what

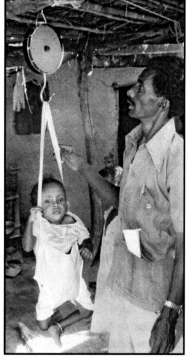

A nutrition surveyor at work, Um Gulja refugee settlement, near Gedaref; November 1988

looked like an enormous fisherman's weighing-scale, with a hook at both ends. One he attached to a wooden roof-bar on the *rakuba*; the bar was a rough stick that had been roped to the uprights in much the same form as it had been taken off the tree. The framework for my own *tukl* roof had been made that way. The surveyor then took the blue plastic shorts and attached the braces to the lower hook on the scales. The child was dropped, protesting, into the shorts. The woman then read off the weight from the scales and noted it down on a clip-board; Salah did likewise.

The child's mother found the Road to Health card and the woman checked the vaccinations. Then they looked at both arms, checking for the BCG scar. After that the team chatted for several minutes with the family before leaving the compound.

"Everything seems all right there," murmured Salah. "Let's see how the next team is doing."

We drove on into the centre of the next allocated cluster. Salah left the car; I was a little late in doing so. He vanished round the corner in pursuit of one of his teams. I followed, but by the time he had turned the corner he was nowhere to be seen. Frowning, I went through the next opening I could see in the mesquite hedge.

Salah was not there. Instead there were four Amhara women of varying ages, sitting around a *kanoon*. A wisp of smoke and a hint of charcoal floated on the thin, warm morning air; and there was a tan-talizing tang of *jebenah* from the round, spouted pot that had just been lifted from the embers. They were just pouring the thick, sweet mix-ture into the *funjals* when I burst through the tattered mequite hedge like a Martian.

They were remarkably unsurprised. The oldest women grinned broadly. "Peace be upon you, *khawaja*," she said in Arabic. "Sit down and have some coffee."

The other women repeated the invitation, also smiling. The *jebenah* smelled so good that I came within an ace of weakening and aban-doning Salah to his hooks and plastic flying-pants. But I put my hand on my heart in the Sudanese manner.

"Thankyou, it looks good but I'd better not," I said in broken Arabic. "Have you seen a man with a machine pass this way?"

They laughed and pointed to the house opposite. Regretfully I took my leave and hurried across the dusty track.

It was another compound of three or four *tukls*, set in a rather dis-organized pattern, with one of the huts being isolated from the oth-

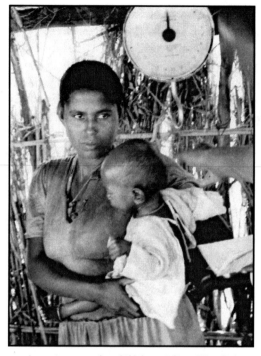

*A woman passes her child for weighing, Um Gulja
refugee settlement, November 1988*

ers and standing at the far end. None of the *tukls* looked in good condition. There was a small group of sheep lying on the ground near the
door, which consisted of a frame of cheap wood into which a corrugated-iron slab had been set, standing proud of the waist-high
mesquite. Nothing seemed to stir, and then I saw Salah going into the
tukl at the far end. I caught up.

The *tukl* was bare, innocent of any sort of furniture; I couldn't
even see a coffee-pot or a mat to sleep on. Inside, the team were
speaking to a woman of about 20. I can see her quite clearly because
I photographed her while she was fetching her child to be weighed,
and the picture is before me now. She had short hair, not braided in
the usual manner, and a rather broad face; her eyes were very clear,
and she looked a mixture of Semitic and African. Her dress was so
plain as to almost resemble sacking. She had a necklace of braided
string hanging in its vee. She looked profoundly tired, and answered
the questions put to her by the team in a listless voice. In her arms
was an infant of about a year. He was thin; his cheekbones were

prominent, and his skull was hairless. In some strange way it seemed to overhang the top of his neck, as if there were no muscle in the latter; almost like a Mekon. I noticed that the surveyors talked to the woman very quietly. They lifted the child into the flying-pants very gently, and it made no sound. As they weighed it the woman reached down and picked up a Road to Health card, which Salah looked at briefly before thanking her and passing it back. They talked to her for several minutes. Salah read off the weight and then made a quick calculation on his clipboard. He leaned forward and pinched the child's flesh. It didn't protest. He watched the mark where he had grasped the waist. The mark did not go away.

"Oedema," he muttered to me without removing his gaze. "Actually this child is severely undernourished in any case, but oedema means severe loss of protein." He had earlier said that if oedema was noticed in more than half a percent of the children surveyed, it would be a serious matter for us.

"What was the height-to-weight ratio?" I asked him as we left the compound.

"It was 75%."

"So what will happen to the child?"

"We've told her that it must go to the SCC clinic daily for a supplementary-feeding programme. It'll be a pre-mix; dura, pulses, oil, sugar, DSM."

"Will she do it?"

He nodded vigorously. "Oh, yes. We find that they almost always do."

If the height-to-weight ratio had fallen under 70%, he told me, the child would at once have been taken into the clinic for a five-meals-a-day emergency therapeutic programme. As it was, the nutrition surveyors would have made a note of the woman's name and the site of her *tukl*. If she didn't turn up at the clinic, the health visitor would come and chase her up. Later in the day, I found one of these health visitors, a splendidly jolly Ethiopian lady in a checked dress and head-scarf. Somehow I could imagine her sitting down to tea and having a damn good natter with her opposite number in a Berkshire village. Salah explained to me that the health visitors commanded enormous respect in the settlements, and were an effective health-care tool.

I wondered about the woman we had just seen. What did she *do*? - there had been nothing in her *tukl*, nothing whatever; just a bare packed-earth floor. There was no weaving-machinery, certainly no sewing-machine, and no evidence that a husband of any kind - who might have been in the fields, working on the harvest - lived there with her. Given the reputation of the area, I wondered if she might have been a prostitute. Salah would not have confirmed such a thing, and I did not ask him. But he went so far as to say that we were in the oldest part of Um Gulja, built in 1976, where he did not expect to find many children because there had been many prostitutes there and they regarded childbirth as an interruption to earnings; probably that was the only context in which they could afford to see it.

The next house was happier; several bouncing children, all of whom wanted me to take their picture, and of course I did so. But the woman with the empty face and the sick child remained in my mind.

There was a COR rest-house in Um Gulja. When we had seen as much as Salah needed to see of the teams at work, we went there to drink tea with Tahir, a man about the same age as Salah and I, and a friend of his. He was the Sudanese store-keeper in the settlement. As the project manager himself, El-Sir El-Mak, was also in charge of the much busier Tawawa settlement, Tahir was effectively responsible for Um Gulja. It had only a few thousand refugees; Tawawa had a registered population of 12,500, although by this time COR had come to suspect that the real figure was closer to 25,000.

Tahir was easy-going but seemed competent. He spoke some English and I spoke some Arabic, and together we had most of a language. He told me why there were so few young men in Um Gulja. About 2,000 feddans had been allocated for refugee agriculture in the camp; these were divided between 1,200 households. So it was enough to feed some but not all of the people, even in a good year. The Sudan Council of Churches, SCC, was planning to buy another 1,000 feddans to divide between 100 more households, which would ease the situation. But domestic farmers were not anxious to lease land to refugees for more than a year at a time, giving little incentive for improvements or crop rotations. In any case, if your land-allocation didn't suffice, there were few ways of making a living in Um Gulja. Many men had packed up and gone, leaving their families in the camp. If those families were lucky, they would receive remittances from the men, who would be working illegally in Gedaref, Kassala, Khartoum and elsewhere.

For those left behind and landless, SCC and SudanAid tried to provide income-generating activities. SCC was providing weaving machines, and I had seen one such in a compound while making the rounds with Salah. SudanAid had imaginatively organized a scheme whereby a man was sent to Port Sudan once a month to bulk-buy kerosene for all the refugees, thus avoiding the heavy mark-up of the local merchants; the charity also organized sports activities including football. Both bodies were involved in vocational training, including textile manufacture and light-industrial work, car mechanics and welding.

Other things were improving in the camp as well. With COR's encouragement, the refugees had formed a security committee which employed a number of settlement residents as guards to check traffic coming in and out at night. This prevented louche Gedarefenes from coming in for drinking and whoring sessions, which caused trouble with the authorities and had led to violence within Um Gulja itself. The scheme had been running for three months, and Tahir was pleased so far. The refugees financed it themselves; every household gave S1 a month and this was sufficient to pay the refugee guards S250-300, or about £20-25. This was enough to live on, albeit not well.

All of this meant that Um Gulja was one of the better settlements in which to live. But it was plainly poor; the baby with oedema had not been an isolated example. As the Twin-Cab bounced back over the dirt road through Tawawa, I asked Salah what his survey teams had been finding over the last few months.

"It's too early to say," he said with professional caution. "We will have to collate all the results before we know." But he clearly knew that all was not well.

*** *** ***

THE REPORT of the 1989 Food Assessment Mission was compiled with an eye to Salah's latest figures, but mainly from work he had done earlier in the year. It reached Hassen's desk a week or two after Salah and I had visited Um Gulja, and it was not long before I got the chance to read it.

"During the year 1988, the health and nutrition status of the refugees seems to have declined significantly," it began. In the reception centres, under-fives malnutrition had hit 18.4% in June 1988, before the rains had really begun to bite. In June 1987 it had been 7.9%. In the permanent settlements (such as Um Gulja), it had risen from 6.5% to 13.4%. During 1988 itself, child mortality in the sttlements - aided by the malaria epidemic as well as other factors - had risen from 0.15% in January to 0.55% in September.

Why more malnutrition? Refugees were still crossing the border from Ethiopia in large numbers, but at nothing like the rate they had in 1984-85, and they were fleeing mainly war, rather than famine as well, as had been the case then. So why was the nutritional status of refugees in Sudan in decline?

Oddly, it seems that the prayed-for heavy rain had something to do with it. I quote from the second edition of *Showak Magazine*, in which I covered the subject:

"Disruption of food deliveries before and during the rainy season due to the non-availability of certain items may... have contributed towards increased malnutrition," says the report. Out of 33 settlements/reception centres, 22 needed at least a three- to four-month stock of food items safely in position before the onset of rains in June [because the roads, unmetalled, became sodden]. *"In 1987-88 WFP* [the World Food Programme] *faced many difficulties in making available food items, particularly the cereals, which are supposed to be obtained from the Sudanese Agricultural Bank." The release of food items, it goes on, needs to be planned to fit in with the distribution plans prepared by COR's Commodity Logistics Unit (CLU) and UNHCR. "If CLU is to have a fighting chance of building up the buffer stocks before the rains, it must get the food on time."*

What had really happened over food distribution had been explained to Berhane by Abdel Jallil, the head of CLU, when it was actually going on the previous summer. WFP had donated more than 3,000 tons of wheat, but as the staple diet of the refugees was dura, the wheat was swapped by the Ministry of Planning. The latter sold the wheat to bakers through the Ministry of Commerce. However, the revenue for these sales apparently never reached the Sudanese Agricultural Bank, vendor of the dura which was to replace the wheat. By the time the rains began in earnest in June, Abdel Jallil already knew that the buffer stocks in the settlements were finished. Why was the revenue from the wheat sales never rolled over into the dura which would top them up? Was it a simple bureaucratic cock-up, or had the rats been at it?

Certainly the rats had been at the dura in a more literal sense. The article continued:

There is another problem. The Mission says that there isn't enough storage capacity in some settlements to hold the needed four-month buffer stock. It identified some of the prefabricated stores as being inadequate... Finally it regarded the stan-

dard of management in some stores as being inadequate and recommended a train-ing programme; in fact, CLU submitted such a proposal to WFP over a year ago.

Without question something did need to be done about this. Robert Ashe, UNHCR's head of office for Showak, told me some months later that he and Hassen had just been to a camp near Girba and had been disgusted by the state of the stores; sacks had burst open and weevil infestation was apparent. The fact was, he argued, that the refugees had to be made to take responsibility for this; they were not even unloading the stuff from the trucks. "It's their *food*," he pointed out. Hassen agreed, and both were committed to reforming the food distribution and storage network and making the refugees do more of it.

But neither man would have claimed that this was the whole answer. My magazine article also said:

The growth in infant malnutrition during 1988 has already been mentioned. Mortality itself has also been on the rise...

Correlating factors like malnutrition and mortality is a complex task, but the Mission did pinpoint a number of factors for both malnutrition and declining health. It was recognized that some of the foods supplied, such as beans, may not be very culturally appropriate-or easy to cook. Fuel may be short. Beans may also be infested. Moreover not all requirements are met in rations. Rises [in malnu-trition] were noted in groups on full rations as well as those that were not...

Sitt Mirghani [Zahra Mirghani, the head of nutrition and Salah's

Hassen Osman with Robert Ashe, early 1989

*Food distribution, Karkora
refugee settlement, 1987 or 1988*

boss] *has suggested another possible
reason for rising malnutrition: the imple-
mentation of recommendations by previous Food Assessment Missions on the
phasing-out of rations and their restric-
tion to vulnerable groups...The report
says: "The extent to which the phasing-
down and phasing-out of general food
rations for those refugees who were moved
to settlements prior to 1984 contributed
to the observed decline is difficult to
determine." It suggests an in-depth
investigation.*

Everything in the FAM report
seemed to suggest that mistakes
by mostly well-meaning officials
in Geneva, Rome, Khartoum and sometimes, I am sure, in Showak
itself led down to the woman with the empty face whose baby had
oedema in Um Gulja.

The business of the vulnerable groups was a prime example. Food
rations were distributed to all those refugees who had been in Sudan
for 12 months or less and who were still in reception centres. They
also went to about 30% of those in proper settlements; single-parent
families and those whose head of household was old, or had TB or
some other debilitating illness. The remainder did not automatically
get anything at all. The idea was that those who could not support
themselves through a land allocation would earn their living through
income-generating projects, backed by vocational training.

Sometimes, this did work. A few months later a new colleague, Ali
Sifori, came from Khartoum to work with me on the magazine; he
proved to be an able and congenial colleague. Early in 1989 he went
to Tawawa to see income-generating projects there. He visited the
World University Service's dressmaking project, where 17 ancient
Singer sewing-machines had been assembled and Tigrayan refugee
women were being taught how to use them. COR had a similar project of its own where 13 Ethiopian women made *toabs*, the flowing
outer garment worn by Sudanese women. They could buy the mate-

rials for S.30 and sell the finished product for S.80; one skilled seam-stress could knock out 20 of these a month, according to Ali. COR charged a modest rent of S.15 a month for the machines themselves. This would have been a good living, but the number of refugees who could do this was limited, inevitably, both by the level of their skills and the size of the market for such products.

Moreover, some of the income-generating projects were cocked up badly. In 1986 a tripartite scheme had been set up by UNHCR, COR and the International Labour Organization (ILO). There were to be 16 projects consisting of 153 units of activities, covering all the settlements as well as the big towns like Khartoum, Kassala, Gedaref and Port Sudan. In the event only eight of the 153 schemes got under-way; they were in brickmaking, bee-keeping and soapmaking. They were not an unqualified success. The whole project had ground to a halt by late 1987, and although I cannot believe that none of the remaining 145 schemes were ever revived, I never heard of any. Of the eight that did get started, the brickmaking factory at Girba did make some progress, thanks at least in part to the VSO attached to it;

Proud of an orange: Hausa refugee at
Humdeit, February 1989

this was despite the fact that the French implementing agency for that component of the project, CEAR, went bust and fled the country without telling either him, or COR. I think the soapmaking activities also got somewhere, but they will only have provided employment for a small number of people. Apart from the three activities, it all seemed to have been a dead loss. "According to one ILO official," we wrote in the Showak Handbook, "the whole programme succeeded only in raising a 'big, ugly hope'."

Two things appalled about the collapse of the ILO project. First of all, it went right to the core of what COR and UNHCR were trying to do: make the settlements self-supporting. If it failed then the outlook was grim, because UNHCR was already withdrawing food support on the grounds that it had no funds, and, as we had seen from the FAM report, that had consequences in itself. Second, the abortive ILO programme cost $20 million (dollars, not Sudanese pounds), some $1 million of which was spent on the feasibility study alone.

In fact, by the time I left Sudan, the ILO's new co-ordinator in Showak, Faisal El-Seid, was determinedly trying to kick life back into the programme. He told Ali that he had arranged loans for more than 280 small schemes without charging them interest, via the ILO revolving fund (revolving: as repayments came in, they would go out to someone else who could use them). It was beginning to look more hopeful, but Faisal told Ali that this programme could only help so many.

"As you can imagine, our assistance is very little when you think that we don't expect to fund more than 20,000 people in our income-generating and revolving funds, in a region facing a burden of more than 600,000 refugees," Ali quoted him as saying. (He was counting the spontaneously-settled refugees in towns and cities, not just those in settlements.) "We have few resources compared with what we want to achieve." Without wanting to criticise UNHCR, Faisal suggested, the stopping of relief assistance to refugees was bound to put the latter in a difficult situation in a country like Sudan which had few resources, and whose own nationals faced unemployment. UNHCR argued that it just did not have the resources.

It might be inferred from all this that the empty-faced woman in Um Gulja and her listless child, the skin hanging in folds from its body, were the victims, somehow, of a wicked and incompetent international bureaucracy. But that would be deeply unfair to UNHCR, WFP and ILO, whatever their shortcomings mght or might not have been; and they all had other heavy commitments beyond Sudan. The real cause of the refugees' misery was the fact that they were refugees, a point that was brought home to me some weeks after the FAM report appeared.

*** *** ***

FAR TOO early one morning at the end of February, I tramped down to the office, camera swinging across my shoulder. The light was still pastel when I arrived at the office gates at seven, to find Yassin and several other colleagues milling uncertainly about around the courtyard. Bit by bit, a small convoy was assembling. Hassen's Mercedes G-Wagen jerked towards the gates; behind it, one of the new Toyota Land-Cruisers, much sought after for their six-cylinder engines, cloth upholstery, air-conditioning, and great chimney-like exhausts that stuck out above the bonnets, away from mud and flood.

We started to haul ourselves into the cars. I settled into the back seat of a Toyota and found myself beside Dr Mekki, who, like me, was yawning and trying to stay awake. Yassin appeared on the other side of me. The convoy rumbled off.

The morning sunlight flooded the cleft in the land cut by the Atbara River. The descent to it took us down the steep, winding track, just wide enough to accommodate a Land-Cruiser, and impassable when wet. An international highway. We speeded up across the long flat beach before the river, tyres humming through the sand, and then drew to a halt; Hassen's G-Wagen was diving into the water, aiming for the first of the Hausa crossing guides, who stood about 20 yards out wearing the usual woolly hat. He waved encouragement at Hassen's driver. Behind us, the white Land-Cruiser carrying Robert Ashe and the UNHCR medical advisor, Bertrand, glided into line. After a minute the Hausa waved us forward and our bows dipped into the water, which looked clear and clean; a million droplets flew into the air from the bow-wave as we gathered speed, catching the morning sun and splitting into the colours of the rainbow. The sky above us was blue; pale blue, but blue, and the clean warmth of the morning started to penetrate my bones and bring the day alive.

Ten minutes east of the river, we stopped briefly at Abuda settlement. There, a full-blown reception committee had been assembled in the shape of all the pupils at Abuda school, who stood in a long semicircle, their shadows long in the still-low light. They sang a song of welcome, and Hassen replied graciously while we accepted offers of tea and Pepsi. Then the line dispersed and we settled back into our seats, knowing that the next stretch would be a long one.

After an hour, we reached the reception centre at Wad el-Hileau. It was large, and intended to house new arrivals from across the border; the prosperity of its souk surprised me, with shop after shop selling soap, cigarettes, dried fruit and other sundries. East German oil lamps and yellow plastic *abriques* hung like bunches of grapes from the shops' shutters. There were many people about, for it was nearly breakfast-time. We skirted the greater part of the camp on what was, for want of a better word, the by-pass; here and there a souk-truck stopped to let us by.

Then the nature of the road changed. It became still narrower, and much bumpier; there were great ruts in its surface where vehicles had churned the earth into deep trenches during the rains the previous autumn, and these were now set as hard as stone. It twisted and turned. Bits of vegetation started to appear; small bushes of mesquite, and then clumps of trees, mostly the silver and red ones from which gum arabic is obtained, and here and there acacias. The traffic dwindled to nothing. On either side we occasionally saw groups of four or five men on camels, watching us. Sometimes they held rifles. A plume of dust rose a quarter of a mile ahead from a Toyota pick-up that had joined us at Abuda; in the back stood three armed soldiers, steadying themselves on the roll-bar behind the cab. I tried to imagine the strain on their stomach-muscles as they kept upright and ready while the car bucked and leaped the moguls of packed dust and the troughs and drifts. Here and there, I saw hub-caps and fan-belts and bits and pieces left over from the long convoys of 1985.

We were all quiet now. It was getting hot, and now and then we glanced behind to see if the white UNHCR Land-Cruiser was still with us. It was; sometimes it would disappear, but then, as we came to the end of a half- or quarter-mile-long straight, we would see the white front of the last car appear at the last bend, or catch sight of the dust-cloud that betrayed its presence, or see the tall chimney-exhaust glinting in the burning sun. Somehow I imagined us fading off the radar-screen into the nothing on the edge of the world.

We were travelling east.

A chorus of approval rose from my companions; for the woods, long-gone around Showak, were thickening and were now more or less unbroken. Once, to my amazement, Yassin yelled that he could

*Newly-arrived refugees from the town of Humera, just
inside Ethiopia, in the Sudanese frontier town of
Humdeit, February 1989*

see a family of baboons disappearing into the silver maze of arid
trees; I missed them, but it was an omen. The suspension crashed, our
shirts stuck to our backs, but bit by bit we were forging our way out
of the Middle East and into the Horn of Africa.

We stopped at an Army outpost for a breakfast of boiled egg and
bread. It was a remote place, this: a stockaded compound outside
which two T55 tanks stood in depressions, their gun barrels pointing
at an acute angle towards the sky. It was only a little further now, we
were told as we drank long draughts of water that the soldiers had
kept cool in an *azir*, the amphora-shaped earthenware pot that allows
water to evaporate a little, and so keeps it drinkable. The convoy
moved off on the last leg of its journey.

The road turned north; the landscape was no longer flat, as it was
all over Eastern Sudan, and the ground fell away into a deep valley,
then rose away into distant hills. On one of the latter, perhaps 20
miles away, I could see plumes of smoke rising high into the air. I
knew what they probably were.

The sight of hills, of valleys, of any relief, excited me after the flatness, the 'stupefying plains' of Sudan. And then I saw what looked like a pillar of salt, about a foot in diameter and five feet high; an anthill, such as you only saw here.

Finally we pulled into the tiny town of Humdeit and stopped next to a church-hall-like building which had probably once been a customs post. We parked the cars in front of it, in a large square shaded by two enormous acacias. Below these was a milling crowd of people, perhaps 600; all tired, their clothes tattered and torn. As Hassen and Ashe left their cars, a ragged cheer broke the air.

*** *** ***

THE ETHIOPIAN town of Humera, just opposite Humdeit, was something of an enclave. Tigray does not quite touch the Sudanese border there, and Humera is in the narrow stretch of Amharic Ethiopia which does so instead.

Humera is an Amhara town, but the country surrounding it is largely Tigrayan. Later in the day, looking across the border some 400 yards from us towards Humera, about seven kilometres beyond it, I could see the mountains of Tigray rising away in the distance.

There had been fighting, and three days earlier the TPLF had descended from the mountains and taken the town from the Ethiopian Army. The latter had withdrawn, but had not taken the Amharic-speaking population with it; instead, it had told them they should walk to Gonder, 400km away, where they would be safe. There was no transport to take them there. The army had taken what little there was. Sirak, a young man of about 30 who had managed Humera's dispensary, and who spoke a little English, told me that the army had removed the ambulance and stuffed it with as many medicines as they could before making their escape. Those medicines that it could not carry, it burned, rather than leave them for the advancing Tigrayans; as a result there were no drugs in the town for the civilians, who, he told me, were weakened by falciparum malaria and some cases of tuberculosis.

If Gonder was 400km away, the Sudanese border was only seven, and it was logical that the town's population should seek safety across it. I spoke to Phillippo, a young teacher with a thin face, dressed in white; he told me that they would simply return across the border to Humera as soon as the fighting stopped and the TPLF, which would probably not try to hold the town, had withdrawn into the mountains.

*Ethnic Hausas at Humdeit, February 1989; no-
one was sure whether they were Ethiopian nationals
or not*

In the meantime, they were wandering back and forth between Humdeit and Humera to collect their possessions.

I told Phillippo I wasn't sure if COR would let them remain in the border area because of the security risk. It was anyway against the 1951 Convention to allow them to do so, because it was not regarded as safe for them.

Phillippo replied that he didn't want to go deeper into Sudan; that had never been the idea. "I want to be able to go back as soon as possible," he told me.

In that case, I asked, what had made them cross the border? As Amharas, did they fear mistreatment at the hands of the TPLF? If it was dangerous to remain, how come they could stroll back to Humera and then across to Humdeit again to collect things they had left behind?

He said that it wasn't the TPLF that was the problem; in fact they had still been in the town when its fighters arrived. Some had had wristwatches or money stolen, but there were no reports of more serious harassment. What the townspeople feared far more was air attack from their own side. The risk was real; the plumes of smoke that we had seen as we came down from the Army post had almost certainly been from Ethiopian air strikes against what they thought were Tigrayan positions. Anyone who thought a regime like the Dergue would be deterred from attacking Humera from the air just because the loyalist population was still there, was being naive.

I was not optimistic for Phillippo. I suspected that if he did not return to Humera now, he would be in Sudan for a long time - perhaps until the end of the war. Probably they would all be taken to Wad el-Hileau, where they would receive full medicals and be granted asylum; then they would be found somewhere to sleep. There they would remain for 18 months or two years until COR could find space for them in one of the permanent settlements.

Couldn't they be repatriated voluntarily? That was what they wanted, and after all Sudan was not at war with Ethiopia. Both countries had UNHCR representatives. I asked Robert Ashe if it could be organized, but he was doubtful.

"I'll approach the Embassy in Khartoum and get the forms," he said. "But nothing will happen for months. It may never happen at all. Their own people have withdrawn to Gonder and abandoned them."

I said goodbye to Phillippo and dove into the crowd of women and children that clustered around one of the great acacias. At its base was a small tent. Outside the tent was a measuring-stand; it was no great surprise to see Salah cherfully slinging babies in and out of the flying-pants while a colleague noted the results on a clipboard. They had already been there and working for 12 hours, Salah told me, having arrived within a day of the first refugee crossing the border. They seemed quite untroubled by the boiling cauldron of humanity around them.

They were not alone. COR's paramedics had arrived from Showak and were inoculating the new arrivals against meningitis and measles, working from an *ad hoc* clinic they had already rigged up in the old customs post. It looked chaotic, but there was a rhythm in the way they were doing it that suggested they knew what they were doing. Above the babble of voices I heard Dr Bertrand yelling some query at Dr Mekki in heavily-accented English. A Sudanese paramedic I recognized from one of the settlements lifted yet another child onto his knee and brandished a needle.

There were a thousand of them. Not all were Amharas; some 300 were Hausas, Nigerian Moslems who had, like their Sudanese counterparts, stopped on their way back from the Haj 40 years earlier. Perhaps their way back then had been blocked by war. Now they were being moved on by another. Intriguingly, they were bilingual in Arabic and Amharic; presumably they spoke Hausa as well. A number claimed to have Sudanese citizenship, although a colleague told me they were thought to have Ethiopian passports, if any, and were therefore refugees. On the way back to the Army post, we visited them; they too clustered round the cars, shouting greetings. I took some pictures of them, and a young boy proudly showed me an orange the Sudanese had given him. Sudan sanctuary.

The Army had rigged up a defensive compound above Humdeit itself, where once more the T55s sat in their lairs, gun-barrels pointing towards Humera, as did the machine-gun emplacements. I stood beside one of the tanks and smoked a cigarette and gazed eastwards across the perimeter fence, past the frontier 400 yards away, and then looked up at the foothills that rose into the mountains that climbed to the ancient kingdom of the Queen of Sheba and its capital at Axum. White smoke still came from the hills. Here it was; the fault line between the Moslem Middle East and Christian Africa, the very ground contours and vegetation changing within the space of a mile or two. It was not in Geneva, Khartoum, Rome or Showak that the empty-faced woman's problems had begun. It was over there.

Summer 1989: *A coup and a departure*

One morning halfway through June 1989 Ali and I went to Gedaref. Ali had some business to do there, and so had I; I wanted to try and persuade the UNHCR office in the city to open their files on protection cases for the third issue of the magazine, which was now well advanced.

At nine, we walked through the industrial souk, or *montega*, towards the house of Ismail Ibrahim, COR's head of Gedaref office, for breakfast. The *montega* was a riot of unguarded welding machinery, rotting cars waiting to be spliced together, and piles of nuts and bolts all over the ground. Among the *montega's* more fun features were large drainage shafts about two feet square, sunk into the middle of the busiest pedestrian thoroughfares. There were no rails or covers of any sort on these, and a pond of black, oily water could be seen about three feet down. That morning I nearly fell down one, much to Ismail's amusement. In fact he was the culprit as he had distracted my attention by telling me the results of the European elections in Britain, which he had heard on World Service that morning. The Conservatives, he was telling me, had taken an almighty pasting. Had I gone down the drainage-shaft, I should at least have died happy.

Politics was also discussed at breakfast. A friend of Ismail's, an Army officer, ate with us; he was reading from the front page of one of the daily newspapers. It seemed that 17 senior officers had been arrested and charged after a failed coup plot against the government of Sadiq had been discovered the day before. There was much speculation as to exactly what was going on.

What was? In the light of what happened two weeks later, it would be fascinating to know. Perhaps it was a feint, designed by the perpetrators of the later, real, plot to lull Sadiq into a false sense of security. Or possibly the later coup was sparked off by a wish to rescue the 17, as much as anything else. In any case, after the arrests, no-one really expected further trouble that month. It was not on my mind at all.

On the night of June 30 several of us gathered over a bowl of punch in the compound. The base for this punch was industrial *aragi*, the taste disguised by karkadee with lashings of sugar. It was

Thursday night; as no-one was working on Friday, that being the Moslem sabbath, this was the night at the pub. It rained heavily. There was much thunder and lightning, and we took shelter in Simon's *tukl*. The dog Shaggy joined us; an unpopular move, as she stank horribly. At about nine, the electricity went off. This was unusual; it had done so far less that year.

At about midnight I decided that I had had enough, and dashed through the heavy rods of rain to my own *tukl*, where I balanced my torch on a shelf and got ready for bed. As often happened during the rains, it was cool. I had a good night's sleep.

I awoke on the morning of July 1 to find the sun shining cleanly; it was hot, of course, but there was a freshness, as the rain in the night had evaporated and cooled the air a bit. Ian was just outside my *tukl*, working on one of the motorbikes.

"Did you hear, there's been a coup or something," he grunted.

"Oh," I said. Then: "Would you like some tea?"

*** *** ***

FRIENDS IN Khartoum were closer to events. As one, an Englishman, explained:

I don't know how your coup went... It was rather bizarre for me. I had gone to bed, as usual, in the front hosh, *completely sober, and about three in the morning was woken by a tremendous rumbling sound which at first I thought might represent the effects of a particularly badly-made fish stew concocted earlier. I rapidly realized, however, that the sound...was in fact caused by the passing of a number of tanks in the street...I attempted to get up to have a closer recce but was...restrained by my mosquito-net in which, in my haste, I got tangled up (James Bond never used a mosquito-net and now I know why). I got to the wall in time to see a British-made Ferret scout car bringing up the rear. It did cross my mind that it might be a coup but it seemed a bit of a cliche to be doing it that way so I put it down to some Sudanese tank commander... going to visit his relatives...*

He went back to sleep.

Information on World Service the next morning was perfunctory. A Brigadier Omer Beshir had broadcast on Radio Omdurman, it was reported; the government of Sadiq, he said, had "beggared the people and made their lives miserable". I have to say that this was true. There was a suggestion that the new military government intended to

222

end the war, then in truce, as quickly as possible. Several senior politicians, including Dr Hassen Turabi of the NIF and Osman Mirghani of the DUP, were known to be under arrest.

The Prime Minister himself was reported by the BBC as having been seen being driven from the palace in the early hours, but over the next few weeks it became clear that he had evaded arrest and was missing. (Like Nimeiry, he spent some years in exile but eventually returned.) The BBC's correspondent in Khartoum, who was Sudanese, was later arrested himself by the new regime.

Savage travel restrictions were slapped in place straight away. It became extremely difficult for a foreign national to go anywhere. The Sudanese themselves found it difficult; the day after the coup Hassen attempted to reach Khartoum for an urgent meeting, and spent 11 hours arguing his way through the checkpoints before he reached the capital. Many of the new ones between Medani and Khartoum itself were manned by paratroopers. Other measures depended on who found himself in charge in a given place. In Kassala, the Army announced that, henceforth, the number of vehicles run by aid agencies would be strictly limited, and some were appropriated. Most were later returned, often with huge mileages racked up; the Forestry Department in Kassala lost one when the Army crashed it, and left it where they'd wrecked it.

House searches began. Europeans appeared to be exempt from this (although apparently not in Port Sudan). However, the searches were methodical and comprehensive, and anyone holding stocks of liquor panicked. I was approached in the street by an Ethiopian refugee who wanted to sell a consignment of Melotti gin at half-price; I thought it safer to decline. In fact, the Army were probably looking for hoarded commodities rather than contraband.

In Khartoum, a curfew was introduced that ran from sundown to sunrise; later this was pushed back by three hours. Extra police-posts in the city ensured that this was strictly enforced. One Englishman attempted to circumvent it one night, wishing to pick up some cigarettes from his house and return to a drinking-party; caught, and drunk, he persuaded the police that he had been going to fetch Tampax for his girlfriend and was therefore on a mercy mission. They let him go. But it was better not to test it; there were penalties for evasion.

In Showak, I was puzzled. Why had the Army staged a coup in a country, and at a time, when power was a poisoned chalice? I did not at the time think it political; the Islamist complexion of the new government was not apparent until later. Indeed, Dr Turabi was in prison with all the other politicians. And the Army appeared to want to end the war in the south, rather than prosecute it with renewed vigour; the truce remained in place for the moment, and there still seemed a good chance that it would become permanent.

I accepted that the Army simply wanted, as Omer Beshir had said in his initial broadcast, to end corruption and the black market and let people eat. For the moment, indeed, his priority seemed to be exactly that. It was soon announced that everything would be sold at the official price, and lists of these prices were posted by order at every shop.

The reductions were dramatic; goods were listed at the level fixed by the State under the old regime, figures which had hitherto simply been ignored. Cigarettes were cut by over 50%. Bread sank to about 15 piastres a loaf; only in Khartoum had I ever seen it on sale that cheaply, and that had been nearly two years earlier. Sugar, a sensitive commodity in a sweet-toothed country, was henceforth also to sell at its official price - that was, S1.30 a kilo instead of the S9 it had been commanding. Before long the shops shut, having nothing left that people wished to buy; or, if they still had it, not willing to sell it at such a loss.

I assumed that, this being Sudan, the goods would simply be kept below the counter and sold to known customers for whatever they were willing to pay. But I was wrong. A few days after the coup, I was sitting in my office when two policemen accompanied by an army officer entered the shop opposite. Beyond the purple shutters I saw the three talking to the shopkeeper, checking the shelves as they did so. The four men then left together, and the shutters were drawn shut, although it was early in the day.

This happened to all the shopkeepers. Many simply remained closed; Beshir, for example. Commodities became scarce. After a few days, a little sugar became available. It had been seized by the Army on the day of the coup. They had checked someone's warehouse and found some 2,000 bags that had been diverted from local cooperatives. Some of this was now sold from the police station at the official price, and everyone waited in line to receive a bag each; it was soon gone. Simon joined the queue with everyone else under the blazing sun, and came back with a kilo in his hand; he waved it around triumphantly. But it was the last we would see for a while. Brewing operations came to a halt. There was barely enough for our tea.

Cigarettes were nowhere to be seen in the shops. The boys who had sold them from blue plywood boxes in the souk were rounded up and chucked off the streets. Ethiopian Nyalas, which had never really been legal, were now available at extraordinary prices if you knew someone who had hidden his stock; after 10 days those prices spiralled to S40, five or six times the fatuous official price for legitimate cigarettes, of which there were none.

I had a new office-boy; he was excellent at finding cigarettes, and went trotting down to the souk for me to interview shopkeepers known to his family. He nearly always returned with something. He and an elder boy had the market sewn up. We let them keep the change, and I think they did very nicely. But two weeks after the coup, these supplies also dried up.

Why the chaos? Other parts of the country were not so badly affected. I heard later that the military commander who had taken control of the region had not been tough enough for the Young Turks of his regiment, and had been disposed of in his turn. His usurpers then decided to take tougher action against the black marketeers.

Soon after the cigarettes finally disappeared, the office-boy disappeared as well. He was often ill and Ali had taken him to see Dr Mekki, who advised him to go to hospital in Gedaref. It seemed he had fallen sick because he and his family were now up at three every morning to queue for bread.

Not long afterwards, I hitched a lift over to UNHCR with Chris and Clare's successor, Barrie Potter, who I knew well. On the way back, we followed the main road into the town centre through the red-light district. The road there was blocked by a large green Magirus lorry, surrounded by troops. Women were being herded out of the *tukls* opposite and onto the back of the lorry, carrying what possessions they had; occasionally a cassette-player, or a bundle or two. They seemed to enter the lorry without fuss, but were heavily guarded.

I mentioned this to a colleague in the office when we got back. He said he doubted if the whores would come to any harm. "Perhaps the army at Girba is having a party," he said with a grin. Then the grin was replaced by a frown.

"You know what all this means for us," he said quietly.

"What?"

"We will have 20 years of this before we try democracy again," he said. "Another 20 bloody years."

I nodded. It was July 17, my mother's birthday; just over two weeks after the coup. So far (it is 20 years later, almost to the day) he has been right.

I crossed the courtyard and mounted the stairs to Hassen's office. His secretary smiled and stood to greet me. I asked her politely if he was busy; I knew that he did not appreciate being disturbed when he was. "Yes, he's there. Go in, Mike," she said. I did so. I rarely went there, for it was the holy of holies. Although spacious, it was plainly furnished. There were a couple of extra chairs, more ashtrays than usual and, for some reason, imitation flowers in a vase on a desk. Otherwise, it looked much the same as any other office in Showak, complete with flat-topped grey-steel desk. Hassen was sitting behind it, writing. He greeted me politely. "Sit down," he said; he looked as completely in control as he had ever been.

"I want to know whether I'm going to print another issue of the magazine," I said. "I didn't ask earlier because I doubted if you'd know yet. And I thought you might have other things on your mind."

"Well, yes, I have." He smiled slightly. "No, you cannot print another magazine. Under the new publications law it would be a capital offence."

I was dedicated to the magazine, but not that dedicated. "I suppose I expected that," I replied. "It occurred to me that I could go to Khartoum and see Ibrahim El-Bagir. He may advise on other work for me."

He was still smiling. He knew that I was only two or three months from completing my posting, and would probably just leave the country from Khartoum. That was my intention.

"Yes, go to Khartoum," he said.

He thought for a moment, and added:

"When you get home, write about Sudan, about refugees, about what you have seen here."

I promised I would. I have.

I stood and we shook hands, and then I left the office. I never saw him again; a few days later I did leave Showak, and Hassen was removed from his post before the end of the year.

*** *** ***

KHARTOUM was full of rumours as usual. The Acropole Hotel seemed to have new staff on duty. I was warned to be careful what I said in the lobby. But there were plenty of cigarettes. I sent 200 back to Showak. And there was food. We had had nothing to eat in Showak since the coup but thin stews made mostly from okra, and even before that our diet had been getting worse.

Ibrahim El-Bagir quickly scotched any notions of my remaining in Sudan. We did not discuss it in detail. He did not say so, but I think he felt that the nature of my work before the coup made it more sensible for me to leave the country. So I went to stay with friends in Khartoum Three, as I had on a previous visit a few months earlier; it was more comfortable than the rest house, and they were congenial company. I set about saying my goodbyes.

Ian arrived in Khartoum a week or so later, having completed his own posting. He was not leaving Sudan permanently, but would have a holiday in Britain before returning to start a new job.

In the early hours of August 8, we went to the airport with one of VSO's drivers. The curfew was being rigorously enforced; there was a checkpoint every 300 yards, and the night-passes for both the car and its occupants were scrutinized with great care. In the airport we went through the usual scrum, fighting to keep our place in the check-in queue; in the departure lounge we stepped over the recumbent forms of over a hundred young men who were waiting for a SudanAir flight to Tripoli, delayed for 24 hours. Finally we trudged across the apron and underneath the nose of the Tristar, then up the gangway, past the Royal Mail crest emblazoned on the fuselage. When the aircraft lifted off into the dawn, I felt a sense of relief.

But it went when the aircraft wheeled around above the Mogren to pick up its course for Aswan. For, as I looked down along the wing, I could see the red-roofed villas set in verdant gardens ringed with date-palms, nestling beside the silver-blue expanse of the Nile. For a moment, I fancied I could see oxen and feluccas, but I think we were too high for that.

*** *** ***

SUDAN was not Ethiopia. There were no week-old corpses swinging from the lamp-posts of Khartoum. But the military government of Omer Beshir continued to prosecute the war; it also adhered to the principles of Islamic law which had, in part, perpetuated that war. And it dealt harshly with those who opposed these objectives.

It was not obvious when I left Sudan that any of this would happen. Indeed, the new government had suggested that the question of Shari'a should be subjected to a referendum. On the face of it, this was reasonable. But human-rights groups outside the country argued that, regardless of their feelings, people would not have voted against Shari'a because they would feel instinctively that this would be a vote against Islam. It may be that the government, knowing this, put the idea of a referendum forward in order to secure the continuation of Shari'a law before revealing its own true colours. To the Western mind, a vote against Shari'a is not a vote against religion, simply a vote against imposing it on others. But it would be unreasonable to expect the Sudanese to feel that way. I can confirm this; staff at the Showak workshop told British volunteers that they could not vote against Shari'a, yet added that they actually thought it should be repealed.

The referendum never took place; in the end the Revolutionary Command Council (RCC), as it called itself, resorted to more direct methods. Some flavour of these in the months after the coup can be had from the following testimony given to Africa Watch in 1990:

The atmosphere in Khartoum is extremely tense. Everyone fears arrest and no-one knows who will be next. The most frightening new development is the mysterious new security agency, with its secret houses. ...Information is gradually coming out about these 'safe houses' but not enough to paint a complete picture...

[They include] the Bar Association club. Other known 'safe houses' include the Central Bank Employees Club, also located on Baladiya Street, and the Journalists' Club on Mek Nimir Street. The choice of these clubs is not accidental, but is intended as a humiliation for the groups who have tried to resist the junta. As a sort of extra humiliation, the military have apparently written 'Human Rights Chamber' on the door of the room at the Bar Association club where they beat people up.

Political prisoners were not the only victims of the new state. Human-rights violations on a more general scale began early. While I was still in Khartoum in August 1989, Ethiopian refugees were told to report to the security offices, where a number of them were arrested and deported to points outside the capital. These were refugees holding permits to live and work in Khartoum, not illegals.

In November 1990, the authorities started to deport displaced southerners (who were Sudanese citizens) as well, dumping them in open country to the south. The combination of the civil disorder that followed, and Sudan's apparent support for Iraq during the Kuwait crisis, finally persuaded Ibrahim El-Bagir to remove the remaining volunteers from Sudan that month. After many years, the VSO programme in Sudan was closed.

But things were much worse in the south, where the army deployed what were called Popular Defence Forces containing numbers of fundamentalist volunteers. Amnesty International reported that in October/November 1989 at least 44 villagers had been killed by pro-government militias in Keiga Alkhel, northwest of Kadugli; this was probably just the tip of the iceberg. However, there were also reports of massacres not connected with the war. Both Amnesty International and Africa Watch stated that the murder of an Arabic-speaking farmer by Shilluk labourers in White Nile province at the end of 1989 provoked, within three hours, a bloodbath in which by the Government's own admission 191 Shilluk were killed. (Amnesty International quoted reports that 500 people died.) Arrests were made, but by mid-1990 no charges had been brought. All of this happened within a year or so of the coup; the conflict in Darfur was yet to come. I wonder what rat-face has been doing, and to whom he has been doing it.

*** *** ***

NOT LONG before the coup I went to the great lake at Khashm el-Girba. Ali and I were researching the income-generating potential of the cooperatives movement, which COR encouraged. The official at Showak whose task it was to do this was badly overworked, but despite this he took us to see some of the projects in which he was involved. He was justly proud of what had been achieved. For example, there was a successful fish-farm near Girba, and we went to inspect it. The project had worked, and now help was being extended to the fishermen who were working around the lake, in the hope that their catch could be more widely sold. It was a valuable source of protein.

So we went to see them, too. Four of us crossed the dam in a Toyota Twin-Cab, and then peeled right towards the forest that lined the shore of the lake. It was a black rim on the horizon, and to reach it we had to travel over several kilometres of open plain. The rains had just begun, and the plain was not yet covered in grass; but a little moisture had softened the earth's crust and the soil crumbled a little under the wheels, making them hiss as we sped along.

We entered the wood quite suddenly, and I gasped, for the grass grew thickly beneath the trees, which were themselves richly clothed in leaves. I felt I wasn't in a desert land any more, but in parkland by an English country house. Yet there was a difference; here, the vegetation, fed by underground water from the reservoir, was so lush and vivid that it almost hurt to look at it. And in the gaps between the trees it was possible to see a sky so blue against the lurid green of the grass that the day has etched itself upon my memory.

The woods were not empty. Rashaida tents, like carpets strung across poles, and camels could be seen; but the human occupants of the tents were hidden. We passed them quietly and continued down to the shore of the lake, finding our fishermen with difficulty.

They had no tent or other shelter, but seemed no less happy for that. They made do with an *anquarayb*, a few pots and pans, a bright yellow plastic *abrique*, and their nets. They slung these last into the back of the Twin-Cab; it was high noon and they would catch little, but they were keen to show us what they could do.

They waded into the water off a shallow beach. One held the shore end of the net; the other swam out a hundred yards or so, and dragged the other end of the net round in a great arc before returning to the beach. It was, as I have said, noon; even so they caught a Nile carp for us and gave it to us as a gift. Ali took it home and got the cook to prepare it in the mess-building where he lived.

At one o'clock we made our way back out through the wood, climbing up and down the hummocks in the earth with care, anxious not to get stuck on the damp earth. We emerged onto the plain below a sky that brought to mind the great vaulted dome of a cathedral. For some reason I found myself thinking of a far-off time and place where other fishermen had left their nets to follow the son of a carpenter.

About the author

Mike Robbins was born in London in 1957. He was brought up mostly in Oxford, where he attended the Dragon School and Oxford College of Further Education. He read History and Politics at the University of Warwick before doing a number of jobs that included spells in music publishing, financial journalism, traffic broadcasting and reporting on the fishing industry. In 1987 he began two years as a development aid volunteer with the Refugee Settlement Administration in the eastern region of Sudan. It was this period that has been described in *Even the Dead are Coming*, which was written soon after he left Sudan.

He served as a volunteer again in the 1990s, this time in Bhutan, and also spent long periods in Syria, Brussels and Rome. In 2002 he moved to Norwich in England, where he was later awarded a PhD by the University of East Anglia for work on the relationship between climate change and agriculture.

LaVergne, TN USA
07 December 2010
207796LV00001B/7/P